British Food Policy During The First World War

Also from Allen & Unwin

Britain, America and the Sinews of War 1914–1918
Kathleen Burk

War and the State
The Transformation of British Government, 1914–1919
Edited by Kathleen Burk

British Economic and Strategic Planning 1905–1915
David French

The Realities Behind Diplomacy
Background Influences on British External Policy 1865–1980
Paul Kennedy

Strategy and Diplomacy 1870–1945
Eight Studies
Paul Kennedy

British Food Policy During The First World War

L. MARGARET BARNETT

Boston
GEORGE ALLEN & UNWIN
London   Sydney

Allen & Unwin, Inc.,
Fifty Cross Street, Winchester, Mass. 01890, USA

George Allen & Unwin (Publishers) Ltd,
40 Museum Street, London WC1A 1LU, UK

George Allen & Unwin (Publishers) Ltd,
Park Lane, Hemel Hempstead, Herts HP2 4TE, UK

George Allen & Unwin Australia Pty Ltd,
8 Napier Street, North Sydney, NSW 2060, Australia

First published in 1985.

Library of Congress Cataloging in Publication Data

Barnett, L. Margaret.
  British food policy during the First World War.
Bibliography: p.
Includes index.
1. World War, 1914–1918—Food supply—Great Britain.
2. Great Britain—Economic policy.   I. Title.
HD9011.6.B37 1985   338.1'941   85-3920
ISBN 0-04-942189-1 (alk. paper)

British Library Cataloguing in Publication Data

Barnett, L. Margaret
  British food policy during the First World War.
1. Food supply—Government policy—Great
Britain—History—20th century
2. World War, 1914–1918—Great Britain   I. Title
338.1'9'41   HD9011.6
ISBN 0-04-942189-1

Set in 10 on 12 point Plantin by Computape (Pickering) Ltd,
North Yorkshire
and printed in Great Britain by Billing and Sons Ltd
London and Worcester

To my parents

Table of Contents

Acknowledgements

During my research I had frequent cause to be grateful for assistance and advice given me by the archivists and staffs of the libraries and record depositories I visited. I also wish to thank the following for permission to quote from papers and manuscripts to which they own the copyright: the Viscount Astor (papers of W. W. Astor); Milton Gendel (E. S. Montagu); Mrs. S. Sokolov Grant (A. Grant Duff); Dr. A. Mackenzie and David Oberlin-Harris (Rev. Andrew Clark); Baron Mottistone (J. E. B. Seely); the Earl of Selborne (Lord Selborne); the Beaverbrook Foundation and the Clerk of the Records, House of Lords Record Office (A. Bonar Law, D. Lloyd George); the British Library of Political and Economic Science (W. H. Beveridge, E. M. H. Lloyd); the Master, Fellows and Scholars of Churchill College in the University of Cambridge (M. P. A. Hankey); the Labour Party (Consumers' Council, War Emergency Workers' National Committee); the London School of Economics and Political Science (the diary of Beatrice Webb); the Warden and Fellows of New College, Oxford (Lord Milner); the Royal Society; Times' Newspapers Ltd. (Lord Northcliffe); the University of Birmingham (A. Chamberlain); and the University of Newcastle (W. Runciman). Transcripts of Crown copyright records in the Public Record Office and elsewhere appear by permission of the Controller of Her Majesty's Stationery Office. Quotations from the diaries of Ramsay Macdonald are made with the understanding that the contents of these diaries were, in Macdonald's words, 'meant as notes to guide and revive memory as regards happenings and must on no account be published as they are'.

This book began life as a doctoral dissertation and benefited considerably from the criticism and suggestions offered by members of my defence committee. The guidance of my department sponsor, the late Professor Stephen Koss, was particularly valuable. I also wish to thank Dr Derek Oddy of the London Polytechnic for his help in locating sources. Finally, my special thanks to my husband.

The research for this book was made partially possible by grants from the Wellcome Foundation and the Center for Food Policy Studies, Columbia University, New York.

Introduction

Assessing the reasons for the Allied victory in the First World War, David Lloyd George picked out civilian food supply as the ultimate deciding factor. It had been the Central Powers' failure to maintain their supply, he wrote in his memoirs, that had lowered their resistance in 1918 and had hastened their defeat.[1] In contrast, successful management of food resources was seen as having sustained the stamina and fighting spirit of the Allied nations, with advantageous consequences for the war effort. This contribution of food supply to the outcome of the war was an indication of how greatly the tactics of war had changed in recent years. In the past, wars between two or more sovereign states were largely confined to the battlefield and the high seas, where traditional military and naval forces fought matters out according to the conventions. Civilians usually had little else to do but offer encouragement from the sidelines, unless, of course, they were unfortunate enough to find themselves in the way of a marauding army or inhabiting a beleagured city. The war of 1914–1918 saw the civilian in the thick of things. The belligerent nations engaged in a no-holds barred contest in which whole economies were mobilized in support of the war effort. The enormous size of the armies fielded and the firepower of the new weaponry used demanded an unusual degree of organization at home to ensure that the military machine was fed and equipped. In addition, when the armies became mired in the futile stalemate of the trenches, all-out economic warfare was the means by which each side hoped to get the edge over the other. The Allies tried to deflect the enemy's seaborne trade by imposing a surface blockade; the Central Powers introduced a newer and more effective means of stopping much needed imports from reaching their destination – destruction of the opponent's merchant ships by submarines. Within a very short time, the war had developed into a mutual siege in which, as Lloyd George pointed out, endurance proved the key to success.

Despite several potent assets in the form of the world's strongest navy, a huge mercantile fleet and great wealth, Britain was the least well-prepared of the belligerents to fight a war of this kind. It was by far the most dependent on imported foodstuffs and other key raw materials and hence the most vulnerable to defeat by severance of its supply lines. Its agricultural sector was tiny and on the eve of war the country was importing over 60 per cent of its total food supply, no less than 80 per cent in the case of the wheat that formed the staple food of the bulk of the population. Stockpiling of supplies had never been thought necessary. Inevitably, food control assumed far greater importance in Britain during the war than in countries that had been self-sufficient or very nearly so in the years before the war.

An analysis of British food policies in the First World War can be read on several levels. It is at once an illustration of the widening scope of warfare in the early twentieth century; a case study of the prevailing attitudes and means that shaped a country's endeavours to bridge the gap between food needs and supply during the emergency; and, in its international aspects, an extension of historical perspectives on the problem of global inequalities in the distribution and utilization of food resources. This book suggests that international co-operation and the sharing of facilities, funds and supplies by the Allied producer and consumer nations provided the key to victory in the First World War, rather than any individual *tour de force*.

Although a number of works dealing with Britain's food supply in the First World War have been published over the years, there is a decided need for a fresh look at the question. No comprehensive study exists. Previous authors have concentrated on particular aspects, such as agriculture or the work of the Ministry of Food, without attempting to draw things together into a whole. The time span of the inquiry needs expanding. Attention has so far focused too narrowly on policy during the second half of the war, yet the debates of the prewar planners and the approach to food problems during the first half of the war form an essential part of the picture.[2] It is also high time that judgements on food policy during the war were revised. The older body of literature, including the highly detailed official history of the Ministry of Food, was for the most part written by men personally involved with the administration of the food supply during Lloyd George's premiership. It tends to be highly laudatory of the way things were handled after December 1916 and dismissive of developments prior to then. While it is not the aim of this book to minimize the importance of food controls in the latter part of the war, it is intended to redress the balance. The impact on policy of social and

political forces operating outside the narrow realm of British government circles, similarly disregarded in the past, also needs to be given
due emphasis.

According to the older histories, food supply in war was not an issue
that attracted much interest before 1914. Confidence in the ability of
the Royal Navy to defend merchant shipping plus the disinclination of
the Liberal government to consider intervention in the economy are
said to have prevented a proper evaluation of the problem. As this
book will show, this was not so. There was a good deal of discussion in
the ten years or so before the war. Resolution of the issue along lines
later deemed to have been satisfactory was prevented primarily by
conflicting opinions as to the nature and duration of a future war and
of the likely social and economic consequences, rather than by
political ideology. Several key policies implemented during the war in
fact originated in ideas aired in this period, notably the central
direction of food resource management, intervention by the state to
facilitate imports, the promotion of agriculture by state subsidies to
farmers and the accumulation of reserves.

The food policies of the two war governments led by H. H. Asquith
(the Liberal government that was in office when war broke out in
August 1914 and the Coalition government that replaced it in May
1915) have also been dismissed as inadequate. Yet it was during this
period that the foundations for the thoroughgoing controls introduced in 1917 and 1918 were laid. While the debate over the validity
of state intervention continued, the Asquithian governments steadily
revised the state's traditional role by becoming increasingly involved
in the organization of the national food supply system. Because
foreign produce figured so largely in the national diet, priority was
given to the maintenance of imports. It was argued that this could be
done best by leaving traders to get on with the job unhampered by
government restrictions, except for a safeguard in the form of a
national insurance plan to compensate for cargoes lost to enemy
attack. But even before 1914 ended, the government had authorized
the purchase, import and stockpiling of wheat and sugar by state
agents and had begun to commandeer and direct the use of transport.
By December 1916, when Lloyd George took over the reins of
government, the state was directly responsible for buying and shipping the bulk of Britain's imported foodstuffs and was engaged in the
regulation of prices and distribution and in conservation. Unfortunately, since the authorities relied on voluntary compliance with food

orders, their intervention in the latter areas was not particularly effective. A central administrative unit, destined to form the core of the Ministry of Food in December 1916, was nevertheless working on these problems. Only in the case of agriculture did the Asquithian governments do less than they should. The much-maligned President of the Board of Agriculture, Lord Selborne, tried hard after May 1915, but agricultural production was not put on a war footing. It will be seen, however, that objections to government interference in this sector came from Conservatives as well as Liberals. Moreover, the enthusiastic response by farmers worldwide to the rise in wheat prices in 1915 seemed to vindicate predictions that 'natural' economic trends would make it unnecessary for the government to step in to encourage production. Finally and most importantly, the potential cost to the nation of state-guaranteed farm prices provoked unyielding resistance from the Chancellor of the Exchequer and the Treasury. The introduction of agricultural controls would undoubtedly have been delayed whoever had been in power. Valuable preparatory work was still done by the Coalition government. Basic units of control, the County War Agricultural Committees, were formed and the policy of agricultural subsidies was fully worked out, providing the next government with a ready-made programme.

Lloyd George replaced Asquith as a proponent of dynamic win–the–war policies, and for many years it was accepted that December 1916 marked the turning point from ineffectuality to forcefulness in the management of the war effort. It is now generally agreed that it was some time before any real changes were discernible. This study argues that in the case of food policy, at least, the turning point was not reached before the summer of 1917. The transitory nature of the period between December 1916 and then is reflected in the absence of any notable departure in food policy. The officials of the new Ministry of Food continued along the path laid down by Asquith's staff. Most regrettably, voluntarism rather than compulsion remained the prime means of regulating prices and consumption. Past writers have blamed this on the eccentric Food Controller, Lord Devonport, with whom several of them had unpleasant working relationships. It is suggested instead that food policy during the first six months of Lloyd George's government was determined almost exclusively by the War Cabinet and that deficiencies and inconsistencies can be traced to the teething troubles of that body. The only major advance in this period was in the area of conservation of grain supplies by such means as closer milling, the compulsory admixture of other types of flour with wheat flour in bread, the diversion of bread grains from animals to humans and the intensive publicity of the need to economize among the general public.

Conservation, it should be noted, has been credited in recent years with tipping the balance between sufficiency and insufficiency of supply. In the past this was attributed to the agricultural campaigns of 1917 and 1918. The Board of Agriculture, with the aid of state subsidies, tried to turn the clock 'back to the seventies'; that is, the 1870s, when Britain produced greater amounts of grain and potatoes and less meat. It has been calculated, however, that farmers succeeded in doing little more in 1918 than restoring total domestic production of food to the prewar level after a disastrous harvest in 1916 and a partial recovery in 1917.[3] Higher output of grain was achieved at the expense of roots, meat and dairy products. Significantly, Britain pursued a different agricultural policy in the Second World War – the overall intensification of existing patterns of production rather than the concentration of efforts on one group of foodstuffs.

Two major determinants of policy during the second half of the war have gone largely unrecognized. These are the pressure exerted by labour and the country's new consumer advocates (with which the labour movement was blended) and the influence wielded by the United States Food Administration (USFA) through the inter-allied trading system that was created after the United States entered the war. Labour agitation, thought by some to foreshadow revolution, was responsible for a major shift in food policy in May 1917. Compulsory price controls and rationing came about in direct response to popular demand and were effective because that demand existed. The USFA was the prime mover in the metamorphosis of a languishing and limited arrangement between the European Allies for joint acquisitions of imports into a complex system of co-operative usage of international food supplies. By the end of 1916 the Americas had become the Allies' main source of supply, so effective had the enemy submarines been in channeling Allied trade to the shorter, but still hazardous, transatlantic routes. This dependency allowed the United States to impose its views not only at the international level but also to sway the domestic food policies of the European nations to a certain degree. Britain found its policy of stockpiling reserves undermined by the United States towards the end of the war, for example. Finances, as well as lack of alternative suppliers, made it difficult for the Europeans to retain the independence a purchaser would normally expect to have in relation to a seller. The exhaustion of their dollar credits turned the European Allies into debtor nations. The United States had moved to the fore of the world's economic powers. Not surprisingly, this development aroused some resentment in Europe and by late 1918 Anglo–American relationships were exhibiting signs of strain, though the war ended before any serious disputes arose. Britain was left in a relatively good position as far as food supplies were concerned. Stocks were high and an expected decline in imports, domestic food production and reserves during 1919 was avoided. The food administrators could claim a success. It is a major argument of this book that that success was qualified.

The progression of food control through its various stages and manifestations provide this book with its central theme. Running through the discussion are subsidiary themes stemming from the wider currents of the war. One of the more interesting trends between 1914 and 1918 was a change in the philosophy of government. The development of food policy reflected the emergence of different attitudes towards the role of the state in economic affairs and its responsibility for the welfare of the people. The Ministry of Food itself is an example of the new methods of government that Lloyd George was primarily responsible for introducing. Officials at the Ministry of Food prided themselves on being pioneers, but they followed in the direct footsteps of their fellows at the Ministry of Munitions, which Lloyd George had created under Asquith's Coalition government. The innovative techniques that proved so successful – such as the incorporation of the existing business network into a state system, which avoided the costly and time-consuming construction of an entirely separate organization, and the recruitment of business experts to fill key executive posts, leaving the usual bureaucrats, the civil servants, with the routine administrative work – were copied, at Lloyd George's specific request, by successive Food Controllers.

Significant changes in social outlooks are also mirrored in the evolution of food policy. At the opening of the war, policy was producer-oriented and paternalistic, the wishes and the voice of the consuming public did not form part of the decision-making process. After May 1917 consumer-oriented policies tailored to popular demand predominated, and representatives of labour and of the 'consumer' were invited to take part in the administration and supervision of food supply. This transformation stemmed in part from recognition of the growing power of unionized labour and of working-class political organizations. At the same time it was a manifestation of a fresh perception of society as an amalgam rather than as a cluster of distinct economic strata. The most important aspect of rationing, and one could say of the orientation of food control in general by the end of the war, was its incorporation of this principle. Much of the success and popularity of Britain's domestic food policies derived from a distinct equalization of experience among the population through the sharing of both resources and sacrifices.

Notes: Introduction

1 David Lloyd George, *War Memoirs* (London, 1933–6), vol. 3, p. 1269.
2 In his book *British Economic and Strategic Planning, 1905–1915* (London, 1982), D. French addresses himself to food issues during this period, but as part of the larger strategy of war.
3 P. E. Dewey, 'Food production and policy in the United Kingdom, 1914–1918', *Transactions of the Royal Historical Society*, no. 30 (1980), pp. 71–89.

British Food Policy During
The First World War

1

Would Britain Starve? The Prewar Debate

The First World War shattered previous assumptions about what an armed conflict between the major powers of the day would be like. None of the nations that took part anticipated four years of muddy misery in the trenches, the development of the submarine into the scourge of seaborne trade, the draining of Europe's treasuries, or the participation in the war effort of entire civilian populations.

Despite the unpredictability of events people in Britain neverthe-less complained – both during the war and during the period of retrospective stocktaking that followed – that the prewar Liberal government had not done enough to prepare the nation for what was to come. It was said that the country's response to challenges posed by the war had been slowed down by the inadequacy of defence planning. Instead of being ready to tackle problems as they arose, the wartime authorities had first to settle not only *what* should be done but *whether* it was up to the government to do anything. Criticism came both from within and without the Liberal Party. David Lloyd George became celebrated for his attack on the government during a Commons debate on munitions production in December 1915 when he charged that 'the footsteps of the Allied forces have been dogged by the mocking spectre of "Too Late"'.[1] The deficiencies in prewar planning were considered greatest in the economic sphere. Never before had the state been forced to assume such extensive powers over finance, trade and transport. The normal play of market forces was suspended during the war, replaced by stringent controls administered by a greatly swollen bureaucracy. The Liberals were denounced as having been overly influenced by political principles. Stubborn adherence to ideals of free trade allegedly prevented serious consideration of war measures involving a high degree of state involvement in economic affairs.[2]

In recent times this critical assessment of the Liberal record has

begun to be revised. The assertion that prewar planning was significantly hampered by political ideology has been refuted. The expectation that Britain's contribution to any future war would follow a
traditional pattern that in the past had had little effect on the
economy, plus confidence that a war would be brief, are considered
reasons enough for the decision to allow business to proceed largely 'as
usual' in the event of war.[3] Had the Liberals nevertheless been guilty
of oversight? Even if convinced that no circumstances would arise that
would warrant government intervention, should they not have discussed the possibility and in the process provided future administrators with a fund of theoretical remedies? In at least one area of the
economy postwar criticism gives the impression that the prewar
government had been affected by severe myopia – food supply.

Of all the belligerents Britain has been said to have been the least
well-prepared to face the changes wrought by the war on food supply
and distribution patterns. The epitaph of 'The Too Late Government'
was, in fact, coined some months prior to Lloyd George's speech by
Sir Joseph Walton, Liberal Member of Parliament for Barnsley,
during a debate on the food supply.[4] According to the official history
of wartime food control published in 1928, government planners
barely touched on the subject of food before the war. The author
pointed out that the War Book, the compendium of contingency
measures prepared by the Committee of Imperial Defence (CID)
between 1910 and 1914, contained only one specific reference to food
– an order to the Board of Trade to begin collecting statistics at the
onset of war.[5]

The picture given by the official history is misleading. The War
Book was intended as a guide to departmental action during the first
few days of war only and cannot be taken as an indication of general
attitudes in the prewar period. As it happens, food supply in the event
of war attracted a good deal of attention from the CID and other
interested parties. Discussion was often spirited and, although few
concrete plans resulted, several key policies adopted during the war
originated in ideas aired at this time.

Given Britain's dependency on imported supplies it would have
been highly surprising had it been otherwise. On the eve of the First
World War two-thirds of Britain's food, measured in calories, came
from overseas. The nation's consequent vulnerability in the event of a
strong seaborne attack was heightened by the fact that the ratio of
imports to home-grown food was highest for the very narrow range of

staples eaten by the working classes, who constituted some 80 per cent of the population at that time. The foodstuff on which people depended most heavily was bread; four-fifths of the wheat eaten in Britain was grown abroad. Of other items that featured largely in working-class diets all of the sugar, four-fifths of the lard, three-quarters of the cheese, two-thirds of the bacon and a half of the condensed milk were imported. What little meat the working classes bought other than bacon also tended to be of foreign origin: frozen or chilled cuts imported from South America and Australasia were considerably cheaper than home-raised meat. British meat and fresh milk were relatively much more expensive before the First World War than they are today and were consumed mainly by the more affluent classes. Even home-produced meat and dairy products were tied to imports, however: Britain had to ship in over half of the barley, oats and oilcake fed to its livestock.[6]

Trends in demography and agriculture since the mid-nineteenth century both contributed to this dependency on imports and made the situation potentially more dangerous. After 1850 the population increased at a faster rate than ever before and became more urbanized. Including figures for predominantly rural Ireland, the population of the United Kingdom rose from 31 million in 1871 to 45 million in 1911. Towns, to which the bulk of the imported food flowed, also expanded at an unprecedented rate. By 1900 three-quarters of the British population lived in urban districts and were thus totally dependent for supplies on retail shops. In 1911 Greater London alone contained over 7½ million people, more than one-fifth of the entire population of England and Wales.[7]

In contrast, the ability of British farms to provide basic foodstuffs declined. In 1872 the United Kingdom had 24 million acres under crops, or 51.3 per cent of the cultivated area. By 1913 this had shrunk to 19½ million acres, or 41.6 per cent.[8] The most alarming aspect of these figures was the shift away from grain production, especially wheat. Some grainlands were used for other crops, particularly vegetables and market garden produce, but much was transformed into pasture. The collapse of world grain prices in the 1870s led British farmers, unprotected as they were by tariffs, to turn to livestock raising. Grazing proved much more remunerative. Prices for home-raised meat and dairy products remained steady in following years while cheap imports forced the prices of home-grown cereals down. Livestock also needed less labour to look after them. Land-

Table 1.1 *Origin of Britain's Wheat Imports (1911)*

Black Sea area (Russia, Turkey, Rumania)	35%
North America (Canada, United States)	30%
India	14%
South America (Argentina)	13%
Australasia (Australia, New Zealand)	8%

Source: The Times, 4 June 1912, p. 6.

lords, happy with the prospect of regular rents, encouraged their tenant farmers to grass over the land by issuing contracts containing penalties for unauthorized ploughing. In the years before the war many farmers let their crop rotations get longer and longer until many 'temporary' pastures became virtually permanent. Once under permanent grass it was unlikely that this land would be reploughed for crops as it would need several years' work to clean it of pests and weeds.

This agricultural transformation had important consequences for the nation's ability to produce food in time of emergency. Apart from the legal aspects and the temporary loss of income that would have been involved in reploughing, farmers would have found it difficult to find the extra men and horses to do the job. The shift to livestock had depleted the rural population at a speed the enclosures had never achieved. In 1871 there were 1,013,150 agricultural labourers in England and Wales; by 1914 only about 668,000 male and 36,000 female workers remained. Horses were the main source of haulage power on British farms in this period, but farmers generally kept only the minimum necessary for normal levels of cultivation and thus could not use their animals for extra ploughing without neglecting other essential tasks.[9]

The changes in agricultural patterns placed a tremendous burden on the nation's shipping. Much of the imported grain travelled extremely long distances. Britain was the greatest buyer of wheat in the world. Its purchases equalled three-quarters of the combined imports of wheat by Belgium, Italy, France, Holland, Switzerland and Brazil.[10] With bread the staple food of the population, there was clearly potential danger in any situation that threatened to interrupt free passage of cargo ships at their normal rate.

Fears about the country's ability to survive a future war with a major maritime power first emerged in the late 1890s. They became more widespread as Germany's naval strength increased in the twentieth century. Fiction communicated the 'starvation theory' to the public. The best-known author of such a work is Sir Arthur Conan Doyle, whose short story 'Danger' appeared in the *Strand Magazine* in July 1914. This gave a vivid account of Britain's abject surrender to a small state after a five-week war during which eight enemy submarines made short work of the country's food ships.[11]

The issue attracted early attention from both politicians and agricultural specialists. In April 1897 the subject was raised in the Commons by two Unionist MPs, H. Seton-Kerr and R. A. Yerburgh; and in September 1898 Professor Sir William Crookes of the Royal Society addressed himself to the problem at a meeting of the British Association for the Advancement of Science. It was not until the Boer War had impressed on the British the full sense of their isolation in the world, however, that a real movement got under way to assess and, if possible, to arrest the decline in domestic food production.

The Boer War confirmed a suspicion held by many in Britain in the latter part of the nineteenth century that the country's powers were in decline. Other, more vigorous, states were pressing forward, eager to assume Britain's role as the world's leading industrial and maritime nation. No longer confident that it could depend for its safety solely on the strength of its own far-flung economic and naval resources, Britain sought to repair its defences during the early twentieth century. The government found the answer in a new system of international alliances that limited Britain's commitments in the world. The long-held policy of 'Splendid Isolation' was jettisoned and diplomatic links forged with France, Russia and Japan. Some people felt, however, that better protection was afforded by stronger ties with an existing multinational association, the Empire.

As a unit, imperialists argued, the Empire could be self-sufficient. What Britain did not produce itself in the way of food or raw materials could be obtained from one of the other member nations, to mutual advantage, but for such a system to be viable, it needed protection from foreign competition in the form of tariffs. Abandoned in the 1840s, preferential tariffs had continued to exert an attraction, especially among Unionists (at core the Conservative Party), though they had not been able to make headway against prevailing free trade policies of both Liberal and Unionist governments in the second half of the nineteenth century. In the aftermath of the Boer War, however, imperial preference took on new lustre and, after some initial hesitation, Unionists rallied strongly to a campaign launched in 1903 by Joseph Chamberlain for tariff reform. Among Chamberlain's supporters were a number of Conservative and Liberal Unionists who were to play an important part in developing Britain's food policies during the war, notably Lord Milner, Lord Selborne and Charles Bathurst.

One early and ardent campaigner for tariff reform was Henry Chaplin, President of the Board of Agriculture in the second Salisbury administration. Chaplin tried to gain sympathy for imperial preference by drawing attention to shortcomings in the national food supply system. In 1903 he chaired an investigation by a committee of the Tariff Commission into British agriculture and produced a report that compared the country's growing dependence on imported foodstuffs with the self-sufficiency of other nations – a situation, the committee argued, that was not only a threat to national security but hurt the industrial worker as well.[12] Chaplin followed up this inquiry by spearheading a campaign for an official study. The organization through which he worked was the Association to Promote an Official Inquiry into the Security of Our Food Supply in Time of War, which attracted the support not only of Unionist imperialists, but of Liberal free traders, businessmen and Labour spokesmen, all of whom were worried about the possible effect on the economy of another war. They had little trouble persuading the government to appoint a Royal Commission to look into the whole question.

The Commission's report, issued in 1905, has been described in a perjorative sense as 'the "Bible" and text-book' of Britain's rulers in August 1914.[13] Since it allegedly threw a pall of restraint over the Liberal government's approach to the food question at the beginning of the war, it should be noted that the inquiry was ordered by the ruling Unionist government. The attitudes expressed by the majority of the Commission were the prevailing sentiments of the time rather than those of one particular political party.

To a certain extent the investigation served the purposes of Chaplin's association admirably. The great dependence of the country on imported supplies and the potential consequences of the situation were thoroughly examined. Yet no practical remedial measures emerged. The Commission concluded that nothing could be done to reverse the trend of agricultural change and that the power of the Royal Navy sufficed to protect the ships that brought in the country's supplies. The sole constructive recommendations made were that better records be kept of food stocks and that an insurance plan be prepared to indemnify shippers against loss by enemy attack.

As would be the case until well into the war, it had proved impossible to discuss the issue solely on its merits. It could not be divorced from the political controversies of the period. The verdict of the Commission was a vindication for the views of the free traders in both major parties. Would their victory have been less complete, one wonders, if the case for preparedness had been pressed by a more moderate advocate than the protectionist Chaplin? Chamberlain's tariff reform initially brought disharmony to Unionist ranks and drove substantial numbers of 'free fooders' into the arms of the Liberals.

Although the outcome of the investigation was disappointing from the tariff reformers' point of view, it provided valuable service for the future by publicly airing a number of ideas. One controversial proposal was the situation of agricultural production by state subsidies in the form of guaranteed prices paid to farmers. This suggestion had been made first in a pamphlet circulated in 1903 by Theodore Angier, a shipowner and vice-president of the Tariff Reform League, Brighton.[14] The Commission considered it socialistic and it received short shrift. Greater interest was shown in the idea of accumulating reserve stocks of wheat as this would entail little direct involvement by the state and was relatively easy to achieve in peacetime. Moreover, although those inclined towards more radical action, such as members of the Central Chamber of Agriculture, wanted national granaries built, others would have been satisfied with the official encouragement of private or village-owned stores. None the less, the Commission ultimately decided against the step on the grounds that reserves might discourage the normal import trade.[15]

In 1903 labour representatives cited the possible 'distress and misery, and semi-starvation amongst the working classes' as their reason for joining the movement to gain an official hearing on food supply in the event of war, and by 1917 the political and social implications of fluctuations in the supply and price of food would be well appreciated.[16] In 1905, however, this aspect of the question was deemed of minor significance. Many witnesses spoke on the subject to the Commission. It was generally recognized that prices would rise sharply at the outset of war, causing hardships to the poorer sector of the community, particularly unskilled labourers. The Commission was warned of riots in cities if bread, especially, was priced out of the

reach of a substantial number of people. Such a situation might force
the government to end a war prematurely to avoid revolution. The
Commission replied that charity would take care of the needy, while
'the working class would bear its privations with fortitude out of
patriotism'.[17]

A trade union representative pointed out at this juncture that the
unionized twentieth-century workman was far different from the
unorganized labourer of the Crimean War period, but his argument
went unheeded. Others shared his suspicion that the Commission
was envisaging not a future war but some conflict in the distant past.
R. E. Prothero, who as President of the Board of Agriculture in 1917
and 1918 was to put into effect several of the suggestions under
discussion in 1905, felt that the Commission was obsessed with the
Napoleonic Wars. The reliance on the Navy to protect imports and
on high prices to curb consumption did indeed invite that comparison. The similarity was not lost on others, but, as one observer later
pointed out, the French blockade had been designed to cut off
imports of merchandize not food. Moreover, the population of
Britain, only 10 million at the beginning of the nineteenth century,
had been almost self-sufficient in food, importing no meat at all and
only 5 per cent of its wheat.[18] The policy of ploughing extra land for
grain, the aim of Angier's state farm subsidy, itself dated back to
Tudor times.

A more modern approach to the food supply question was introduced into the hearings by the nutritionist, Dr Robert Hutchinson,
who stressed that any adequate assessment of the issue must be based
on the physiological needs of the community. The aim should be to
maintain the army and workforce at their most efficient and productive level. Food was the fuel of the soldier and factory worker in the
same way that ammunition and coal served the military and industrial machines. He urged government intervention to assure a steady
flow of the cheapest, most efficient source of human energy – bread.
Next in importance were protein sources such as meat, supplies of
which should also be regulated. In the light of subsequent events, it
is interesting to note that Hutchinson deprecated early attention to
sugar. Despite its high calorie content, he pointed out, other foods
were far more essential. His testimony went totally disregarded. This
was not really surprising. The members of the Commission, to one of
whom the term 'calorie' had to be explained, lacked the scientific
knowledge necessary to appreciate his advice. Indeed, the concepts

he raised were so new that only a minority of the medical profession subscribed to them fully.

At the end of 1905 the Unionists were swept out of office by the Liberals and legislators were soon absorbed in social welfare schemes and naval estimates. It was several years before supply in war again attracted official attention. In January 1909 H. H. Asquith, the Liberal Prime Minister and head of the CID, received a letter from Sir Frederick Bolton, a shipowner and former chairman of Lloyd's. Bolton was concerned about the possible effect of a war on the economy in general and about the danger to the country's food supplies should a war with Germany result in the closure of Britain's eastern ports. He urged the government to prepare plans for that contingency.[19] The possibility that Germany might blockade the North Sea ports had been considered before. Only the previous September the director of naval intelligence had produced a memorandum on that very subject.[20] It was not thought likely that Germany would take such a step, however, and Bolton's suggestion met with a cool response.

At the start of 1909 the Prime Minister, like most members of his party, viewed the threat of war with Germany as remote. Leading Liberals condemned such predictions as utter nonsense spread for political reasons by the Opposition. The President of the Board of Trade, Winston Churchill, speaking at Swansea on 17 August 1908, declared himself 'astonished and grieved' by the 'wild language' of people who ought to have known better. 'I think it is greatly to be deprecated', he said, 'that persons should try to spread the belief in this country that war between Great Britain and Germany is inevitable'.[21] It was only because of pressure from the Unionists that Asquith agreed to a review of defence preparations by the CID that year. In contrast to A. J. Balfour, the Unionist leader who had founded the CID, Asquith lacked interest in questions of defence and in the activities of the CID in general. He was not prepared to launch an official defence programme on the basis of Bolton's letter alone. The CID, itself a product of the spate of concern about national safety that had followed the Boer War, was, in addition, not designed to make a study of the matter at that time. It was not until the end of 1910, after several years of skirmishes between the CID and both the Admiralty and the War Office over strategic policy, that the CID was transformed into a body of technical committees that routinely took on investigations into a wide range of defence questions.[22]

Asquith had no objection, however, to Bolton conducting a private inquiry. Bolton's report reached the Prime Minister the following December. It outlined weaknesses in transport and dock facilities in the west and south of the country that could lead to the collapse of distribution if too much traffic was diverted to them from the east. The effect that could have on the big industrial cities, he stressed, was dreadful to contemplate. London's warehouses normally contained only a one-week reserve of provisions.[23]

Asquith was impressed enough with Bolton's findings to circulate his report to the members of the CID for discussion on 24 February 1910. However, in a typical response to possibly controversial matters, the Prime Minister took steps to delay a decision on it. After conceding that the maintenance of food distribution in time of war was of great importance, he read to the committee a letter from Sir George Murray, Joint Permanent Secretary of the Treasury, suggesting the need for further information before acting on Bolton's data.[24] In intervening, Murray was only doing his job. Examination of the CID's proceedings was undertaken routinely by the Treasury. It was a means of controlling government spending by challenging at their conception schemes necessitating a high degree of involvement by the state. The Treasury had been given this task in 1905 by the Unionists, who at this time were more opposed than the Liberals to the state taking on extra responsibilities. Government spending had risen rapidly since the turn of the century, prompting fears that it would soon outstrip national revenues. In 1910 the Treasury was the hub of the administrative system. Its nineteenth-century ideals of retrenchment were gradually being undermined by twentieth-century calls for social welfare programmes and higher defence spending, but it still retained the power to curb government expenditure in areas not sponsored strongly by members of the Cabinet. Murray, who with his co-Secretary Sir Edward Hamilton has been described as 'as firmly Gladstonian' as the Treasury itself, carried a good deal of weight with the CID, which readily endorsed the appointment of a sub-committee to consider whether the matter of food supply should be pursued.[25] The ensuing delay proved short, however. In June Colonel J. E. B. Seely, the Under Secretary of State for the Colonies, was asked to head an inquiry into the safeguarding of the distribution of food and raw materials in time of war.

While Seely's committee, of which Bolton was a member, deliberated at some length, two incidents occurred that made the inquiry particularly timely. From June to August 1911 Britain was racked by labour disputes of such intensity that it was feared they would escalate into a national strike. The greatest alarm was occasioned by a railway strike in mid-August that brought the entire transport system of the industrial Midlands and north of England to a halt. Since the railways were the main carriers of food to the cities at this time, the consequences could have been serious if the strike had not been called off after forty-eight hours. Meanwhile, in July of the same year Germany dispatched a gunboat to the Moroccan port of Agadir, arousing widespread fears in Europe that war was imminent and causing the Liberal leadership to revise its thinking on defence.

Churchill, now Home Secretary, underwent a complete change of heart about a threat from the east. The violence that had accompanied the summer's strikes also foreboded ill for a disruption of food supplies in a national emergency. A long talk with Bolton had convinced him, Churchill wrote to Reginald McKenna, the First Lord of the Admiralty, on 13 September, that 'the maintenance of the food supply in time of war and the prices resulting from its insecurity, touch public order very closely'. Order, he continued, depended 'almost exclusively on the poorer people being able to purchase a certain minimum amount of the staple foods, especially bread, at prices which they can afford; and the Government will be forced to secure them this ration at all costs, paying themselves the difference in some form or another between the normal and war prices'.[26] He urged McKenna to help Bolton campaign for contingency plans.

Seely's committee made its first report in November 1911. It had concerned itself mainly with the capabilities of the railways, but it had some important comments to make on the overall preparedness of the nation to maintain its food supplies in war. The committee recommended that firm action be taken to minimize the impact of war by improvements to the transportation network, the collection of data on agricultural production and the preparation of plans for the regulation of cereal supplies. If the government was not prepared to control food distribution in time of war, the committee warned, the country could face a severe domestic upheaval.[27] The final report, issued in June 1912, went further. It advised that a central office be set up to handle all questions of food if a war occurred. The responsibility should devolve first on the Prime Minister, who would then delegate the matter either to the Board of Trade or preferably to a standing co-ordinating body.[28] These reports were not well-received by some

members of the CID. The Prime Minister declared himself unable to
make head or tail of the interim report and this 'muddleheaded
document', as one staff member called it, was 'unmercifully damned
in a trenchant minute' by the First Sea Lord Sir Arthur Wilson.
However, Seely's friend Winston Churchill argued so persuasively in
the report's favour at the meeting of the CID called to discuss it that
the Treasury was immediately alerted to the need 'to put on the
brake'.[29]

The reports had several noteworthy consequences. Although no
mention of it was made in the War Book, the standing co-ordinating
body that Seely called for – the Cabinet Committee on Food Supplies
– started work immediately war broke out. It was probably in
response to this suggestion too that responsibility for sugar supplies
was assigned to the Home Secretary. McKenna, who exchanged
offices with Churchill at the end of September 1911, was ready to take
over the importation of sugar on behalf of the state at the very
beginning of August 1914. Two important steps on related questions
were also taken as a result of the Seely committee's findings. Asquith
speedily endorsed Seely's recommendation that plans be prepared for
the regulation of railway traffic in the event of war. The Treasury
heartily approved too, and Seely was asked to supervise the drafting of
a scheme. The revival of the proposal for a national insurance plan for
shipowners met with considerable opposition, however, particularly
from the Treasury. It was nevertheless agreed to appoint a sub-
committee led by Churchill to look into the question. In addition,
Seely felt that the committee's mandate had not allowed the subject of
how the civilian population would be fed if seaborne supplies were
disrupted, to be fully explored, and he was able to persuade Asquith
not to let the matter drop after the committee presented its final
report, but to appoint a body to keep the question under continuous
review.[30] A standing sub-committee headed by Walter Runciman,
the President of the Board of Agriculture, took on the job in August
1912.

While the factors affecting imported supplies tended to monopolize
the CID's attention, the other side of the food question – agricultural
production – had not been neglected. The revelations about the
decline of British agriculture made after the Boer War spurred a
number of studies that provided a wealth of statistics and an improved
understanding of problem areas without which later efforts to increase
output would have been much more difficult. The studies included a

report on the loss of employment in agriculture, which appeared in 1906; a report on agricultural education, published in 1908; the country's first-ever comprehensive statistics on agricultural output, issued in 1912 covering 1908; data on the types of work done by the Board of Agriculture; a private series of investigations by a group of agricultural specialists, published between 1910 and 1912; and the examination of agricultural conditions by both the Unionist and Liberal Parties.[31]

In 1912, the year following Agadir, both parties decided to revise their agricultural policies. The Unionists were the more daring. In August 1912 the Committee on Unionist Land Policy voted to include in their 1913 political manifesto proposals for the state maintenance of food supplies in wartime, the control of food prices (especially bread), and the promotion of cereal production by a guarantee to farmers of a minimum price of 35/- per quarter for wheat.[32] The Unionists' plan of action, which became known as 'The Blue Pamphlet', was a response to their opponents' Rural Land Policy prepared by the Liberal Land Enquiry Committee. With the exception of the measures cited above, the two programmes were very similar. The aim was a general stimulus for farming. Among the promises made were a minimum agricultural wage, regular hours of labour, better housing in rural areas, the allocation of allotments, and security of tenure for tenant farmers.[33]

Competition for the rural vote accounted in part for this heightened attention to agriculture. Politics were in the doldrums. Elections held in January and December 1910 had left the two main parties with roughly equal representation in Parliament. This doomed the Liberal government to dependency on Labour and Irish Home Rule MPs to stay in office, and the Unionists to frustration at their continued failure to regain the reins of power. The Unionist Party especially needed to renew its basis of support in the country. Imperial preference, which had been adopted as an official plank in 1907, was now causing division within Unionist ranks because of its failure to win votes. An increasing number of Unionists wanted the party to widen its appeal to the electorate by adoption of a fuller political programme. State support for agriculture, it was hoped, was the way to satisfy the die-hards of tariff reform and to attract voters at the same time. The opportunities were there. Farmers were complaining that Parliament was ignoring their interests. Tenant farmers, who had banded together in 1908 in the fast growing and aggressive National Farmers' Union, were particularly under-represented in the House.

Table 1.2 *Production of Staples*

	United Kingdom			Germany		
	1893	*1913*	*Per cent Change*	*1893*	*1913*	*Per cent Change*
Area under cultivation	13,987,000 acres	12,797,000 acres	−9	42,175,000 acres	45,414,000 acres	+8
Wheat (quarters)	7,597,000	7,175,000	−6	14,523,000	20,023,000	+38
Barley (quarters)	9,617,000	7,276,000	−24	13,338,000	19,186,000	+44
Oats (quarters)	21,023,000	20,600,000	−2	33,505,000	60,187,000	+80
Potatoes (tons)	5,634,000	5,726,000	+2	27,539,000	49,403,000	+79

Source: National Unionist Association, *Gleanings and Memoranda*, Vol. XLIII (July–December 1914), 52–33.

Growing distrust of Germany's intentions also focused attention on British farming methods. Recent research has challenged suggestions that Germany purposely adapted its agricultural sector for war in the years before 1914. It is maintained that German policies were dictated by internal politics.[34] None the less, contemporary observers in Britain and France found it ominous when the German government openly took steps to make the German Empire as self-sufficient in food as possible. Behind a wall of tariffs that protected them from international competition, German farmers were encouraged by their government to produce food that provided the highest *calorie* output possible. British farmers, under a *laissez-faire* system, concentrated on making the most *profit* per acre. Production of staples was much higher in Germany. Of the cultivated area, 46 per cent was under grain and 10.5 per cent under potatoes in Germany compared to 19.5 per cent and 1.5 per cent in Britain.[35] Germany's farmers were told to raise the most economic animals. Scientists had found that 44 per cent of the calories eaten by pigs were returned as human food; calves and cows also gave good returns. German farmers were therefore discouraged from raising beef cattle and sheep, the animals most kept by British farmers. Agricultural yields had been rising steadily in all the developed countries for decades, but the concentration of scientific research on this problem had given Germany a clear lead over Britain. By 1914 Germany was producing nearly 90 per cent of its food.[36]

The Germans were jubilant at the success of their agricultural policy and talked openly about the significance of the development. Prince von Bülow, described by one British diplomat as the country's bitterest enemy, made sneering comparisons between the German achievements and Britain's performance, and the German economist

Dr Felix Somary predicted that physical sustenance would be the most vital issue in the next European war. Germany later defended its submarine attacks on Allied merchant ships on the grounds that before the war Britain and France had frequently referred to the idea of 'starving Germany out,' but Germany made similar threats against Britain. At the Annual Congress of the Pan German League at Erfurt in September 1912 Admiral von Breusing stated that 'in case of war with Great Britain the interception of the British food supplies must become one of the first objects of Germany'.[37]

Confidence that the might of the Royal Navy would safeguard the British merchant fleet from such an attack had been the basis of British defence policy for years and was a major reason why contingency plans covering supply rarely got further than discussion. It contributed strongly to the outcome of the Royal Commission's inquiry into supply in 1905. Some extravagant statements were made at that time. Citing the American Civil War, Commander-of-the-Fleet Sir John Hopkins declared blockades to be out of date, and a former director of naval intelligence, Sir Cyprian Bridge, assured the Commission that one British cruiser could deflect any enemy attack on commercial shipping.[38]

Such complacency began to be challenged in 1907 when a long-running feud between Admiral Lord Charles Beresford and the First Sea Lord, Admiral Sir John Fisher, erupted into a controversy involving the Admiralty, the War Office, the CID and the Cabinet over naval preparedness for a future war and Beresford's proposals for an Admiralty War Staff.[39] The dreadnought debates of 1908 and 1909 similarly focused attention on the question of naval defences. After Agadir, when suspicions of Germany's intentions were at their height, doubts about the Royal Navy's capability to come up to expectations were being voiced in several quarters. In its interim report the Seely committee questioned whether the Navy could adequately safeguard even coastal shipping. The Unionists brought up the subject regularly in Parliament and at public meetings. A major shortcoming, they charged, was the Admiralty's possession of only 115 cruisers to protect trade routes although one naval expert had estimated that the country needed 180 to protect merchant shipping and another 100 to serve the fleet.[40] A committee of inquiry appointed by the London Chamber of Commerce early in 1913 raised much the same points. Changes in the relative strength and disposition of the British fleet, it warned, merited the most serious attention. The committee cited inadequate protective measures taken by the Navy, the lack of cruisers available to protect trade routes, and the failure to equip liners with defensive weapons as some of the reasons for concern.[41]

The Navy did not lack champions and criticism of it paradoxically tended to weaken the hand of those hoping to commit the government to food controls in the event of war. Legitimate doubts about the Navy's ability to protect imports got lost in a concurrent argument between the naval and military chiefs of staff over whether Britain should support its continental allies by sending a large conscript army to the battlefront or whether the Navy would provide the country's main contribution in a future war as it had traditionally done in the past. Navalists used the issue of supply as a weapon against the militarists. In March 1913, for example, the Secretary of the CID, Maurice Hankey, warned Seely, then head of the War Office, that the raising of a continental-sized army could subject the British population to destitution and starvation by withdrawing supplies from the civilian market. The country should rely as usual on a strong Navy, which would protect both supplies and the country from attack.[42]

This loss of focus on food supply as a distinct issue in its own right was reflected in the report of the final CID sub-committee to consider the matter before the war, the standing sub-committee appointed in August 1912 to pick up where the Seely committee had left off. It was headed by Walter Runciman, an able but lack-lustre administrator who embodied the old Liberal doctrine of 'Peace, Retrenchment and Reform'. Despite the Agadir incident, he believed a war with Germany to be unlikely. Indeed, he told a public meeting on 25 October 1912 that he saw no reason for Britain to be involved in a war anywhere in the world in the forseeable future.[43]

The Runciman committee conscientiously assessed the capacity of all the major ports in the south and west to handle cargoes diverted from the east, gathered accurate statistics on imports and weighed the consequences of a suspension of trade with Baltic and North Sea countries. More than a quarter of imported foodstuffs were found to come from these sources, but since these accounted for a negligible amount of wheat and only 10 per cent of imported oats, their loss was not judged to be of significance. The committee's report, issued in February 1914, was an expression of its chairman's own strong navalist views. It returned the position on supply to where it had stood in 1905. Referring to the recent experience of the Balkan nations, the committee advised the government not to fix food prices in time of war. The higher prices expected in the initial war period would fall as new sources of supply were found; in past wars the country's trade had always increased. 'By maintaining a general control of sea communications,' the committee contended, 'this country should, in the future as in the past, be able to bear the exhausting consequences of war ... better than continental countries.'[44]

During the last few months of peace the sessions of the CID sub-committee all too often ended in trivial discussions of chimerical cure-alls. One subject on which too much time was spent was the Channel Tunnel. It was believed that the tunnel would take only three years to build and its supporters claimed that it would enable Britain to tap the resources of the Mediterranean and the Black Sea overland. Whether the French railways could support such a burden and what might be happening in northern France in a future war apparently did not occur to the project's proponents.[45]

The debate on the food supply was still in progress when war was declared at the beginning of August 1914. Although the country's administrators did not totally lack guidance – the Cabinet Committee on Food Supplies, McKenna's sugar purchasing organization and various other committees got to work immediately – no overall scheme for putting the entire food supply on a war footing had been prepared. It is impossible to say whether later difficulties might have been avoided or mitigated if plans for food control had been drafted before the war. The probability is that they would not. Germany's experience was to show that years of agricultural development and speedy introduction of controls over prices and consumption were no guarantee of success. Under war conditions Germany's production and distribution patterns broke down more quickly than Britain's. Britain benefited not only from the lessons offered by the German food administration, but from the British government's procrastination in regulating supplies. Public opinion was always well ahead of legislation and this provided an atmosphere of acceptance that eased the introduction of controls and made them more likely to be effective.

Notes: Chapter 1

1   D. Lloyd George, *The Great Crusade* (New York, 1918), p. 16.
2   E. M. H. Lloyd, *Experiments in State Control at the War Office and the Ministry of Food* (Oxford, 1924), p. 21.

3 For a discussion of this theme see D. French, *British Economic and Strategic Planning, 1905–1915* (London, 1982).

4 S. J. Hurwitz, *State Intervention in Great Britain: A Study of Economic Control and Social Response, 1914–1919* (New York, 1949), p. 205; *Hansard*, vol.74 HC Deb., 5s., 23 September 1915, col. 630.

5 Sir W. H. Beveridge, *British Food Control* (London, 1928), p. 5.

6 Ibid., p. 359; E. H. Whetham, *The Agrarian History of England and Wales*, vol. 8, *1914–1939* (Cambridge, 1978), p. 15; P. Mathias, *Retailing Revolution* (London, 1967), pp. 17–26.

7 Mathias, *Retailing Revolution*, pp. 4–7.

8 Sir A. D. Hall, *Agriculture After the War* (London, 1920), p. 85.

9 Board of Trade, Industrial (War Inquiries) Branch, *Report on the State of Employment in Agriculture in Great Britain at the End of January 1919* (London, 1920), p. 3; Whetham, *Agrarian History*, p. 59.

10 Sir R. H. Rew, 'The prospects of the world's food supplies after the war'. *Journal of the Royal Statistical Society*, vol. 81 (March 1918), p. 43.

11 For more on the starvation theory see V. R. Easterling, 'Great Britain's peril and the convoy controversy: a study of the intended effects of unrestricted U-boat warfare and the convoy system as a countermeasure, World War One'. PhD thesis, University of Colorado, 1951, p. 49.

12 W. A. S. Hewins, *The Apologia of an Imperialist: Forty Years of Empire Policy*, vol. 1, (London, 1929), p. 107.

13 Royal Commission on the Supply of Food and Raw Material in Time of War, *Report*, Cd 2643, *Evidence*, Cd 2644, *Appendices*, CD 2645 (1905); F. H. Coller, *A State Trading Adventure* (London, 1925), p. 4.

14 T. V. S. Angier, *Our Food Supplies in the Time of War* (London, 1903), p. 9.

15 Sir. W. Crookes, *The Wheat Problem* (London, 1918), p. 93; Sir J. Rennell Rood, *Social and Diplomatic Memories*, vol. 3 (London, 1922–5), p. 191.

16 Royal Commission on the Supply of Food, Cd 2645, *Appendix 49*, 'Papers issued by the Association to promote an official inquiry into the security of our food supply in time of war', p. 356.

17 Cd 2645, p. 43.

18 R. E. Prothero (Lord Ernle), 'The food campaign of 1916–18', *Journal of the Royal Agricultural Society of England*, vol. 82 (1921), p. 10; C. H. Firth, *Then and Now: or A Comparision Between the War With Napoloen and the Present War* (London, 1918), p. 20.

19 Report of sub-committee to consider the desirability of an enquiry into the question of local transport and distribution of food supplies in time of war, 22 March 1910, Appendix 1, Sir Frederick Bolton to the Prime Minister, 19 January 1909, CAB 38/16/5, Cabinet Papers, Public Record Office (PRO).

20 French, *British Economic and Strategic Planning*, p. 55.

21 Quoted by R. S. Churchill, *Winston S. Churchill*, vol. 2 (Boston, 1966–7), pp. 493–4.

22 N. D'Ombrain, *War Machinery and High Policy: Defence Administration in Peacetime Britain 1902–1914* (London, 1973), pp. 250, 264.

23 Report of sub-committee, 22 March 1910, Appendix 2, Preliminary report by Sir Frederick Bolton, 7 December 1909, CAB 38/16/5.

24 Minutes of 105 meeting of the Committee of Imperial Defence (CID), 24 February 1910, CAB 2/2/105.

25 R. Jenkins, *Asquith* (London, 1964), p. 160.

26 Quoted by R. S. Churchill, *Winston S. Churchill*, vol. 2, pp. 514–5.

27 Report of a sub-committee of the CID on the local transportation and distribution of supplies in time of war, 1 November 1911, pp. 3–4, CAB 38/19/51.

28 Report of the standing sub-committee of the CID on the internal distribution of supplies in time of war, 20 June 1912, Appendix 10, Internal distribution of supplies in time of war, p. 51, CAB 38/21/22.

29 Major Adrian Grant-Duff, Journal entries for 13 November 1911, 1 December 1911, 16 December 1911, 19 December 1911, Grant-Duff Papers, Churchill College, Cambridge.

30 J. E. B. Seely to H. H. Asquith, 14 September 1911; Asquith to Seely, 15 September 1911; M. Hankey to Seely, 2 July 1912; A. Grant-Duff to Seely, 9 August 1912. All in Box 11, Mottistone Papers, Nuffield College, Oxford.

31 Whetham, *Agrarian History*, p. 1.

32 H. Hayes Fisher to W. H. Long, 1 August 1912, 27/1/17, A. Bonar Law Papers, House of Lords Record Office.

33 'The blue pamphlet', *Liberal Magazine*, vol. 21 (November 1913), pp. 641–2.

34 G. Hardach, *The First World War 1914–1918* (Berkeley, CA, 1977), p. 111.

35 Editorial notes, Board of Agriculture, *Journal*, vol. 25 (February 1919), p. 1261.

36 G. B. Roorbach, 'The world's food supply', *Annals of the American Academy of Political and Social Science*, vol. 74, no. 163 (November 1917), p. 3.

37 Sir. C. Spring-Rice to Sir A. Chamberlain, 9 January 1908. Quoted by Chamberlain, *Politics From Inside* (New Haven, CT, 1937), p. 95; C. H. Kenderine, *Food Supply in War Time* (London, 1913), footnote, p. 8; Professor P. Eltzbacher, *Germany's Food: Can It Last?*, S. R. Wells (ed.), (London, 1915), p. 2; C. Bathurst, *To Avoid National Starvation* (London, 1912), footnote p. 7.

38 Royal Commission on the Supply of Food, Cd 2643, *Report*, pp. 28–9.

39 D'Ombrain, *War Machinery*, pp. 231–4.

40 *The Times*, 25 January 1912.

41 London Chamber of Commerce, *Report of the Special Committee to the Council of the Chamber: Food Supplies in Time of War* (London, 1914), pp. 8–9.

42 Hankey to Seely, 15 March 1913, Box 12, Mottistone Papers.

43 *The Times*, 26 October 1912.

44 Report of the standing sub-committee of the CID on supplies in time of war, 12 February 1914, pp. 25–6, CAB 38/26/7.

45 Ibid., and subsequent meetings; Sir A. Conan Doyle, *Great Britain and the Next War* (London, 1913), p. 41.

2
Initial Responses to War. The Focus on Supply

The motto 'Business As Usual' has become indelibly associated with that period of the First World War between August 1914 and May 1915. Although used disparagingly to describe the policies of the incumbent Liberal government, the phrase originated not in the economic philosophy of one political party but in general contemporary ideas about the position of civilians in wartime. In 1914 most people were of the opinion that war was not something that closely involved the ordinary person. War was waged by professionals, usually far away. The best help the public could give in the emergency was to continue conscientiously with its normal daily routine. Conversely, it was the duty of the government to retain the greatest possible semblance of normality in everyday life. Those unavoidable expansions of the state's authority brought by the war to domestic areas such as finance and shipping were not expected to touch the life of the average citizen to any inconvenient extent.

As the prewar debate indicated, opinion was not unanimous. A minority of concerned individuals believed that the government should do more to organize the domestic economy for war than tradition dictated. On what should be done and how far the government should go, there was little agreement. People who advocated an increase of the state's powers in one area did not necessarily approve interference in another. Nor was support for government action confined to any one political party or group. Interventionists could be found in Liberal ranks as well as among the Unionists and Socialists. It has been said that attitudes towards state intervention during the early part of the First World War fell into two groups – 'freedom' and 'organization'.[1] Thinking on the issue tended to end more frequently in varying degrees of ambivalence, however, than to crystallize into two clearly opposed points of view.

The evolution of food policies during the first six months of the war reflected this fluidity of opinion. Contrary to the picture presented by postwar critics, the Liberals were by no means uniformly *laissez-faire* in their approach, nor did their political adversaries press for intervention in all areas of food supply that were ultimately subjected to state control. It was a transitional period in which some of the problems that were to beset the country's food supply started to develop. Not yet at such a critical stage that they warranted unquestionable large-scale intervention by the government, these problems nevertheless stimulated experimentation with a number of nontraditional solutions.

The question of how much the government was prepared to do was closely linked to estimates of how long the war would last. Since the war was expected to be soon over, the authorities believed that intervention was justified only where it was likely to be short-term and the effect on the economy transitory. Importation of wheat and sugar on state account met these requirements. The Liberals refrained, on the other hand, from long-term commitments that could have a lasting impact on national life, such as the subsidization of agriculture.

The administrative machinery for handling the food supply followed the same pattern as that devised to organize the war effort in general. The declaration of war on 4 August was followed by a flurry of activity as *ad hoc* committees were appointed to carry out emergency procedures. There were two types of committee: Cabinet committees, consisting of varying numbers of Cabinet ministers with civil service and civilian advisors at their disposal, and advisory committees, made up solely of outside experts. Cabinet committees were an established means of spreading the government's workload and possessed the authority to draft official policy for Cabinet approval. Advisory committees were either just that, as in the case of the Consultative Agricultural Committee, or bodies formed to execute orders emanating from the Cabinet. The number of committees grew rapidly: there were twenty on 20 August, thirty-eight by 1 January 1915. No less than five of these dealt with some aspect of the food supply.[2]

Chief among these food committees was the Cabinet Committee on Food Supplies. It was chaired by Reginald McKenna, the Home Secretary, who was assisted by Walter Runciman, now President of the Board of Trade, Edwin Montagu, Financial Secretary at the Treasury; and Lord Lucas, previously Parliamentary Secretary to the

Board of Agriculture under Runciman and the latter's successor there. Little is known about the day-to-day workings of this committee. As was the case with the Cabinet itself at this time, the committee kept no records of its meetings and issued no reports. This dearth of documentation led to assumptions that the committee ceased to exist after February 1915, but in fact it continued work until the formation of the Ministry of Food in December 1916.

The Cabinet Committee's purpose was to oversee the various steps being taken to maintain the supply and distribution of foodstuffs and to devise general food policy. In theory, its powers were impressive. The Secretary of the CID, Maurice Hankey, whose job it was to co-ordinate the work of the war committees to the best of his abilities, described the Cabinet Committee on Food Supplies as 'practically an executive body ... with full discretion to take action without reference to the Cabinet'.[3] In reality, because the Prime Minister insisted on all major decisions being sanctioned by the whole Cabinet, and because the Committee lacked the authority to enforce the co-operation of other units dealing in foodstuffs, such as the War Office, the Cabinet Committee's ability to direct and control was limited.

It was Asquith who delineated its first goal: a constant supply of food at cheap or reasonable prices.[4] This intrinsically desirable aim posed a problem. The last sub-committee of the CID to consider food supply before the war – the Runciman committe – had warned the government not to do anything that might discourage importers. This especially meant not limiting prices in Britain to levels lower than those prevailing in the world market. Government spokesmen were already assuring business men publicly that no official action would be taken that would interfere with the free play of market forces. All four of the Committee's members adhered to these general principles. Thinking as they did, could they fulfill both parts of the Prime Minister's instructions?

The committee decided to concentrate on supply, and by this they meant imported supplies. They believed that reasonable prices would automatically follow if a constant supply of goods was maintained. Runciman outlined this policy in the Commons on 8 August. Far from being deprecated, he said, rising prices should be welcomed for the attraction they offered to importers and 'speculators' to provide the country with supplies.[5]

Postwar writers criticized this decision as inappropriately stemming from peacetime economic orthodoxy. This was blamed largely on the President of the Board of Trade, who was said to have determined the approach of the Asquithian governments to food supply questions until December 1916.[6] To suggest that Runciman was responsible for whatever shortcomings in the handling of the food supply were later felt to exist is not only unfair but inaccurate. Runciman generally acted as the Cabinet Committee's spokesman and consequently came to be associated most closely with its decisions, but his statements represented the collective view of the Committee and were firmly backed by the Prime Minister and the majority of his colleagues. The policy of placing supplies first was sound common sense, given Britain's high proportion of foreign-produced foodstuffs. It was endorsed by a number of contemporary experts. J. M. Keynes, a young economist attached to the Treasury, pointed out that to curb prices before supplies were assured would result in a disastrous diversion of trade away from the United Kingdom. Herbert Hoover, wartime Food Administrator of the United States, similarly placed supply before prices. One can even find a measure of sympathy on the left: Sidney Webb admitted that prices had to be kept attractive to importers.[7] Germany's experiences from very early in the war plus the situation in Britain in 1917, when prices were fixed before controls over supplies had been fully established, bear out the Cabinet Committee's caution.

The activities of the Cabinet Committee on Food Supplies and other official bodies connected with food supply show that behind a façade of 'business as usual', which was there to sustain confidence among the general public, the authorities were quick to divest themselves of qualms against interference in the economy where a shortfall in supply appeared likely if free trade continued. In only one area of the economy did the government show an uncompromising reluctance to intervene and to continue in this policy past the point where prudent caution gave way to lost opportunity or, in the minds of some, negligence. This was agriculture.

It has been commented that what Britain lacked at the beginning of the war was not strictly a food supply policy but a food production policy.[8] In fact, by 24 August the government had been presented with one by the Agricultural Consultative Committee, which had been formed on 10 August to offer advice to farmers on how they could best help the war effort and to recommend general agricultural policy to the government during the emergency. No government officials sat on the committee, which was purely advisory. Its chairman was Sir Ailwyn Fellowes, an important Conservative landowner and former President of the Board of Agriculture. Experts from all parts of the country, including the tariff reformers Charles Bathurst and Christopher Turnor, were brought in to assist.

Part of the committee's brief was to consider the need for plans to control all home-grown food supplies. It was decided that such plans were unnecessary at the present time. The committee reported themselves 'strongly in favour of maintaining the comparatively normal market and commercial conditions in agriculture now prevailing until the last moment consistent with national safety'. Fearing, however, that bread prices could become prohibitive for the working classes, the committee urged that a scheme be worked out for the state to take over all mills, bakehouses and supplies of wheat and flour in the country, and to be ready to distribute bread at subsidized prices if necessary. They also recommended the preparation of a comprehensive plan for the control of all food supplies. As far as agriculture was concerned, farmers should be encouraged to increase their acreage of wheat at the expense of permanent grass by a state guarantee of a minimum 40/- per quarter for 1915. It was stressed that this must be done soon if the 1915–16 harvest were to be affected.[9]

The Cabinet Committee discussed the report several times but took no steps to follow up the suggestions. The report was also kept secret. Committee members in Parliament tried in vain to bring the matter into the open. Week after week Bathurst and others requested the Board of Agriculture to tell the Commons what the government had decided to do to induce farmers to grow more grain. Finally, when it was already too late to sow wheat, they asked the government to release the report to Parliamant, only to be told that it was 'private and confidential'.[10]

Two factors account for the government's reluctance to make the contents of the report known. Firstly, for various reasons, all official dealings in matters of supply were shrouded in secrecy. This stemmed partially from a desire to censor any news, however innocuous by later standards, that might cause alarm within the country or give encouragement to the enemy. It was taken to excessive lengths, involving not just a curb on the press but the withholding of information from Parliament. In the case of the agricultural report, censorship was totally unnecessary. The weak points of British agriculture were well known and the committee's deliberations had been accompanied by the open discussion in the press and farming circles of the need to restore the grasslands. When Bathurst 'inadvertently' leaked the committee's opinion on a state subsidy for wheat farmers during a Commons debate in February, the news caused no stir. As far as the enemy was concerned, as Lord Milner said later in the war: 'everything which makes the enemy think we are afraid of the truth is of course undeniably an encouragement to the enemy'.[11]

Another probable deterrent to publication of the report was that this would give official airing to proposals that formed part of the prewar campaign for tariff reform. Not surprisingly with Bathurst and Turnor at work, the committee had resuscitated some of the Unionists' earlier suggestions for agricultural development. It would have been impossible for the Liberals to consider such action at the end of August. At that time the war was expected to last only a few months; the government could not possibly commit itself to an opponent's policy involving an overhaul of the national farming system that would take years.

Even if the Liberals had overcome their political scruples, strong resistance to an attempt to reduce herds by promoting grain production would have come from the farming community, who had a tremendous amount of money tied up in livestock. Farmers initially resisted suggestions from the government that they should sow more grain. On 24 February 1915, shortly after Bathurst's revelations in Parliament, the National Farmers' Union rejected by a large majority a motion censuring the government for refusing to offer a guaranteed wheat price.[12]

As discussed in chapter 1, subsidiary problems also hindered the adoption of new farming techniques. Wheat drains the soil of nutrients more thoroughly than most other crops. Besides extra men and horses for ploughing, farmers would therefore need larger supplies of fertilizers than usual. These were not available. Before the war British farmers used much less fertilizer than their German counterparts and since August 1914 usage had fallen along with supplies due to the loss of chemicals from Central Europe and competition from the munitions factories for nitrogen and sulphuric acid. Typically, exports of fertilizers had not been banned. In addition, farmers hesitated to make changes until the legal issues had been resolved. Most English farmers were tenant farmers with leases that contained clauses governing the usage of the land. The Agricultural Holdings Acts of 1908 and 1910 had given tenants the freedom to decide what crops to grow, but the landowner could still specify the amount of arable under certain crops in the last year of a lease. Tenants could be prosecuted by their landlords for breach of contract if they ploughed more than the agreed acreage. Penalties of up to £50 per acre or a sum equal to the full capital value of the land existed in most agreements. Although the National Farmers' Union asked the government in September whether it contemplated legislation to protect tenant farmers against suit, the Board of Agriculture would give no assurances.[13]

The government's avoidance of intervention in agriculture was less justified once hope of a short war had gone. By the spring of 1915 Unionist campaigners were hopeful of concessions. The Board of Agriculture put speculation to rest on 15 March, however, when it declared that 'it would be criminal on the part of the Board of Agriculture if at the eleventh hour we suddenly reversed a settled policy which has been adopted by the Board since the matter was first raised in September, and certainly anything in the way of a bounty or a guarantee is not considered by the Board to be either possible or desirable'.[14]

The Board's war-related activities consisted primarily of collecting statistics on domestic production, publishing a series of leaflets on increasing output in conventional ways, and some listless work by the education and research departments. With a meagre grant of £669 for extraordinary investigations, few new projects associated with war needs could be undertaken. A potentially valuable step was the allotment of vegetable plots in urban areas. Land was set aside for this purpose early in the war, but it was intended not as a food production measure but to provide occupation for the unemployed. When the latter failed to materialize, so did the garden produce. The only other action of note was the passage in October of a Slaughter of Animals Act designed to protect Britain's herds of cattle by curbing the exuberant marketing of immature animals that had been encouraged by rising food prices.

That so little was done was blamed on the President of the Board of Agriculture, Lord Lucas. His performance satisfied neither the Opposition nor his own colleagues. Charles Hobhouse, a member of Asquith's Cabinet who kept a record of events in a diary, described Lucas as 'a good example of a Liberal peer – industrious after 11 a.m.', and observed that after seven months in office Lucas still had not 'found his legs'.[15] Although Asquith liked Lucas, he recognized that his 'angularity of vision' made it difficult for others to work with him. The Prime Minister ranked him last but one in a 'Tripos' evaluation of his government that he drew up for his confidante Venetia Stanley on 26 February 1915.[16] Significantly, Lucas was the only one of the four members of the Cabinet Committee on Food Supplies to be replaced when the government was reshuffled in May 1915.

Lucas's political opponents considered him totally inept. He simply did not seem to understand the seriousness of the war. Bathurst thought Lucas's grasp of affairs was too pitiable for words. Lord Milner, a strong advocate of agricultural reorganization and of intervention of the state in wartime, recalled later: 'When I called attention in August [1914] to the vital necessity of increasing our home-grown food supply, Lucas blew me away with a few remarks of amazing superficiality. He assured his fellow peers that a rise in the price of wheat was a bogey. Why trouble growing it when you could import any amount you wanted?'[17]

Lucas's confidence on this point perhaps accounted for his support of one of the Agricultural Consultative Committee's recommendations – the accumulation of a reserve of wheat. The committee had been divided over the means to achieve this. The majority wanted a bonus to British farmers to keep wheat off the market on stacks on the farms; a minority urged the purchase by the government of three million quarters of foreign wheat. It was this latter suggestion that most appealed to the Cabinet Committee on Food Supplies. It had come at a timely moment. Members of the grain trade had already asked for government help in maintaining imports, as some exporters in North America had used the war as an excuse to break contracts or to demand special arrangements for payment. With shipments likely to fall unless the government stepped in, the circumstances certainly came under the Cabinet Committee's mandate to protect supply. It also entailed limited intervention in the marketplace and was designed to supplement normal trading rather than to supplant it. The Committee decided to buy a reserve large enough to see the armed forces through to the summer and therefore appointed in October a Grain Supplies Committee with orders to obtain unobtrusively two million quarters of wheat. Headed by Sir Henry Rew, Assistant Secretary at the Board of Agriculture, the committee consisted of representatives of the Board of Trade, the Treasury, the Admiralty and the War Office.[18]

But where should they buy? Markets were already tightening.

Russian and Balkan supplies from the Black Sea region had been lost when the enemy closed the Dardanelles. Winter brought bad news from other areas: the Australian crop failed and the Government of India, which requisitioned the entire surplus of that country, announced in November that it would keep most of its supplies off the market in an effort to curb rocketing prices there. It was also rumoured that the United States was going to place an embargo on exports to safeguard its own supplies. Less was coming onto the world market at the very moment when all were anxious to buy more. The situation was aggravated by unusually large purchases by Scandinavian countries and Italy. France too, usually self-sufficient, was buying to compensate for loss of productive land in the war zone.

Fortunately, harvests in the northern hemisphere had been abundant in 1914. Britain began the cereal year (1 September to 31 August) with a healthy twenty-one week stock. But shortages were expected to appear in the spring. In September statisticians at the Board of Trade produced a report giving estimates of wheat stocks over the next two years. Even without considering possible attacks on trade by the enemy, stocks at the end of May 1915 were expected to be down to eight weeks, with further reductions likely before August.[19]

The purchasing committee started operations in December. For fear that the market would be shaken by the participation in the bidding by the British government, the Grain Committee's activities proceeded in secret. To maintain the fiction of normal trading the committee worked through an agent, Messrs Ross T. Smythe of Liverpool, who was authorized to sell as well as buy. By March 1915, 2,839,6000 quarters of wheat had been bought. The experiment, in Rew's opinion, was a success. Few agreed with him. 'Unbusinesslike, wasteful, and unnecessary' was the professionals' verdict when the news leaked out in February.[20] The government too had misgivings. In January, operations were temporarily suspended to assess the situation. Smythe's had been instructed to buy heavily in Argentina, the most expensive market of the time, and had acted clumsily, buying at higher prices than other merchants and then selling at less than the normal price. The Treasury, not surprisingly took alarm, warning the committee that the situation was not drastic enough to warrant government buying and selling at a loss.[21] The Cabinet agreed and ordered trading to stop in both Argentina and the United States, where prices were also high. Another factor also entered into their decision. All the Allied governments were competing for extra supplies, forcing up prices in the process. Since these purchases were largely financed by loans from the British Treasury, the effect of all this counterbidding was felt primarily by Britain. It was ludicrous that secret British purchases were compounding the problem.

Buying resumed the following month and further blunders brought disclosure of the government's venture in an embarrassing manner Announcement of the bombardment of the Dardenelles coupled with a confident prophecy of success by the Prime Minister had immediate repercussions on grain prices, which fell by 5/- a quarter in expectation of a flood of backed-up shipments from the Black Sea. Most traders suspended operations until the trend of events became clear. One buyer alone persisted in the Argentine market – Ross T. Smythe. Questions were asked and the truth came out. It was awkward for the government. In addition to telling the Commons that 'governments cannot buy half so well as private individuals'. Runciman had met a suggestion by Andrew Bonar Law that reserves be built up by government purchase with the response that such a move would be inconsistent with the government's policy of trusting to private enterprise.[22] The government now had to mollify angry deputations from the grain trade with promises that its forays into the market would cease. There was no intention of keeping this promise. The Cabinet Committee had already decided to buy the Indian surplus and were soon making arrangements to ship some 2½ million quarters of wheat. This time, six firms acted on the government's behalf and as the purchasing committee negotiated a price well below current market rates, no charges of wastefulness were forthcoming.

The government's participation in the grain import business sustained objections to interference in the economy. The transactions had dislocated normal business activity. By early April the importation of wheat had practically come to a standstill. Everyone was watching Messrs Ross T. Smythe. It was argued that if the government was not buying, it was because they knew something the public did not, namely that the market would soon fall suddenly. The Cabinet Committee on Food Supplies decided that the only way to reassure the trade was to resume purchases on a modest scale.[23] The damage was done, though, and to the end of the 1916, when the Wheat Committee began operations, the import trade in wheat was sluggish. Far from improving matters, the Grain Supplies Committee contributed to the fall of wheat stocks to eight weeks at the beginning of April instead of the end of May as originally calculated. In the opinion of the next President of the Board of Agriculture, Lord Selborne, it was only the purchases of Indian wheat that averted a crisis in 1915. Moreover, the experience cost the country £5¼ million.[24]

Another venture was also raising doubts about the worth of state trading. The Royal Commission for Sugar Supplies, officially created by the Cabinet Committee on Food Supplies on 20 August 1914, had been buying sugar on state account since the very beginning of the war. In this case, transactions were open from the start and the trade was not disrupted by odd purchases but was taken over in its entirety. A proclamation of 26 October gave the Sugar Commission a monopoly on imports, but dealings by private individuals had already ceased in accordance with an informal agreement made between the refiners and the government early in August.

Of all the foods necessary for life, why should sugar have been singled out for full control at this early date? It is generally agreed that the move was taken to protect the refiners. The United Kingdom consumed more sugar per head than any other nation in the world and imported its entire supply. In addition, London was the seat of the most important international sugar market. As more than half of the country's supplies came from Germany and the Austro-Hungarian Empire before the war business would have been severely curtailed without the government's help.[25]

The monetary side of the question should not lead one to overlook, however, the importance that was almost universally attached to sugar as a food at this time. It was a common preservative and was also thought to be of special nutritional importance. Scientists had revealed that the value of food lay in its role as the body's fuel and that this fuel was stored in the shape of calories. They had constructed tables showing the number of calories contained in various foods that could be bought for a penny. Sugar was high on the list; *ergo*, sugar was an essential food. It was commonly believed by the working classes that children would die unless they ate a pound of sugar a week. Health workers reported mothers feeding babies up to two pounds a week. This misconception was not confined to the un-educated. Christopher Addison, a physician and future head of the Ministry of Health, blamed the poor health of his children in 1917 on the shortage of sugar. Sir Alfred Mond, Liberal MP for Swansea and vice president of one of London's infants' hospitals told the Commons that the government should consult 'skilled hygienists' about the detrimental effect that the shortage of this 'valuable food' was having on growing children. Had they been consulted, the 'skilled hygienists' would have supported the assertion. In 1918 influential members of the Royal Society railed against the government's 'stupidity' in shipping in cereals when they should have been concentrating on sugar.[26]

According to the official history of food control, the Sugar Commission was a great success, but the records do not sustain this claim. The complaints began as soon as the Commission started work.[27] Owing to very large purchases at the beginning of the war – nearly 1 million tons or half the annual consumption – supply was no problem until the end of 1915. The price trend, on the other hand, was most unsatisfactory. During the first week of the war, the retail price soared 80 per cent. As the initial panic buying subsided, the price dropped, but as late as 1 January 1915 it still stood 67 per cent above the prewar level.[28] Its record was considerably worse than that of food in general. Why was this so? Refiners' profits were not the answer. Control of the entire supply allowed the Sugar Commission to limit profit margins to 1/- per hundredweight. As with wheat, the trade's normal buyers alleged that lack of business acumen on the part of the Commission's agents was at the root of the problem.[29]

The Commission was forced by the war to rely on distant suppliers of cane sugar, such as Cuba, Java, Mauritius and the Philippines, instead of the European suppliers of beet sugar. The long journey plus higher freight charges added to the price. The Commission's critics argued, however, that these costs accounted for only a fraction of the increase. It was reported that although the Commission's agents, Henry Tate and Sons, were the sole buyers in some markets they had paid prices far in excess of what the regular trade would have given. In Java, for example, with no competition, the Commission bought at 12/- per ton at the beginning of August and 19/- at the end of the month.[30] It was later charged that in its haste to secure supplies at whatever the price, the Sugar Commission cost the country £2 million by June 1915. In fact, until the end of the war the Commission operated in the black, its profitability sustained by the high prices paid by the consumer. Uneconomic trading was only one reason for the high retail price of sugar. The Treasury found the national sweet tooth an ideal source of additional revenue. The import duty on sugar was raised several times during the war. Moreover, the Commission set a minimum retail price and let it be known that they would cut off supplies to any shopkeepers selling below the minimum. This had no effect on consumption. Usage continued high as long as supplies were maintained.

Three other examples of government trading in food also date from very early in the war, all of them units set up by civilian departments to obtain supplies for the armed forces. Their history properly belongs to military studies, but some mention is due because of the contributions they made to the eventual establishment of full controls over civilian supplies. Military provisioning had several consequences for civilians. Because of the quantity of supplies needed by the unusually large army Britain sent to the continent and because of some international political factors, the armed forces could not be fed and equipped without the aid of civilian government departments. This forced the latter to become involved in state trading when they otherwise would have held back. Military provisioning brought a significant amount of foodstuffs – mostly imports – under immediate regulation. It also withdrew supplies from the general market, prompting the civilian authorities to intervene increasingly to ensure that the public did not go short. Some of the machinery set up to handle supplies for the armed forces was then used for civilian shipments as well. Finally, the military purchasing units provided techniques and experienced personnel for the future Ministry of Food.

After the war broke out the Army Contracts Department was overwhelmed by work, so the War Office requested assistance with food purchases. Domestic orders were handled by the Board of Agriculture, which formed a department to buy forage, wool, and other agricultural produce for the army direct from the farmer. This agency started operating in September and by the spring of 1915 it was functioning smoothly. The country was divided into districts and a government agent was appointed for each. All local contracts were declared void and standard prices were applied to the whole country. The army benefited from punctual, regular supplies at economical prices. Farmers had the satisfaction of receiving the whole of the profit made.

The Board of Trade organized the other two schemes, which covered imports. At the onset of war the War Office immediately requisitioned all the meat on the London market and sought contracts with Argentine shippers for frozen meat. The Argentine government was reluctant to negotiate with the British military authorities, however, for fear that this would constitute a breach of neutrality.

They therefore asked that the contracts be taken out in the name of a private concern. There were financial obstacles to this. Private businesses were experiencing trouble obtaining currency and negotiating bills of exchange in Argentina. Credits established by the government allowed business to resume after a few weeks, and it was decided to accede to the Argentine government's request and buy military supplies through an agent attached to the Board of Trade. The transactions were to be kept secret. The British too wanted to keep the matter from the Germans. The amount of meat ordered might permit the enemy to calculate the size of the armed forces in Britain, as well as submit shipping sailing from South America to great danger of enemy attack. The secrecy of the arrangement created a minor problem for the Cabinet Committee on Food Supplies, however. It meant that the agreement between Britain and Argentina could not be submitted to Parliament for approval, yet without this the purchases were illegal – a potential source of parliamentary disputes.[31]

Sir Thomas Robinson, the current Agent-General for Queensland, was appointed to represent the government on 20 October. He initially placed orders for 15,000 tons of meat a month, of which the War Office needed about 10,000 tons, leaving a surplus for the civilian market. During the following months the amounts bought on government account were increased and gradually the Board of Trade became responsible for all imports of frozen meat from South America. Early in 1915 contracts were signed with Australia and New Zealand, which had requisitioned their entire exportable surpluses of agricultural produce at the beginning of the war and had offered them at fixed prices to Britain.[32]

Later in the war, the food authorities made it their policy to co-ordinate the acquisition of food at an international level. The first steps towards this goal were taken during this initial war period, although not consciously with that aim in mind. Credit for this belongs to the French government. On 5 August the French Ambassador in London approached the Foreign Office about purchasing supplies in Britain for the French army. Flour, grain, frozen and tinned meat, and forage were all needed. It was decided that since British stocks were not sufficient to support any additional demand, an international purchasing board should be established to obtain supplies for both forces. The Commission Internationale de Ravitaillement (CIR), composed of representatives of the French government, the Admiralty, the War Office and the Board of Trade, was thus set up under Board of Trade auspices on 17 August.[33]

Although they agreed to pool their orders, the two countries were left free to obtain supplies wherever they could if they wished. Civilian supplies did not come under the contract. The adverse effects of this loose agreement were soon felt. It was initially intended that the CIR would buy frozen meat for France, but the French soon started trading on their own account. This helped drive up prices and led to prolonged Anglo-French talks in December and January, after which France transferred responsibility for its meat imports to the Board of Trade's unit. A short time later the Board took on purchases for the Italian army too. The CIR, whose only dealings in foodstuffs now were in grain, similarly extended its services over the next two years to the other Allies.

The creation of so many independent state purchasing committees inevitably led to duplication of effort, conflicting methods of approach and the dispersal of expert advice, not to mention the effect that competition had on prices. By the end of 1914 there were a host of agents working the international markets, supposedly representing one country but bidding against each other for the same items. It was so bad in the United States that in November Theodore Roosevelt offered his services gratis to help the British government set up a single buying commission there.[34] His offer was not accepted and the confusion was not fully cleared up until the United States entered the war in 1917.

In August 1914 it had been decided that the Cabinet Committee on Food Supplies would give first consideration to supply. This had resulted in the state assuming responsibility for certain imports. In the main, however, the government had stood back and allowed the businessmen to get on with their work unhindered. Confidence that a relatively free market would bring in the goods was not misplaced. Trade continued at a satisfactory level throughout the first year of war.

For the first six months merchant ships sailed in general safety. In August 1914 few believed that the submarine posed any great threat: its short range capabilities limited it to the North Sea and its construction and size made it vulnerable to attack itself. The German government had no plans to use the submarine as a regular tool of commercial warfare. In September two German U-Boat commanders took it on themselves to sink several British warships, but his did not awaken either the Germans or the Allies to future possibilities. Admiral of the Fleet Sir John Jellicoe, for one, still felt that the submarines were powerless to hurt Britain's overseas trade as long as the Navy remained superior to all others.[35] Indeed, the Navy proved well able to meet any conventional challenge. In the course of the first year of war it successfully cleared the seas of the enemy's warships, bringing the threat of a surface blockade of Britain to an end.[36]

For the most part, Britain's importers had no trouble bringing in supplies. During the first three months of the war imports of primary foods were actually higher than normal, although shipments of some subsidiary foods from the east – preserved eggs from Russia, for instance – declined.[37] Stocks were supplemented in August and September by nearly half a million tons of cereals and an indeterminate amount of other foodstuffs confiscated or bought from vessels diverted from North Sea and Baltic destination into British ports under an order of 4 August that declared all foodstuffs conditional contraband. This diversion of shipping was quickly abandoned following strong protests from neutral countries, especially the United States, one of Britain's most important sources of supply. The rate at which imports were arriving allowed the government to declare that these controversial seizures of cargo were unnecessary anyway.[38]

In one vital area, however, the Cabinet Committee's expectations proved false. A constant supply of goods did *not* guarantee stable prices. It had been predicted that the price of food would rise at the start of war, so when this happened the Committee were not concerned. They expected the cost of living to fall back to a relatively normal level by the end of the year by which time, it was said, the war would be over. Price rises in the first week of war were due partly to financial dislocation in overseas markets and partly to panic buying at home, which allowed shopkeepers to name their own prices. People brought dustbins, buckets and tubs to the stores and filled them with provisions. One woman was said to have bought £270 worth of food in one day including 144 pots of jam and one and a half tons of flour. Long queues of motor cars driven by the chauffeurs of the wealthy were seen parked outside grocery shops where they had come to carry off as much as they could persuade the shopkeepers to part with.[39] On 10 August the government passed an anti-hoarding Act to deal with the phenomenon but it was not enforced. The panic died down spontaneously. Prices soon fell but not to the prewar level. They were expected to decline further, however, as confidence was regained in the markets.

By the turn of the year it was clear that this was not going to happen. Food prices had continued to rise. Wholesale prices for December were 22 per cent above the index for June, while retail prices were 16 per cent higher than in July.[40] Agitation in labour circles was vociferous and well-organized. The War Emergency Workers' National Committee (WNC) – formed on 5 August by the larger trade unions, the co-operative movement and various socialist political parties – announced the establishment of a special committee to inquire into the cost of living and mounted an anti-inflation campaign complete with public meetings and massive demonstrations. Although outwardly professing calm, the government took alarm at the unexpected state of affairs. Montagu wrote to each of his colleagues on the Cabinet Committee on Food Supplies urging them to devote their attention to the second part of the goal outlined by the Prime Minister. They had failed in their set task, he told them. It was now their duty to tackle the pressing problem of prices.[41]

Postwar accounts tended to make light of the prices issue, treating it as separate from the food question. A report written for the CID in 1923 made no mention of prices. 'Everything went more or less according to plan', the author wrote, 'and for the first two years of the war the food supplies were maintained without any great difficulty.' The matter was similarly downplayed in the official history of wartime food control: 'So far as the food problem was remembered at all, it was merged in the larger question of the race between prices and wages. For the most part it was forgotten.'[42]

To the mass of the population, however, rising food prices were the outstanding problem of the war and one which they had no trouble remembering. It has been calculated that they constituted the most discussed topic among the trades councils, local working-class organization affiliated with trades unions.[43] This was understandable given the high proportion of the average income spent on food at this time. Working-class families spent about two-thirds of their weekly wages on food. A rise of only a few points on the price index had a much greater impact than it would today. Owing to their habit of buying in small quantities, poor people already paid more per pound for food items than the wealthy. During the first week of August 1914, for example, colonial bacon was supposed to fetch about 1/4d per pound according to the Board of Trade, but working-class customers were being charged 1/10d per pound for quarter-pounds.[44] To make matters worse the cost of cheaper foods was increasing at a faster rate than the more expensive items. On the average, beef rose 16 per cent between July and October but high quality domestic meat rose only 7 per cent and lower quality domestic (still relatively expensive) 11 per cent, whereas better quality imported frozen meat rose 16 per cent and lower quality imported 30 per cent.[45] The disproportionately sharp rise in the cost of lower-grade beef was brought about by the channelling of supplies to the armed forces. The surplus could not satisfy the civilian demand and the consequent competition among retailers for supplies drove up prices. Due to its normally low price, imported frozen meat was consumed almost exclusively by working-class families. The less affluent thus had no cheaper substitutes to turn to when prices rose as did those who were better off. If they could not afford better cuts of meat, they had no alternative but to reduce purchases. Price rises, therefore, represented a supply problem for some groups.

Labour representatives saw a solution in 'maximum prices' for the basic necessities of life. What they had in mind were prices fixed by law in the interests of the consumer. The Cabinet Committee on Food Supplies did discuss a fixed price for bread several times between August and October but decided it would not be practicable.[46] Lists of so-called maximum prices were, however, published by the government, the first appearing in August. One of the first steps taken by the Cabinet Committee was to invite the retail provision trades to form advisory boards. They considered such committees an ideal way to control prices without officially interfering in the market. Business was to regulate itself. The committees were asked to calculate the price for each basic commodity above which a 'fair profit' turned into 'profiteering'. Not surprisingly, this exercise proved useless in curbing prices. In the absence of proper cost accounting, the prices were rough estimates based on what the trades themselves considered 'proper' returns. And since they were drawn up by representatives of only the larger retail organizations they were not accepted by those, such as the co-operative societies, whose opinions had not been sought.

Publication of the price lists merely increased labour dissatisfaction. It was charged that prices were set in the interests of the producer – too high. Spokesmen for the government countered that they had received many letters from small shopkeepers complaining that the maximum prices were set too low for them to make a living. Since the prices were not legally binding, the argument may appear to be academic. But the results of this policy were concrete enough. Despite official denials, many retailers understood the 'maximum' price to be the 'government' price and charged accordingly. The maximum soon became the minimum.[47]

The maximum price venture only helped to accelerate the upward trend in the cost of living. The experience seemed clearly to indicate that official interference in business matters did indeed have undesirable results and the government abandoned the price lists after October. They were influenced in their decision by reports from Germany, where price controls had been in effect since August in some districts. Wholesalers were sending their supplies to whichever locality paid the highest price, bypassing towns that had set lower prices. Despite Germany's vaunted superiority in food production Berlin was already experiencing a shortage of breadstuffs.[48] Maximum prices continued to be a vexing issue throughout the war. They needed a good deal of planning, a large staff of accountants and control over distribution to make them work, as later experiments were to show.

The government was not yet ready to venture further into this quagmire, but it was forced to concede in January that it would have to take some action. The upward trend in the cost of living plus the realization that the war would last longer than first thought had led to general questioning of the government's handling of the food supply. Although one contributor to *The Times* observed on 19 January that 'fortunately the question of principle – as between State action and *laissez-faire* – is no longer in dispute', the extent to which the government should step in was by no means clear.[49]

Not unexpectedly, the loudest calls for intervention came from the Socialists and other spokesmen for the working classes. The Women's National Council handed McKenna a petition signed by 20,000 women demanding lower food prices. The Management Committee of the General Federation of Trade Unions urged the government to go in for state trading. The WNC and W. Pember Reeves, Director of the London School of Economics, both saw a solution to the problem in the control of shipping and the importation of wheat at cost by the government. More restrained advice came from the *Estates Gazette*, a journal devoted to the landed interest, and from Professor Sir William Ashley, an economist to whom the government turned for help later in the war. The *Gazette*, warning that 'we must keep our heads cool', suggested that while the high prices would right themselves as larger supplies became available, much might be achieved by the co-ordination of the government departments concerned. Ashley, observing in *The Times* that state action was acceptable only for the most important foodstuffs, warned that high prices encouraged the enemy. Both agreed that an official inquiry into the causes of the problem should be undertaken.[50]

This was already under way. A Cabinet Committee headed by the Prime Minister began inquiries into the cost of living in January. It went into the question in detail, commissioning reports on any factor that might have contributed to inflation, such as freight charges, the rate of wheat imports, the functioning of the railways and employment levels at the docks and in the merchant marine. Although this resulted in some useful statistics, no fresh approach to the problem ensued. Since Asquith included on the committee Runciman – 'the best member' in the Prime Minister's opinion – and Keynes, policy not surprisingly remained the facilitation of the flow of supplies.[51]

Some of the factors considered by Asquith and his colleagues, such as extra competition for supplies, hoarding and transportation problems, had indeed contributed to the price increases and their ultimate control was to have beneficial effects. But historians agree that they did not constitute the main source of inflation during the First World War. Much of the blame has been assigned to the country's financial policies, which allowed war expenditure to soar. The huge deficit that soon existed between government outlay and revenues was met primarily by loans rather than by heavier taxation and enforced savings by the public, as in the past. Lloyd George's first war budget of November 1914 did little to curb purchasing power in the country. Income tax rates, which only applied to incomes over £150 a year, were doubled, but only for the last four months of the fiscal year. Duties on sugar, tea and beer were increased too; but the revenues provided in this manner were a drop in the ocean compared to total war expenses. The issue of a new paper currency to replace gold sovereigns, government guarantees of national credit arrangements and large loans advanced to Allied governments likewise encouraged spending and a concomitant upward trend in prices.[52]

The government's investigation into the cost of living, as with its other activities connected with the food supply, was veiled in secrecy. As far as the public was aware, the authorities were doing nothing. Unhappiness with this state of affairs came to a head in February. The House of Commons debated on the 11th and 17th a resolution tabled by J. R. Clynes, the Labour MP for North East Manchester, calling on the government to fix effective maximum prices for essential foodstuffs and to take control of all commodities whose supply had been disrupted by the war. The motion was supported by the Unionist Business Committee, formed by back-benchers in January to provide a voice for the Opposition despite a wartime truce on intraparty controversy agreed to earlier by the Unionist Party leadership. Ultimately this group came to include all of the Conservative MPs not serving in the trenches, but initially it was dominated by relics of the prewar imperialist and tariff circles. Labour demands for state intervention on behalf of the food supply gave an opportunity for earlier Unionist proposals for the abandonment of free trade to be revived.[53]

Asquith's response at the debate, according to a Labour source, made 'perhaps the most definite contribution of the Government to the subsequent Labour unrest'. The Prime Minister rejected maximum prices on the grounds that they had failed miserably in Germany. He professed sympathy for working people but pointed out that the cost of food was no higher than during the Franco–Prussian War and asked Labour to wait until June before raising the issue again.[54] February marked the end of the industrial truce that had operated since the start of the war. After only ten trade disputes in January and a loss of 55,900 working days, forty-seven new strikes, involving 209,000 working days, broke out in February.[55]

At the same time, pressure was also being exerted on the government from within. The First Lord of the Admiralty, Winston Churchill, whose interventionary propensities had already been displayed to the Cabinet in the matter of conscription, temporarily focused his attention on the food supply. In January the Admiralty's Director of Trades issued a report which Churchill circulated to the members of the Cabinet on 12 February. Tables prepared for the Cabinet Committee on Food Supplies indicated that the supply of imported wheat available to Britain during the remainder of the cereal year would more than meet requirements. Admiralty statisticians, however, predicted a deficit. They calculated that the Allies and neutral countries would need 6.8 million tons of wheat between January and June 1915 compared to available supplies of 6.6 million tons. A survey by the United States showed a worse gap: 5.5 million tons available versus 6.0 million tons needed. If the supply flow decreased rather than increased, prices would not fall of their own accord.[56]

The announcement by Admiral von Tirpitz on 4 February that from 18 February German submarines would be used in an unrestricted campaign against merchant ships gave additional reason for concern. Recent technological advances had greatly increased the submarine's capabilities. It could now travel further and in waters previously too rough for its own safety. On 3 December 1914 a German submarine had got very close to the British warships anchored off Scapa Flow before it had been detected and chased away. Jellicoe wrote to the First Sea Lord, Admiral Sir John Fisher, to warn him that Germany now possessed an enormous advantage over British shipping.[57]

The choice of February for the beginning of the submarine campaign was ominous. Argentina began selling its new wheat harvest that month. If the attacks on shipping were successful, merchants would demand extra payment for risking the journey to South America. Every penny on the loaf represented an extra burden of £10 million a year on the working classes, the Admiralty warned. The price of bread could soon be out of reach of a large proportion of the population, creating what was termed an 'artificial' famine – that is, one caused by maldistribution rather than sheer lack of supplies.

The remedies suggested by the Admiralty entailed greater involvement by the state. The government should build up reserves to maximum storage capacity (then twenty-one weeks for grain and eight months for meat) and ban all exports of food immediately (over 34,000 tons of grain had been exported to Allied countries in December alone). The government should encourage the domestic production of food and demand more enterprise by those government departments dealing with internal affairs. Demonstrating a considerable loss of prewar confidence the Admiralty complained: 'The national idea is that the Navy, and the Navy alone, ensures the country against famine, and it has never been pointed out that any further action on the part of any Government Department is required.' The Director of Trades asked for the control of distribution and the requisition of the entire mercantile marine at set rates. Although not supportive of the first of these, Churchill campaigned 'violently' (according to Hobhouse) for the latter at the Cabinet meeting held on 2 March.[58] Montagu, who was more inclined towards state intervention than his colleagues on the Cabinet Committee on Food Supplies, had also raised the subject of controlling all shipping and limiting owner's profits to a reasonable percentage, but the other members of the Committee opposed the idea. Runciman and McKenna believed that to place all shipping under control and force it to carry goods only to and from British ports would deprive the nation of foreign currency earned through trade between neutral ports.[59] The scheme was therefore not approved. However, the Cabinet was not unsympathetic to the need for greater regulation of merchant shipping.

After discussing prices several times in January, the Cabinet had concluded that high freight charges caused by a shortage of shipping plus irregular deliveries due to congestion at the ports were the prime causes of the rise in the cost of living. A survey revealed that some 3,000 of the world's 20,000 steamers over one hundred gross tons had been permanently withdrawn from trade either through military requisitioning or by being bottled up in German ports. The efficient working of the rest was hampered by temporary requisitioning, from which they were released in inconvenient parts of the globe, and by overworked ports, which led to slower turn-rounds.[60]

The effects of requisitioning were compounded by its haphazard application. There was no proper planning of shipping usage. The War Office refused to provide information on its projected troop movements even to the Admiralty; and except where only a specialized vessel would do, the Admiralty was indiscriminate in its choice of ships. No attempt was made to assess the relative value to the war effort of a carrier's present use before it was commandeered. The need for better co-ordination of military and civilian needs became more pressing as the various state trading units stepped up their activities during the winter of 1914–15. The Admiralty Transport Department was given the responsibility of finding carriers for the Sugar Commission, Sir Thomas Robinson's meat department at the Board of Trade and the CIR. Importation of supplies for the Allies proved an unwelcome burden that took tonnage away from British civilian imports. Having been largely self-sufficient in agricultural produce before the war, France had little shipping capable of carrying food and was particularly deficient in refrigerated tonnage. Goods bought on French account thus had to be carried mainly in British vessels. Similarly, by February 1915 most of the steamers carrying food to Italy were also British. The demand for refrigerator ships was a problem in itself and frustrated legislation limiting freight charges on government charters. A fixed tariff of fees (the 'Blue Book' rates) officially covered requisitioned vessels, but the Admiralty Transport Department was frequently forced to pay shipowners more in order to secure the use of carriers in high demand. Lacking the machinery and staff for full compulsion, the Admiralty too often had to rely on co-operation.[61] The Cabinet Committee on Food Supplies could not rectify the system because it lacked the authority to enforce the co-ordination of national requirements. It was also hampered by both the reluctance and the impotence of its members to interfere with the war departments or to get help from them.[62]

Some curbs on Admiralty freedoms with civilian shipping were nevertheless forthcoming. On 13 January the Cabinet requested the Admiralty to release all ships not urgently needed and to show speed in converting captured vessels to food carriers. A month later came an order to interfere as little as possible with ships carrying food supplies and especially to avoid the requisitioning of tonnage chartered to carry grain.[63]

Despite the public outcry, the rise in the cost of living had little effect on consumption patterns. In most cases incomes were sufficient to allow purchasing power to remain steady and, in the case of the poorest working people – casual labourers and their families – even to increase. The mass unemployment predicted before the war failed to materialize and societies formed around the country in August 1914 to relieve hardship caused by the war soon dwindled away. The departure from the workforce of large numbers of men for the armed services plus growing demand from industries servicing the war effort quickly mopped up the unemployed and gave more regular employment to the casual worker. For poorer people a rise in income meant more food bought. The sharp increase in the price of frozen meat resulted in some falling off in consumption – total purchases fell 6 per cent during the first year of the war. In general, however, only those very badly off and public institutions on fixed budgets, such as Poor Law Schools and workhouses, restricted food purchases.[64] Most people seemed more inclined to follow the admonition of an enterprising baker in Chelmsford, who had his paper bags printed with the Union Jack and the message: 'The Nation's Watchword – Buy As Usual'.[65]

The relatively normal rate at which imports arrived in the country allowed consumption to remain unchecked. That it would be to the nation's advantage to discourage consumption and thereby save shipping space and reduce international competition for supplies was a thought that seemed scarcely to arise in official circles at this time. Only one conservation measure was considered and that attracted only passing interest. This was the obvious and easy method of stretching wheat supplies by extracting more flour from the grain. In the autumn of 1914 Lord Lucas held a sampling session in his office of breads made with various types of flour. It was decided to shelve the survey, however, and the British enjoyed their usual white loaves, made with only 70 per cent of the kernel, until November 1916. The satisfactory flow of supplies plus the belief that the war would soon be over almost certainly accounted for the government's lack of concern for economy, rather than ideological objections to interfering in people's private lives, for the Cabinet Committee on Food Supplies were to issue frequent appeals for restraint later.

Although 'Business As Usual' remained the ideal, the Liberal government had diverged significantly from peacetime modes of official practice by the spring of 1915. They had taken a big step on the road to control of the food supply by becoming partially or totally responsible for the acquisition of three important imported foodstuffs – wheat, meat and sugar. This has provided a nucleus of administration that was to feed the future control mechanism. The government had also defined and taken tentative action on two major problem areas – prices and shipping. Their inquiries had contributed to the amassing of detailed statistics that served as the foundation of subsequent measures of regulation. The coming of spring, however, refocused attention on one matter that the Liberals had been adamant in avoiding – domestic agricultural production. The time was ripe for a change of outlook. The opportunity to provide this came in May 1915, when Asquith surrendered to the reality of a long war and formed a coalition government. The Unionist Lord Selborne, well-known for his support of wartime 'organization', took Lucas's place. The stage seemed set for some more dynamic action at the Board of Agriculture.

Notes: Chapter 2

1   A. J. P. Taylor, 'Politics in the First World War', in *Politics in Wartime* (London, 1964), p. 76.
2   Committee of Imperial Defence (CID) Paper 2145B, List of committees appointed to consider questions arising during the present war, 1 March 1915, CAB 42/2/2.

3 Ibid.
4 E. S. Montagu to W. Runciman, 12 January 1915, Box 136, Runciman Papers, University of Newcastle-upon-Tyne.
5 *Hansard*, vol. 65 HC Deb., 5s., 8 August 1914, col. 2213.
6 Sir W. H. Beveridge, *British Food Control* (London, 1928), p. 6.
7 J. M. K[eynes], Wheat prices, 25 January 1915, CAB 37/123/51.
8 T. H. Middleton, *Production in War* (London, 1923), p. 2.
9 Agricultural Consultative Committee, Report of the committee to the Board of Agriculture and Fisheries with relation to the expediency of any measures for the conservation, increase and control of the supply of home-grown foodstuffs, 24 August 1914, Box 160/19, Milner Papers, Bodleian Library, Oxford.
10 *Hansard*, vol. 70 HC Deb., 5s., 2 March 1915, col. 651.
11 *Hansard*, vol. 20 HC Deb., 5s., 3 November 1915, col. 128.
12 National Farmers' Union, Minutes of annual meeting, 24 February 1915, NFU Papers, University of Reading.
13 E. H. Whetham, *The Agrarian History of England and Wales*, vol. 8, 1914–1939 (Cambridge, 1978), p. 50; National Farmers' Union, Minutes of general purposes committee, 15 September 1914, NFU Papers.
14 *Hansard*, vol. 70 HC Deb., 5s., 15 March 1915, col. 1893.
15 E. David (ed.), *Inside Asquith's Cabinet: From the Diaries of Charles Hobhouse* (London, 1977), entry for 23 March 1915, p. 231.
16 H. H. Asquith (Earl of Oxford and Asquith), *Memories and Reflections 1852–1927* vol. 2 (Boston, 1928), pp. 21. 23; R. Jenkins, *Asquith* (London, 1964), pp. 340–1.
17 C. Bathurst to Bonar Law, 22 May 1915, 50/3/34 A. Bonar Law Papers, House of Lords Record Office; Lord Milner to Lord Selborne, 4 April 1915, Box 12/246, Selborne Papers, Bodleian Library, Oxford.
18 R. H. R[ew] to the President [Lord Lucas], 8 April 1915; Lucas, Note on the wheat position, 10 April 1915; Memorandum on the wheat supply 1914–15, n.d. All in Box 92, Runciman Papers.
19 Board of Trade, Special Enquiries Branch, Wheat (including flour). Theoretical stock, 22 September 1914, Box 92, Runciman Papers.
20 R. H. Rew, Interim report of operations in wheat and flour, March 1915; Shipton, Anderson and Company to Runciman, 6 April 1915. Both in Box 92, Runciman Papers; R. H. R[ew], Note on the wheat position, 14 June 1915, PRO 30/30/4, Milner Papers, Public Record Office (PRO).
21 J. M. K., Wheat prices, 25 January 1915, CAB 37/123/51.
22 *Hansard*, vol. 70 HC Deb., 5s., 17 February 1915, col. 1179.
23 Rew to Lucas, 8 April 1915; Lucas, note, 10 April 1915; Ross T. Smythe and Company to Rew, 9 April 1915. All in Box 92, Runciman Papers.
24 Selborne, Memorandum to Cabinet, 21 July 1915, CAB 37/131/30; Rew, Interim report, March 1915, Box 92, Runciman Papers.
25 A. Marwick, *The Deluge: British Society and the First World War* (London, 1970), p. 162; S. J. Hurwitz, *State Intervention in Great Britain: A Study of Economic Control and Social Response, 1914–1919* (New York, 1949), p. 72; R. J. Hammond, 'British food supplies, 1914–1939', *Economic History Review*, first series, vol. 16, no. 1 (1946), p. 4.
26 C. S. Peel, *How We Lived Then 1914–1918* (London, 1929), p. 82; National Health Insurance, Medical Research Committee. Special Report no. 68, H. Corry Mann, *Rickets* (London, 1922), p. 49; C. Addison, *Four and a Half Years*, vol. 2 (London, 1934), p. 422; *Hansard*, vol. 83 HC Deb., 5s., 21 June 1916 cols. 174–5; W. B. Hardy to Sir K. Anderson, 2 January 1918, Box 527, Royal Society Food (War) Committee Papers, Royal Society, London.
27 Beveridge, *British Food Control*, p. 125; Marwick, *Deluge*, p. 161.

28 S. Litman, *Prices and Price Control in Great Britain and the United States During the World War* (New York, 1920), p. 28.
29 Graham, Rowe and Company to Bonar Law, 25 November 1914, enclosing copy of petition to McKenna, 17 November 1914, 35/3/68, Bonar Law Papers.
30 *Hansard*, vol. 74 HC Deb., 5s., 29 September 1915, col. 864; Litman, *Prices*, p. 114.
31 The Board of Trade and meat supplies, September 1915, MAF 60/93, Ministry of Agriculture, Fisheries and Food Papers, PRO.
32 For a detailed discussion, see E. M. H. Lloyd, *Experiments in State Control at the War Office and the Ministry of Food* (Oxford, 1924).
33 *Commission Internationale de Ravitaillement*, Establishment and functions, n.d., MAF 60/190.
34 T. Roosevelt to B. P. Blackett, 27 November 1914, Box 26/180–1, Asquith Papers, Bodleian Library, Oxford.
35 Sir J. Jellicoe to Churchill, 30 September 1914 in A. T. Patterson (ed.), *The Jellicoe Papers*, vol. 1 (London, 1966–8), p. 71.
36 A. Salter, *Slave of the Lamp* (London, 1967), p. 60.
37 Sir R. H. Rew, *Food Supplies in Peace and War* (London, 1920), p. 42; Ministry of Food, *Monthly Office Report* (London, December 1918), Table D: Stocks of the principle foods in the United Kingdom.
38 CID, Report on the opening of the war, 1 November 1914, CAB 17/102B.
39 Peel, *How We Lived Then*, p. 16; *Daily Mirror*, 5 August 1914; *Hansard*, vol. 65 HC Deb., 5s., 8 August 1914, col. 2213.
40 Litman, *Prices*, pp. 13, 25.
41 Montagu to Runciman, 12 January 1915, Box 136, Runciman Papers.
42 CID, Food supplies in war, August 1923, MAF 60/89; Beveridge, *British Food Control*, p. 9.
43 A. Clinton, 'Trade councils during the First World War', *International Review of Social History*, vol. 15 (1970), part 2, p. 221.
44 Peel, *How We Lived Then*, p. 54.
45 F. Wood, 'The increase in the cost of food for different classes of society since the outbreak of war', *Journal of the Royal Statistical Society*, vol. 79 (July 1916), p. 504.
46 Montagu to R. W. Matthew, 26 October 1914, Montagu Papers, Trinity College, Cambridge.
47 A. W. Flux to J. S. Middleton, 31 August 1914, Box 11/58, War Emergency Workers' National Committee (WNC) Papers, Transport House, London; *Hansard*, vol. 65 HC Deb., 5s., 8 August 1914, col. 2215; Open letter to the Home Secretary from Miss Margaretta Hicks, Mrs Despard, Mrs Julia Scurr and Miss Susan Ebury, *Daily Herald*, 25 August 1914.
48 G. Hardach, *The First World War 1914–1918* (Berkeley, CA, 1977), p. 116; Memorandum on German 'maximum prices', n.d., Box M/13/7, Crewe Papers, University College, Cambridge.
49 *The Times*, 19 January 1915.
50 *The Times*, 18, 19 and 21 January 1915; *Estates Gazette*, 23 January 1915; *Daily Citizen*, 20 January 1915.
51 Various reports in Crewe Papers, Box M/13/7; Asquith, *Memories*, vol. 2, p. 74.
52 H. Roseveare, *The Treasury: The Evolution of a British Institution* (New York, 1969), pp. 240–1.
53 W. A. S. Hewins, *The Apologia of an Imperialist. Forty Years of Empire Policy*, vol. 2 (London, 1929), p. 13.
54 *Labour Year Book* (London, 1916), p. 43; *Hansard*, vol. 69 HC Deb., 5s., 11 February 1915, col. 758.

55 N. B. Dearle, *An Economic Chronicle of the Great War for Great Britain and Ireland 1914–1919* (New Haven, CT, 1929), pp. 25, 29.
56 Memorandum on the wheat requirements of the United Kingdom, 1 February to 31 August 1915, n.d., Box M/13/7, Crewe Papers; Admiralty memorandum for the Cabinet, 15 January 1915, CAB 37/123/49.
57 Jellicoe to Fisher, 5 December 1914, Patterson (ed.), *Jellicoe Papers*, pp. 103–4.
58 David, *Inside Asquith's Cabinet*, p. 225, entry for 2 March 1915.
59 Montagu to McKenna, 12 January 1915, Montagu Papers; D. French, *British Economic and Strategic Planning, 1905–1915* (London, 1982), p. 104.
60 Asquith to the King, 13 January 1915, CAB 41/36/1; Shortage of merchant shipping, January 1915, Box 89, Runciman Papers; Sir G. Paish, 'Prices of commodities in 1915', *Journal of the Royal Statistical Society*, vol. 79 (March 1916), p. 190.
61 CID, Food supplies in war, August, 1923, MAF 60/89; J. A. Salter, *Allied Shipping Control* (Oxford, 1921), p. 8; J. M. Keynes, Extract from 8 February 1915 memorandum by Port of Plymouth Chamber of Commerce, 15 February 1915, Box M/13/7, Crewe Papers.
62 Montagu to Asquith, 21 January 1915, Montagu Papers.
63 Asquith to the King, 13 January 1915, CAB 41/36/1; Directions from the Cabinet Committee on Food Prices to the Transport Department, Admiralty, 10 February 1915, Box 27, Asquith Papers.
64 E. S. Pankhurst, *The Home Front* (London, 1932), p. 113.
65 Bag included by Reverend A. Clark in diary, entry for 25 January 1915. Ms. Eng. Hist. e.97, Bodleian Library, Oxford.

3

An Uphill Struggle. Lord Selborne at the Board of Agriculture

In May 1915 the 8 year old Liberal government succumbed to a political crisis brought on by general unhappiness with the conduct and duration of the war, a scandalous shortage of ammunition and an irreconcilable dispute between Churchill and Fisher over policy at the Admiralty. Its place was taken by a coalition headed by Asquith. Forming this government, Asquith later confessed, was 'the most uncongenial job' he had ever been required to take on.[1] Distasteful as he found it, he went about it with some shrewdness, devoting his not inconsiderable talents to using the event to refurbish his own and his party's reputations.

Although he disliked the idea of a multiparty administration, Asquith recognized that the co-option of the Opposition into the governing process could be advantageous. By spreading the responsibility for war policy among all parties, the Liberals could expect a diminution in the parliamentary censure they had endured in recent months. A display of unity by the nation's political chiefs would no doubt be welcomed by the country and should give a psychological boost to the war effort. The Prime Minister's own position as leader of a united nation organized for victory could raise him even higher in the public esteem. Who better qualified than he to make a success of such a challenge? Asquith was renowned for his skill in moderating assemblies of people of disparate political backgrounds.

Opinion has varied over the years as to what Asquith had in mind when he distributed the offices in the coalition. Earlier observers focused on the Prime Minister's reservations of the key posts for his own party. Liberals held twelve of the twenty-two Cabinet positions including the Treasury, the Foreign Office, the Home Office and the new Ministry of Munitions. This was interpreted as a deliberate attempt to perpetuate Liberal supremacy.[2] More recently, it has been suggested that Asquith's motives were more subtle. He himself told Herbert Samuel that he was aiming at an ideological balance between the advocates of *laissez-faire* government and those who wanted to see an extension of state controls in wartime, whichever party these men belonged to.[3] Although personally inclined towards the views of the former, Asquith was not a doctrinaire champion of free trade and he recognized that the continuation of the war would bring increased calls for intervention. He wanted to regulate the pace of this change. As mediator between two evenly balanced groups, he would be well placed, the Prime Minister believed, to ensure that progress along the interventionary path was made in an atmosphere of moderation and continuity.

Asquith's efforts to 'pair off' the members of his cabinet did not produce the right atmosphere for efficient government. The Cabinet never worked well as a team and the conflict of interests led to frustration, loss of enthusiasm, and a decline in the Prime Minister's reputation. The new President of the Board of Agriculture found the going particularly hard. The Earl of Selborne belonged to an active group of Unionists who had been calling for some time for the government to gear up the economy for war. He had told a correspondent in April: 'Personally I do not think that we shall get through this war without compulsion. It should take the form of national mobilisation, which would cover the organisation of our industries as well as the supply of the army.'[4] In Asquith's system Selborne was balanced by Runciman, who continued to provide a more restrained presence at the Board of Trade. As far as agriculture was concerned, however, there was no question of an equilibrium. Opinion within the Cabinet was heavily weighted in favour of non-intervention, not least because of another of Asquith's appointments. As a counterweight to Lloyd George, who was permitted to give free rein to his enthusiasm for strong war measures at the Ministry of Munitions, Asquith promoted one of his most valued colleagues, Reginald McKenna, to the Treasury – an office that carried with it considerable authority over war policy. McKenna continued to chair the Cabinet Committee on Food Supplies, which meant that Selborne was not only outnumbered there by people holding different views than himself but had to deal with a Chancellor of the Exchequer who could bring to discussions weighty financial arguments why the state should not increase its commitments.

Such difficulties were not readily apparent when Selborne first took office and he and his supporters had no doubt that they could bring about a speedy reorientation of agricultural policy. Asquith's choice of candidate could well be taken as a tacit admission that he wanted more vigorous attention paid to this sector of the economy: a contemporary hailed Selborne's appointment as 'the beginning of a new era in the relationship of agriculture to the government'.[5] This proved not to be. The new era did not arrive for another eighteen months. Until his resignation from the government in June 1916, however, Selborne worked hard to bring it about.

Circumstances appeared auspicious. He enjoyed the goodwill of the farming community, which considered him ideal for the post. On hearing of his appointment the parliamentary correspondent of the *Mark Lane Express*, the official organ of the National Farmers' Union, wrote: 'we ought as farmers and agriculturalists to be grateful to Mr Asquith . . . for giving us such a statesman and administrator as Lord Selborne to preside over the Board of Agriculture.'[6] Selborne also had a valuable ally in his long-time friend and political associate, Lord Milner. Milner considered Selborne the most fortunate of all the new ministers, for, he believed, agriculture offered greater scope for big changes than any other branch of government.[7] The Board of Agriculture was an office that Milner himself would not have refused, but his outspoken contempt for the Prime Minister and the Liberal war record left him with no place in Asquith's dream of balance and moderation. Equally anxious to avoid serious clashes, the Unionist leadership did not press for his inclusion.

Milner had no intention of sitting passively on the sidelines, however, and Selborne's friendship allowed him to assume a leading role in yet another attempt to get the tariff reformers' prewar land proposals accepted as official policy. On 17 June a departmental committee of the Board of Agriculture chaired by Milner began 'to consider ways to maintain and if possible increase food production in England and Wales'. Similar bodies were appointed a few days later by the appropriate authorities for Scotland and Ireland. Since the subject had been studied by the Agricultural Consultative Committee less than a year previously, a full investigation might well be thought unnecessary. Time was of the essence. The new cereal year would be starting in September and if preparations for next year's harvest were to be influenced, Parliament would have to pass the appropriate legislation before the summer recess. The investigation, readily endorsed by the Prime Minister, bore all the marks of a typically Asquithian delaying tactic, but Selborne himself asked for a new report, presumably to back his proposals with the weight of an up-to-date and 'impartial' verdict on the need for action.

It was Milner's job to ensure that the verdict would be both favourable and unanimous. This was not easy. The committee contained representatives of all three political parties, including Liberals like Sir Henry Verney and F. D. Acland, the past and present Parliamentary Secretaries to the Board of Agriculture, who did not bother to conceal their repugnance to the idea of state interference in agriculture. 'A set of men more absolutely divided, not only on first principles, but in their appreciation of the facts with which they had to deal were never seated round one table', Milner complained. Nevertheless, he achieved a unanimous report, although only 'by expressly disclaiming any opinion as to the extent of the danger, and saying that *if* any emergency existed, such and such steps were best calculated to meet it'.[8]

The Milner committee's interim report, presented on 17 July, was all that Selborne could have wished. Like the Agricultural Consultative Committee's report before it, it recommended a state guaranteed minimum price for wheat, this time, in deference to wartime inflation, of 45/- per quarter to run for four years. Although Milner had promised a report that would be a challenge to the government, he attempted to minimize potential objections by attaching conditions to the guarantee. To allay fears that the scheme might involve the state in unnecessary expenditure for few returns, the guarantee would only apply to farmers who either increased their arable acreage by at least one-fifth of that tilled in October 1913 or who had a minimum of one-fifth of their total acreage under wheat. Most importantly, farmers were put under no obligation to increase arable acreage – the guarantee was merely an inducement to plough more land voluntarily.[9]

Of the three studies the Milner Report was expected to carry the most weight, not only because of the reputation of its redoubtable chairman but because any substantial increase in the production of wheat would occur in England. On average, during the ten year period before the war, 92 per cent of the land under wheat in the United Kingdom was located in England, primarily east and south of the Pennines.[10] Nonetheless, Selborne depended on the Scottish and Irish committees to corroborate the Milner committee's recommendation of long-term government support for agriculture. Their reports disappointed him. Both committees were primarily swayed by realistic appraisals of agricultural conditions in their own countries. With 31 per cent of their grasslands under temporary pasture that could easily be readied for grain and root crops, compared to only 9 per cent in England, neither country needed to encourage widespread ploughing of permanent pasture. Moreover, wheat production was already intensive wherever the soil permitted. The Scottish committee opposed a guarantee for wheat. They felt it would only encourage the sowing of inferior land that was best used for oats. If the state was going to interfere, the Scots preferred help with other problems such as the agricultural labour supply.[11] Some support for Selborne's aims came from the Irish committee, a large and poorly co-ordinated body torn by internal dissensions whose report was described by one of its members as the worst piece of work he had ever seen done by any serious body of men. The members could not agree about what could be done to increase output nor on the need or advisability of government intervention in Irish agriculture. The obligation to come to some decision produced a recommendation for a guarantee to wheat growers, but only for one year.[12]

The Scottish and Irish reports detracted from the impact of the Milner Report. No matter that the latter was unanimous: two out of three independent surveys had declared long-term intervention to be unwarranted. The separation of the question into three areas of research had been a fundamental mistake.

Despite the conflicting reports, Selborne and Milner were still confident at the end of July that the Cabinet would accept the English committee's suggestions. *Some* action had to be taken, Milner reasoned, and the opposition had not come up with alternatives. [13] While Selborne circulated the reports among his colleagues in the Cabinet, Milner canvassed them privately for support. It was all for nothing. On 5 August, the day after the Cabinet discussed the matter, the Prime Minister reported to the King that 'Lord Selborne's proposal ... found little favour and will probably not be discussed again'.[14]

The Cabinet's rejection of the wheat guarantee was the first and greatest of Selborne's disappointments during his term in office but not the last. He was so unsuccessful in bringing about any 'big changes' in farming that one recent historian has described him as 'outstanding among the covey of incompetent administrators which was the parting gift of the old world of Edwardian England to the new world of total war'.[15] In the main, however, it was factors beyond Selborne's control that robbed him of success.

Certain facets of Selborne's personality did lessen the chance that he would do well in a government of this type during a time of national emergency. His memoranda reveal a diffidence in presenting his own case and a deference to the views of others that spoiled the thrust of his arguments and gave less inhibited opponents the advantage. This was compounded by a circumlocution of prose that occasionally made it difficult to discern exactly what he meant. A telling example of this occurred in November 1915 when Selborne explained the government's reception of the Milner Report to agriculturalists in Newcastle. The next day, to Milner's horror, the *Morning Post*, a Unionist paper presumably sympathetic to the President of the Board of Agriculture, quoted Selborne as saying that the Milner committee had only recommended the wheat guarantee on the assumption that the Admiralty declared it necessary and that in his view the conditions attached to the guarantee had provided justifiable arguments for its rejection. 'I had to rub my eyes when I read that,' Milner wrote incredulously to Selborne. It was a bit much, he objected, if a minister not only had to accept a Cabinet ruling but make a public declaration that he thought it right. Selborne was aghast at the incident and claimed that his words had been distorted by the extreme condensation of the *Post*'s article.[16] Judging from written records, it is quite conceivable that Selborne had spoken ambiguously enough at Newcastle for the *Post*'s reporter to have misunderstood him.

Asquith's cabinets were no place to display such deficiencies. They were notorious for their lack of order, formless discussions and decisionless adjournments, a situation for which the Prime Minister's reluctance to engage in unpleasant and divisive issues was much to blame. Asquith made little effort to monitor proceedings and frequently wrote letters while his ministers argued among themselves. The all too frequent result, according to one member of the Cabinet, was confusion. Meetings often ended with those present unsure whether anything had been decided and time was then wasted debating matters all over again at a subsequent session. Since however minutely a subject had been discussed in committee action could not be taken on it without the approval of the Cabinet, little could be achieved in case of deadlock unless the Prime Minister took the trouble to bring the matter to conclusion. Getting him to do this was not always easy. Selborne described Asquith during this period as 'always courteous and pleasant except when pressed for a decision when he became awkward and dour'. Opposing factions were generally left to settle matters as best they could. 'The Prime Minister's methods of driving an awkward team,' McKenna's biographer has remarked, 'was to throw the reins on the horses' necks.'[17] Little wonder that the course was erratic or that less senior members of the Cabinet were unable to grasp the initiative.

Selborne's position was weakened considerably by a lack of backing from his own party leadership. Had he been able to count on their support at the debate on the Milner Report on 4 August, he might have been able to carry the day. Instead both Bonar Law, the Unionist leader, and his predecessor Arthur Balfour showed a dismaying reluctance to take a stand. The Liberals had been amazed in April by Bonar Law's restraint in demanding concessions from Asquith as the price for Unionist participation in the coalition. What was perhaps even more unusual was that the Unionist leadership maintained this compliant attitude in the months that followed. One explanation advanced for this has been Bonar Law's tangential connection with a criminal lawsuit which, it is said, lessened his bargaining powers with the Liberals.[18] But even before this he had avoided intraparty confrontations as damaging to public morale in wartime. Now, although Selborne was presenting proposals akin to the Unionists' own prewar agricultural policy, Bonar Law told Milner shortly before the Cabinet met that despite sympathy with the report's aims he would not press for its acceptance. Balfour, the First Lord of the Admiralty, similarly refused to make an issue out of the food supply. Despite several appeals by Selborne he would not commit himself even to acknowledge at the Cabinet meeting that a wheat guarantee would be a wise precaution in view of Germany's submarine campaign against Allied shipping; nor would he bring up the matter again in the Cabinet two weeks later when twelve cargo ships were lost in two days. The following March, when Selborne tried to amend agricultural policy for 1916–17 Balfour voted against him. This disloyalty from his own party so upset Selborne that he was still smarting from it over twenty years later.[19]

In circumstances such as these Selborne's personal inadequacies counted for less. In his *War Memoirs* Lloyd George refuted the suggestion that either Selborne or his successor, Lord Crawford, were responsible for whatever weaknesses existed in agricultural policy during this period. Lloyd George condemned the coalition as a whole; its negative attitude towards the war, according to him, ruined all hope of success. 'Looking back on that period', he wrote, 'one could almost imagine that a powerful junta within the government had made up their minds that we could not win, and that the War must therefore be brought to an end as early as possible, and that for this reason they opposed any plans which might encourage its prolongation.'[20] The Milner committee's recommendations for increasing the production of food clearly fell into this category.

Since Lloyd George had personal reasons for portraying the management of the war before December 1916 in an unfavourable light, his explanation of the Cabinet's unwillingness to endorse the state support of wheat production is rather suspect. Besides objections arising from the scheme itself, at least one other factor could have fostered an unfavourable atmosphere for presentation of such a proposal. Sides were already being taken on the raising of a conscript army. The issue had split the Unionist contingent in the Cabinet, Bonar Law and Balfour disagreeing with energetic efforts by their party colleagues (Selborne among them) to commit the government to compulsion. One can only speculate whether these party divisions had any bearing on the Unionist leaders' attitude to the Milner Report, but all parties concerned might well have been reluctant to become embroiled in another controversy about an interventionary measure before the matter of conscription was settled.

The official reasons given for the rejection of the wheat guarantee gave no hint of any tension within the Cabinet. Addressing a meeting of farmers and agricultural experts at the House of Lords on 26 August Selborne blamed the decision on four factors: a reduction in German submarine activity, an increase in the acreage planted with cereals in the world, an anticipated increase in the army's enlistment of agricultural labourers and the expense of such a subsidy.[21]

The first of these, the recent lessening of German submarine attacks on Allied shipping, figured largely in the Cabinet debate. In his accompanying memorandum to the Milner Report Selborne had endorsed the wheat guarantee as a 'war necessity' in view of the damage being inflicted on British trade by the submarines. Consequently, Selborne told Milner, Balfour's refusal to admit that submarine warfare posed any real threat was regarded as a 'clinching argument' by the rest of the Cabinet against the proposal.[22] There are strong indications, however, that the Cabinet's decision did not rest on confidence about the safety of Allied shipping. Although the German blockade had eased after the sinking of the passenger liner *Lusitania* on 7 May, the situation was still causing disquiet in government circles. British tonnage sunk in the spring of 1915 was minor compared to later losses (29,000 gross tons in April, 92,000 in May and 90,000 in June) but these figures included an increasing number of vessels used to carry grain. Between January and March only one consignment of wheat was lost; seven were destroyed in the second quarter. Nine other ships carrying maize and barley had also gone down. Sir Henry Rew told the Cabinet Committee on Food Supplies on 8 July that attacks on grain ships had recently become more insistent, and in August twelve cargoes were lost in two days.[23] The Cabinet was far from sanguine about the sinkings and Asquith reacted swiftly and disapprovingly to an unauthorized public statement by Selborne – who maintained that he had no option but to explain the Cabinet's decision so – that the government considered the submarine menace to be 'well in hand'. Balfour too was taken aback: 'I cannot conceive what Willie Selborne meant by saying that,' he wrote to his sister. 'He didn't get that from me.'[24]

A better argument can be made for the influence of the superabundant harvest in 1915. Encouraged by soaring prices, farmers around the world had increased their acreage under wheat. A good growing season had also brought higher yields than usual. The United Kingdom produced 31 per cent more wheat that year than the average for 1904–1913. The news from North America was even better. The Canadian harvest of 11.6 million metric tons was more than double the prewar average, and the United States' production of 27.9 million tons, compared to an average of 19.8 million in 1904–1913, was a record yield. Of the United States' crop 66 per cent was for sale abroad.[25] The North American results were all the more impressive because they were achieved without reducing the output of other crops. In the United Kingdom, on the other hand, the extra wheat had been grown at the expense of barley and important root crops. The net increase in food production was therefore small and, since the soil had been deprived of the beneficial action of the roots, future yields on those acres could be expected to fall. None the less, the news that so much extra land had gone under wheat was greeted with pleasure by the Cabinet and the fact that it had happened with no other inducement than a high market price was 'worked very hard', according to Selborne, at the meeting on 4 August. At least one member of the

Cabinet, Lewis Harcourt, gave this as his reason for opposing the guarantee and others surely agreed with him that intervention by the state at this stage was simply unnecessary.[26]

One matter on which all were agreed was the difficulty in finding the manpower for an extensive agricultural programme. The Board of Agriculture reported in June that about 16 per cent of the country's male agricultural workers had already enlisted, 19 per cent in the case of England. It was thought that farmers would be able to hire enough women and militarily unfit men to do unskilled jobs, such as weeding; but where would they be able to find the able-bodied, skilled plough-men they needed or for that matter the extra horses and tackle? The War Office had already siphoned off the agricultural surpluses of men, horses and equipment and were now stepping up their drive for recruits. The death toll on the Western Front that spring had been heavy and plans were being made for a big campaign in 1916. Despite the competition for labour between the armed forces, the munitions works and the farmers, however, recent analysis of agricultural labour patterns in the First World War reveals that far from suffering a debilitating decline in its ranks, agricultural manpower in England and Wales dropped by only 7 per cent from its prewar level in 1915, and if temporary assistance from the military and other sources is included, farmers had at their disposal 94 per cent of their normal labour supply. The Board of Agriculture had included in its calculations too many farms with a larger than average hired workforce; smaller, family-staffed farms predominated in England and Wales.[27] While manpower was adequate for normal farming activity, however, farmers would still have been hard put to undertake an extensive ploughing programme. The work was done later at the expense of basic farm tasks.

Of the various reasons given by Selborne on 26 August in explanation of the government's stand, the reluctance to incur the associated expense of a guarantee has attracted little comment. Yet monetary considerations had a most decided impact on policy at this time, and it is probable that this, and not the intensity of submarine warfare, was the 'clinching argument' against the guarantee.

By mid-1915 the rising cost of the war was causing considerable alarm among the government's financial advisors. From the beginning Britain had been spending more on the war than either France or Russia. Not only was it subsidizing its allies in traditional fashion, but it had deviated from past practice and had embarked on an expensive continental venture. At the time of the first war budget in November 1914 the war was costing Britain between £900,000 and £1 million a day. This rose to an average of £2.9 million a day in the second quarter of 1915, £4.2 million in the following three months and reached £5 million a day by September. On 4 May the then Chancellor of the Exchequer, Lloyd George, estimated the budget deficit in the coming year at £865,400,000, more than £200 million higher than the national debt before the war.[28]

To many concerned observers the figures bore out allegations of wild and irresponsible spending by government departments acting with little regard either for each other or for the aggregate resources of the country. Lloyd George had not shown much energy in either controlling spending on the war or improving war revenues to narrow the gap between income and outlay. When McKenna took over the Treasury, he made it clear that the country could expect more stringent attention to fiscal questions. He hoped to make the war 'pay for itself' even if it meant scrapping for the duration certain hitherto inviolable Liberal tenets. McKenna's first war budget, presented in September, raised income taxes and duties on consumer goods and introduced two new sources of revenue: the Excess Profits Duty, which tapped the soaring incomes of firms benefitting from the war, and a series of new and, to traditionalists, shocking import duties on 'luxury' items. Drastic as these measures seemed to contemporaries they came nowhere near solving the problem. Expenses for 1915–16 were expected to exceed income by more than £1,000 million.[29] Increasing revenue, however, was only one side of the coin. McKenna proposed to curb spending by both bureaucrats and public. A general economy drive was announced by the Prime Minister on 26 June and a Committee on Retrenchment and Public Expenditure was formed to debate ways to effect cutbacks in civil spending.

These efforts to 'balance the books' at home coincided with a crisis caused by the increasing level of Allied spending abroad. The assistance given by Britain to foreign governments included in addition to advances for purchases in Britain credits for use in North America. At the beginning of the war this service was easy to provide. The Treasury possessed an estimated $4,500 million in dollar credits in the United States and $2,500 million in Canada.[30] The balance of trade with both of those countries had run in Britain's favour before the war and continued to do so for several months after August 1914. Initially, sterling gained on the dollar. In December 1914, however, the exchange reversed itself along with the balance of trade. Imports of raw materials from North America had increased while exports had decreased, partly because of greater demand for British goods by the Allies and partly because factory output had fallen due to the transfer of labour from general industry to munitions works and the army.

The resultant shrinkage of dollar credits was mitigated by the assistance of J. P. Morgan and Company of New York who in January 1915 became the official financial agents of the British and French governments for war contracts in the United States. Morgan's help was invaluable. It possessed branch offices in London and Paris, which allowed effective co-ordination of business, and it was the largest merchant bank in the United States, able through its services to other banks to tap private resources otherwise out of reach of the Allied governments. The Wilson administration, citing American neutrality, would not permit the Allies to float public loans in the United States to cover the widening gap in the exchange. By June 1915, however, Morgan's was finding it difficult to arrange private funding for Allied purchases and in July suggested that the Allies renew negotiations for issue of an American War Loan. In anticipation of success, Morgan's stopped supporting sterling, which dropped suddenly on the international market.[31]

On 22 July, the day after Selborne circulated the Milner Report, McKenna – his nerve shaken by a fiscal analysis prepared by Keynes, according to Lloyd George – reported to the Cabinet that the Treasury had insufficient dollar credits to settle the Russian account in New York. Two days later Lord Cunliffe, the Governor of the Bank of England, received word from Morgan's that one quarter of all new orders placed in the United States by the British government had to be paid in cash before any contracts could be signed. The Treasury needed $65 million immediately to break the impasse. With the help of the Prudential Assurance Company, which placed its own American securities at the disposal of the government for use as security against a loan, the Chancellor of the Exchequer resolved the matter quickly, but it was clear that the shortage of exchange would remain a continual problem in the future.[32]

Under the circumstances, it is not surprising that McKenna showed 'an invincible repugnance' to Selborne's proposals for increasing wheat production. Milner found the Chancellor of the Exchequer 'very hot against the whole proposal' and assured of the determined backing of the Treasury 'pundits', when he talked to him at the end of July. Despite the conditions attached to the wheat guarantee, the measure could involve substantial expense, especially if, as some members of the government still believed, the Dardanelles were to be opened in the near future. The arrival of freed Black Sea area grain would inevitably cause prices to plummet, leaving the Treasury to subsidize farmers for the next four years. So unattractive was this prospect that Selborne could not even win McKenna over by pointing out that an increase in food grown at home would mean 'more than £10 million of goods . . . transferred to the right side of the balance sheet by substitution from American to British production'.[33]

What little support Selborne received in government circles did, however, derive from this possibility of reducing American imports. On 27 July Lord Kitchener, who had all along pressed for a 'nation in arms', issued a memorandum stating that 'the War Office recognises the necessity of developing sources at home to replace U.S. sources as soon as possible'. He saw an immediate solution to the problem of exchange in the curtailment of orders for breadstuffs, bacon, sugar and tobacco.[34] Hankey, who had communicated his own fears about the financial outlook to the Prime Minister earlier, was positively enthusiastic: 'I am absolutely convinced that we must place ourselves beyond dependence on foreign supplies for the necessities of existence,' he wrote to Selborne, 'and the steps you propose as an *ad hoc* measure will, I hope, lay the foundation of a great national system which may be a safeguard to us in years to come.'[35]

One of the Milner committee's lesser recommendations did, however, find favour with both McKenna and the Treasury: that another attempt be made to establish a reserve of wheat. Selborne would rather this be done by limiting the amount of wheat British farmers could put on the market between August and May, thus setting aside a predetermined proportion of the harvest for the summer months when stocks were always at their lowest. He advised against a repetition of the government's import schemes, warning the Cabinet that further discouragement of normal trading would lead inexorably to a complete takeover of the grain trade by the state, which he considered an expensive and administratively difficult undertaking. McKenna, however, would only approve the accumulation of a reserve on condition that the wheat be obtained from Australia. Selborne found the Chancellor of the Exchequer's decision illogical given the latter's determination to reduce spending. 'I wonder that you regard with so little apprehension the prospect of the possible results of a further purchase of wheat on government account,' he told McKenna a few days later. 'The danger exists that we might have to take over the corn trade and that might be a very serious matter indeed for the *Exchequer* [his italics].'[36] McKenna was not to be swayed and on 17 August Asquith authorized Selborne to revive the Grain Purchasing Committee. The aim was a thirteen week reserve of Australian wheat.

The desire to build up stocks was not the sole reason behind McKenna's stand. It was hoped the scheme would help to soothe hurt feelings in the Dominion. The Australians had found it increasingly difficult to dispose of their produce since shipping started to concentrate on the shorter and, at first, less hazardous runs across the Atlantic and had been complaining for some time that the mother country was insensitive to the plight of Australian farmers. Besides, the Treasury possessed ample credits to expend on Australian wheat, which had the added attraction of being cheaper than that grown elsewhere.[37]

Despite his misgivings, Selborne entered confidently on the project, promising the Prime Minister first a full year's reserve, then revising this to a more 'moderate' estimate of a six-month's stock a few days later.[38] Headed by Sir George Saltmarsh, who had been in charge of the shipment of Indian wheat earlier in the year, the Grain Purchasing Committee ordered large quantities of wheat which they arranged to place in private mills around the country, the Cabinet having parsimoniously ordered that the creation of the reserve had to be achieved without building new storage facilities. The government later claimed that the scheme resulted in a safe margin of wheat for the country by 1916. In fact, only some 2,250,000 quarters of wheat, or two to three weeks supply, were bought under the plan, none of which found its way into permanent storage. Neither Selborne nor Saltmarsh were to blame for this. A shortage of shipping worked against them. The Australasian route had been particularly inadequately served for months before the decision to buy in that market and at the beginning of October 1915 the Australian government had been unable to book a single steamer to ship its grain crop to Britain.[39]

The inability to build a reserve from imports led Selborne to believe that the time was ripe for another attempt to gain approval for his ploughing policy. So confident was he that circumstances now favoured his cause that in March 1916 he not only revised the subject of the wheat guarantee but proposed drastic new powers for the Board of Agriculture to compel farmers to break up pastures.[40]

The War Committee, the inner sanctum of the Cabinet met to
discuss Selborne's proposals on 10 March and, as he expected, proved
far more ready to consider intervention than the Cabinet had been the
previous August. A memorandum by Saltmarsh circulated two days
previously had prepared the ground. Based on the current stock
position and expected reductions in shipping availability in the
immediate future, predictions were that supplies of wheat would fall
below the danger limit of eight weeks by 1 May. Saltmarsh suggested
that the only way to remedy the perpetual problems with grain
supplies was to institute bread rationing.[41] Although both Runciman
and McKenna thought that the adversities had been overstated,
neither they nor anyone else questioned Selborne's assertion that the
outlook for the next six months was not auspicious. Further tipping
the balance in Selborne's favour, exceptionally strong support came
from Lloyd George, then in the thick of a challenge by a party faction
to Asquith's leadership and doubtless welcoming the opportunity to
compare the timidity of present policies with the 'win the war' energy
that could be brought to the endeavour. Lloyd George called for an
end to sporadic efforts to amass stocks of wheat and demanded a
concrete plan for the whole food supply. He applauded Selborne's aim
of self-sufficiency in wartime and endorsed his suggestion that the
Board of Agriculture be given new powers to enforce production.
Lloyd George's eloquence undoubtedly swayed the War Committee,
which requested Selborne to draft for subsequent discussion two
alternative schemes for increasing agricultural output in 1916–17, one
based on the Board's possession of compulsory powers and the other
without.[42]

The question of compulsion dominated the debate when the War
Committee met on 23 March to consider the schemes. The radical
nature of such a step in an area of the economy so bound by tradition,
plus the abrupt departure it would entail from the current position,
caused even the interventionists to pause. Faced with a choice
between compulsory and voluntary expansion of cultivation even
Lloyd George and Selborne preferred that the state try the induce-
ments of a guaranteed wheat price first. Given their views on the
desirability of interference in the economy by the state, it was not
surprising if Liberals objected to such a tremendous increase in the
Board of Agriculture's authority as the compulsory powers scheme
entailed. But the most vehement denunciation came not from them
but from Balfour, who called compulsory ploughing 'the wildest thing

ever proposed' and declared indignantly that 'it would be better to take over the land and run it on Socialistic principles'.[43] Given the strong reaction from all sides against compulsion, the War Committee might well have approved the wheat guarantee as the lesser of two evils had the discussion continued that day. However, due to the pressure of time, the session was adjourned; it was to be two months before the War Committee returned to the subject and by then the situation had changed considerably.

Asquith left England on 25 March for an official visit to France and Italy, returning on 7 April to face two crises that dominated the political scene for weeks to come. The Prime Minister's time was divided between coping with the parliamentary fracas surrounding the settlement of the conscription issue and the suppression of the revolt in Ireland. It was not until after the passage of the Conscription Act at the end of May that Asquith agreed to put agriculture on the War Committee's agenda again.

In the meantime the Unionist leadership let Selborne down once more. As the weeks went by the President of the Board of Agriculture became increasingly angry about the lack of opportunity to bring the government to a decision regarding agriculture and about the Prime Minister's apparent disregard for the wishes of his Unionist ministers. Bonar Law turned a deaf ear, however, to Selborne's observation that the deferral of the debate on agriculture and other questions of interest to the Unionists were sufficient grounds for withdrawal from the coalition, and he would not even respond to an appeal for an official protest at the delay. It was only after several weeks of procrastination that Bonar Law passed on to Hankey, who set up the War Committee's meetings, Selborne's request for a further hearing.[44]

As Selborne suspected it would, the passage of time proved fatal to his proposals. By the time the War Committee finally took up the question again on 26 May it was possible to argue that it was now too late for a compulsory plan to be put into effect before the start of the next agricultural year, even if one were to be approved, so the wheat guarantee was again discussed solely on its merits. Without the threat of a more radical alternative, however, the measure held fewer attractions than it had in March. Moreover, by May the danger to the food supply seemed to have diminished. Stocks of wheat had remained stable for the past two months, and Runciman reported that since the note sent by the Americans to the German government on 18

April protesting the sinking of the unarmed French steamer *Sussex* very few wheat cargoes had been lost to enemy action.

The War Committee not only decided that further action on agricultural development was unnecessary but that restrictions placed on the military requisitioning of grain ships could be eased. It was at this point, in Lloyd George's opinion, that the spirit shown by the coalition sank to its nadir. The record of the debate ended: 'On a general view of the situation, the War Committee take the view that if the submarine menace should become so serious as to cut off our food supplies, a mere increase in the quantity of food raised at home could not avert disaster.'[45]

Only one of Selborne's projects came to fruition, the creation of County War Agricultural Committees, the backbone of the food production campaigns of 1917 and 1918. Again a suggestion of the Milner committee and approved by the Cabinet on 4 August 1915, the scheme was outlined to agriculturalists at the beginning of September. Each county was asked to appoint a committee made up of local landowners, farmers and agricultural labourers who would be responsible for the transmission of data to the Board of Agriculture on the county's needs of fertilizer, machinery, feed and so on, and in return would disseminate official guidance on the agricultural programme each area should follow to obtain optimum national output. The committees were also to curb enlistment of agricultural workers with the assistance of the district labour exchanges and recruiting offices and to discuss ways in which food production could be increased in the light of local conditions. In large counties, sub-committees were to maintain links with local communities.

The project had real potential. Even without compulsory powers over land usage the County War Agricultural Committees could have co-ordinated domestic patterns of cultivation to make better use of the land. Until the change of government in December 1916, however, the committees did not live up to expectations. The most frequent complaint made of them is that they were too large to be efficient: one of the first steps of the Board of Agriculture's Food Production Department in 1917 was to appoint smaller executive boards. This weakness would have been less important had the Board of Agriculture issued firm guidelines in 1915, but apart from the restoration of the grainlands Selborne seemed to have no clear idea of how production should be amended. Asked in September 1915 what advice the committees should give to farmers, Selborne said that meat, milk, cheese, wheat and oats were all needed. During the Second World War the authorities did in fact obtain good results by encouraging farmers to maintain a balanced output rather than persuading some to choose between grain and animal products, but there is no indication that Selborne was thinking along these lines in 1915. A week later he tried to be more explicit, urging farmers to plough as much land as in 1895; that is, an additional 700,000 acres. He then muddled the issue again by declaring that meat was just as important as wheat and issued an order banning the slaughter of immature animals.[46]

This had a negative effect on attitudes, as the secretary of one County War Agricultural Committee explained: 'When the President of the Board of Agriculture says to us, "Go home and work out your own salvation," we feel lost, and do nothing or very little.' The reluctance of committee members to take their duties seriously was indeed marked. Commenting in December 1916 on the committees' lack of progress, the *Mark Lane Express* reported that farmers had shown 'a spirit of apathy which . . . has knocked the life out of . . . these bodies'.[47]

This inertia stemmed only partially from inadequate guidance from above. The conservatives of the farming community and landed interests had much to do with it. After decades of bureaucratic controls over the farming industry, it is difficult for a modern observer to imagine just how shocking Selborne's creation of the committees was to some of his contemporaries. Although the National Farmers' Union initially sponsored the committees as a means of assisting the nation in a time of trouble, the farming community in general considered them 'a very daring experiment'. The novelty made many members, themselves often chary of interference by the state, reluctant to become fully involved.[48]

Lord Selborne resigned his post in June 1916 in protest against the government's Irish policy. He was not to hold high office again and his parliamentary career thus ended on a note of failure. Yet his year at the Board of Agriculture was not entirely wasted. The County War Agricultural Committees fulfilled their potential during the food production campaigns of the following two years and the Milner Report provided the next government with a ready-made agricultural policy that could be introduced immediately. Not least, Selborne had helped to break down prejudice against state intervention in agriculture. He had brought over to his views the person within the government who could soon make best use of them, Lloyd George, and had at least accustomed agriculturalists to the idea of state supervised production. Had this transitionary period not occurred, the production programme of 1917 and 1918 would surely have experienced even more resistance than they did from all concerned.

Notes: Chapter 3

1   H. H. Asquith, *Memories and Reflections 1852–1927*, vol. 2 (Boston, 1928), p. 120.
2   Lord Beaverbrook, *Politicians and the War* (London, 1960), p. 130.
3   S. Koss, *Asquith* (London, 1976), p. 189.
4   Selborne to Jellicoe, 28 April 1915, A. T. Patterson (ed.), *The Jellicoe Papers*, vol. 2, p. 158.
5   B. H. Hibbard, *Effects of the Great War upon Agriculture in the United States and Great Britain* (New York, 1919), p. 183.
6   Lobbyist, 'The Earl of Selborne', *Mark Lane Express Agricultural Journal and Live Stock Record*, 31 May 1915.
7   Milner to Selborne, 6 June 1915, Box 12/246, Selborne Papers, Bodleian Library, Oxford.
8   Milner to Selborne, 17 July 1915, Box 12/258–9, Selborne Papers.
9   Board of Agriculture and Fisheries, Departmental Committee on the Home Production of Food (England and Wales), *Interim Report*, Cd 8048, *Final Report*, Cd 8095 (1914–16); Milner to Selborne, 17 July 1915, Milner to Selborne, 17 November 1915, Box 12/288, Selborne Papers.
10 C. S. Orwin, 'The reports of the departmental committees on the home production of food', *Economic Journal*, vol. 26 (March 1916), pp. 105–13.
11 Scottish Departmental Committee on Food Production, *Report on the Question of Maintaining and if possible Increasing the Present Production of Food in Scotland, First Report* (August, 1915).
12 Sir H. Plunkett to A. D. Hall, 6 August 1915, Box HALL.9, Plunkett Papers, The Plunkett Foundation for Co-operative Studies, Oxford; Department of Agriculture and Technical Instruction for Ireland, *Report of the Departmental Committee on Food Produciton in Ireland*, Cd 8046, *Minutes*, Cd 8158, (1914–16).
13 Milner to Selborne, 30 July 1915, Box 12/271, Selborne Papers.
14 Asquith to the King, 5 August 1915, CAB 41/36/37.
15 A. Marwick, *The Deluge: British Society and the First World War* (London, 1965), p. 172.
16 *Morning Post*, 8 November 1915; Milner to Selborne, 17 November 1915, Box 12/288, Selborne Papers; Selborne to Milner, 18 November 1915, Box 12/290, Selborne Papers.
17 A. Chamberlain, *Down The Years* (London, 1935), p. 111; Selborne, personal notes, 1916, Box 80/285, Selborne Papers; S. McKenna, *Reginald McKenna 1863–1943* (London, 1948), p. 179.
18 R. Jenkins, *Asquith* (London, 1964), pp. 369–70.
19 Milner to Selborne, 30 July 1915, Box 12/271, Selborne Papers; Selborne to Balfour, 20 and 30 August 1915, 49708/262 and 264–5, Balfour Papers, British Library, London; Selborne, personal notes, 1937, Box 191/68, Selborne Papers; War Committee, Minutes, 23 March 1916, CAB 42/11/9.
20 D. Lloyd George, *War Memoirs*, vol. 3, p. 1274.

21 'Lord Selborne's food supply meeting', *Journal of the Board of Agriculture*, vol. 22, no. 6 (September 1915), pp. 489–503.

22 Selborne, Memorandum, 21 July 1915, CAB 131/30; Selborne to Milner, 4 August 1915, Box 350/248, Milner Papers. Bodleian Library, Oxford.

23 R. E. Prothero (Lord Ernle), *Whippingham to Westminster* (London, 1938), p. 274; Sir R. H. Rew, Note on wheat position, 8 July 1915, Box 92, Runciman Papers, University of Newcastle-upon-Tyne; Selborne to Balfour, 20 August 1915, 49708/262, Balfour Papers.

24 K. Young, *Arthur James Balfour* (London, 1963), p. 357.

25 T. H. Middleton, *Production in War* (London, 1923), pp. 112, 160; Hibbard, *Effects of the Great War upon Agriculture*, p. 24; L. H[arcourt]., Wheat, 14 August 1915, CAB 37/132/19.

26 Selborne to Milner, 4 August 1915, Box 350/248, Milner Papers; L.H., Wheat, 14 August 1915, CAB 37/132/19.

27 *Hansard*, vol. 72 HC Deb., 5s., 17 June 1915, col. 777; P. E. Dewey, 'Agricultural labour supply in England and Wales during the First World War', *Economic History Review*, vol 28, no. 1 (February 1975), pp. 100–12.

28 F. W. Hirst and J. E. Allen, *British War Budgets* (London, 1926), pp. 14, 21, 26, 80.

29 E. V. Morgan, *Studies in British Financial Policy, 1914–25* (London, 1952), pp. 91–2.

30 S. Pollard, *The Development of the British Economy 1914–1967* (London, 1969), p. 72.

31 K. M. Burk, 'The Treasury: from impotence to power', in Burk (ed.), *War and the State: The Transformation of British Government, 1914–1919* (London, 1982), pp. 89–90; R. A. Dayer, 'Strange bedfellows: J. P. Morgan & Co., Whitehall and the Wilson administration during World War I', *Business History*, vol. 18, no. 2 (July 1976), pp. 128–30; J. M. Cooper, 'The command of gold reversed: American loans to Britain, 1915–1917', *Pacific Historical Review*, vol. 45, no. 2 (May 1976), p. 211.

32 D. Lloyd George, *War Memoirs*, vol. 2, pp. 683–4.

33 Ibid., p. 964; Milner to Selborne, 30 July 1915, Box 12/271, Selborne Papers; Selborne to McKenna, 6 August 1915, Box 81/73, Selborne Papers.

34 Note by the Secretary of State for War on 'The Financial Situation', 27 July 1915, D/24/6/1, Lloyd George Papers, House of Lords Record Office, London.

35 Hankey to Selborne, 13 July 1915, Box 80/14–16, Selborne Papers.

36 Selborne, Memorandum (accompanying interim report of Milner Committee), July 1915, AC 19/3/13, Austen Chamberlain Papers, University of Birmingham.

37 Selborne to W. H. Long, 7 February 1916, Box 82/121, Selborne Papers.

38 Selborne to Sir M. Bonham Carter, 14 October 1915, Box 15/30, Asquith Papers, Bodleian Library, Oxford.

39 *Hansard*, vol. 86 HC Deb., 5s., 17 October 1916, col. 502; Rew to the President [Selborne], 4 October 1915, Box 92, Runciman Papers.

40 Selborne, Food supply and production, 2 March 1916, CAB 42/10/2.

41 Sir G. Saltmarsh, Food supplies, 1 March 1916, CAB 42/10/4; War Committee, Minutes, 8 March 1916, CAB 42/10/8.

42 War Committee, Minutes, 10 March 1916, CAB 42/10/9.

43 Selborne, The food supply of the United Kingdom, 16 March 1916, CAB 42/11/3; War Committee, Minutes, 23 March 1916, CAB 42/11/9.

44 Selborne to Bonar Law, 8 May 1916, Box 80/161–3, Selborne Papers.

45 War Committee, Minutes, 26 May 1916, CAB 42/14/11.

46 Selborne, A scheme to encourage and assist the farmers of England and Wales to maintain and if possible to increase the production of food during the war, 7

September 1915, and Report of a Conference of representatives of the county councils of England and Wales, of agricultural colleges and institutions, &c, &c, &c, 7 September 1915, MAF 53/6/146; Report of a conference at the University of Bristol between agriculturists of the counties of Gloucestershire, Somerset, Dorset, Herefordshire, Monmouthshire, Warwickshire, Worcestershire, and Wiltshire, and the Earl of Selborne. The steps to be taken to maintain and if possible increase the production of food during the war, 16 September 1915, MAF 53/6/147.

47 *Mark Lane Express*, 27 March 1916, 25 December 1916.
48 Ibid., 27 September 1915; *Hansard*, vol. 82 HC Deb., 5s., 22 May 1916, col. 1847.

4

Shipping and Prices: Incentives for Control

Lord Selborne has been censured for not living up to expectations. His counterweight in the coalition government, Walter Runciman, has suffered the same fate for allegedly doing the exact opposite. His critics have complained that the President of the Board of Trade proved all too graphically how right Asquith was to depend on him to defend the *laissez-faire* principles of Liberalism against the onslaughts of the incoming Unionists. In recent times Runciman's contributions to the coalition have been summed up as consisting primarily of opposition to every creative suggestion that might have led to an improvement in national efficiency.[1] Contemporaries were sometimes no kinder. According to Christopher Addison, one of those participants in the Lloyd George coalition who heartily condemned members of the previous administration in postwar memoirs, Runciman's attitude had a particularly stultifying effect on shipping operations during the first two years of the war. Displaying an 'utter lack of foresight and courage', Runciman was said to have maintained an obstinate prejudice against intervention by the state in civilian sectors of the economy, while his timidity in introducing controls over shipping and his laxness in replacing lost tonnage by new construction left the nation inadequately prepared to cope with the war at sea. If there was one administration that deserved to be pilloried by posterity, Addison charged, that was the Board of Trade under Runciman.[2]

Because of the large proportion of imports in Britain's food supply how shipping was used or misused had important consequences. By the end of 1915 the shortage of shipping serving the civilian market had developed into one of the most serious challenges to the nation's ability to feed itself. As the year progressed the pool of merchant vessels free to carry commercial cargoes shrank swiftly due to the depredations of the enemy and the military requisitioners. The latter

Table 4.1   *Merchant Shipping Under Requisition*

1 January 1915	3,176,051 tons
1 September 1915	5,321,432 tons
1 December 1915	6,202,875 tons

Source: J. M. Keynes, 'The Freight Question', 18 December 1915, *Collected Writings*, Vol. 16, p. 152.

Table 4.2   *Shipping Losses*

	War Losses	Net Difference Between New Construction and War Losses
1914 (August to December)	252,738 tons	+231,000 tons
1915	885,471 tons	− 63,000 tons
1916	1,231,867 tons	−687,000 tons

Source: J. A. Salter, *Allied Shipping Control*, pp. 355–7, 363.

were particularly voracious. By 1 December 1915 nearly one third of the merchant fleet had been withdrawn from commercial service.

Since the Admiralty was in charge of both military requisitioning and shipbuilding, it may be asked why Runciman should be blamed for this situation. Addison considered this question himself, concluding that 'it was for the President of the Board of Trade to be the alert and aggressive custodian of the vital interests of overseas supplies and of the Mercantile Marine'. In his opinion, Runciman simply had not stood up for the civilian sector as he should but had weakly allowed things to drift until the mercantile fleet was dangerously depleted.[3]

Not everyone was so disparaging about Runciman's performance at the Board of Trade. Several of his colleagues thought that he had done well: in 1917 Asquith declared Runciman to be 'an indispensable member of any really capable Administration'; Hankey considered his knowledge of shipping matters 'exceptional'; and Lords Grey, Crewe and Hardinge all commented favourably on his work. Selborne, who might have been expected to have been critical of a political opponent with views so different from his own, felt that Runciman had run the Board 'quite admirably'.[4] In fact, Runciman's record was not as barren as his critics claimed. During 1915 and 1916 the web of controls over shipping used to import foodstuffs was extended significantly. It is true that not all of the advance occurred under Board of Trade auspices – the Admiralty played a larger role than some considered appropriate in a matter affecting civilians – but in every instance the action taken was either initiated or endorsed by Runciman. However insufficient these measures seemed in retrospect, they represented a comparatively more radical step forward – given the resistance of shipowners to interference in their affairs at this time – than later controls, which went into effect in an atmosphere of greater acceptance. More could have been done, especially with regard to shipbuilding. Nevertheless, the ground was prepared well enough during this period for a smooth and quick transition to the Ministry of Shipping's more inclusive jurisdication in December 1916.

Under the Asquith coalition government, the Cabinet Committee on Food Supplies remained true to the policy laid down by the Liberals of concentrating on the maintenance of imports. The dwindling pool of shipping inevitably made it increasingly difficult to carry out this policy without the introduction of measures assuring sufficient tonnage to service food importers. Additional inducement for the government to step in came from the complaints of the state purchasing units that the shortage of transport was making it impossible for them to fulfill their assignments. The problems experienced by the Grain Purchasing Committee during the winter of 1915–16 have already been described. The Sugar Commission fared only a little better. The Admiralty Transport Department, which was responsible for requisitioning transport for the Commission, was simply not providing all the shipping the Commission required. The huge stocks of sugar built up in the autumn of 1914 began to fall swiftly during the summer of 1915. On 1 March 1915 the country possessed 427,000 tons of sugar, enough to last three months; by 1 March 1916 only 59,000 tons were in storage.[5]

The supply of meat was similarly adversely affected by transport problems. In April 1915 the Board of Trade gave up persuasion as a means of inducing shipowners to make refrigerated tonnage available and adopted a more forceful approach. All British steamers with insulated space trading with South America, Australia and New Zealand were ordered to give priority to the carriage of meat purchased by the Board. Shipowners were required to form two organizations, the River Plate Refrigerated Tonnage Committee and the Australasian Refrigerated Tonnage Committee, which operated under the guidance of the Board without direct interference in how a ship itself should be run. In June the Board made it mandatory for these ships to carry meat for civilians in any excess insulated space they possessed on their homeward journey. As more and more ships were withdrawn from service by requisitioning, the owners of the rest found it more profitable to concentrate on the shorter crossings to the Americas. A single ship could carry three times as much freight as it could in the time it took to make the round trip to Australia. As a result, the produce of Australia and New Zealand was not being shipped. In June 1915 some 2 million carcasses were glutting cold storage units in New Zealand, at the very time that statisticians in Britain were forecasting a deficit in civilian meat supplies of 133,000 tons for the year, even allowing for a 15 per cent decrease in consumption since the start of the war.[6]

It was believed that these transportation problems could be alleviated by directing available tonnage into specific areas of trade. After some hesitation, Runciman gave his backing in November 1915 to a proposal by Bonar Law for two civilian committees possessing wide powers under Orders in Council to secure shipping for the carriage of imported food. In an effort to co-ordinate their work, both committees were to consist of the same people.[7]

The goal of the Ship Licensing Committee was to harness all British vessels into the service of the import trades by limiting the employment of ships currently used only between ports outside the British Empire. Through the refusal of licenses, it was hoped to pressure the owners into bringing these ships home. The immediate result was disappointing. The number of ships affected by the order was less than expected. Licensing was an important step in the control process, however, and the committee was to play a useful role in subsequent years as an executive body that could quickly commandeer transport needed by various government departments for special purposes.[8]

The Requisitioning (Carriage of Foodstuffs) Committee, as its name suggests, was designed specifically to obtain tonnage for food importers. It had one major flaw; its activities were not co-ordinated with those of existing government agencies handling food supplies. Without consulting anyone else, the committee decided to give preference to wheat shipments in the winter and spring of 1915–16. It proposed to increase imports to 800,000 quarters a week and effect a reduction in freight rates (and hence the price of imported wheat) by providing more competition among carriers. The committee's powers allowed it to order a shipowner to charter in a particular market. As a first step, the committee tried to increase trade with North America, a decision that did not help Saltmarsh to bring over the Australian crop and that hardly fitted in with McKenna's plans to reduce the demand for dollar credits. Since the free enterprise system attracted more ships to the North Atlantic routes than the wheat trade needed, the committee's efforts in the first seven weeks of its existence were superfluous and had no effect on either the number of vessels serving those routes or freights. After February 1916, however, when wheat trading in the north routinely slackened off, the committee ordered more ships westward than the market would have attracted unaided. As a result, imports from North America were higher than usual in the early spring of 1916 and freight rates did decline. This success encouraged the committee to expand its geographical scope and to begin organizing similar services for France and Italy.

The drawback was that nothing had been done to increase the share of shipping serving the food trades as a whole. Consequently, the committee's concentration on finding ships for the wheat trade reduced the amount of tonnage available for the shipment of other foodstuffs. Imports of meat and sugar continued low while freight rates and retail prices climbed higher.[9] The experience showed that with demand for tonnage space exceeding supply, any special project to increase imports in one area could only succeed at the expense of others. To ensure that this did not deprive the country of commodities that it could ill spare, the relative importance of imported goods had to be assessed and shipping allocated accordingly. Runciman therefore proposed to the Cabinet on 17 January 1916 the long-term planning of allied import programmes and the allocation of transport based on properly calculated forecasts of needs.[10] This job was assigned to a new Shipping Control Committee, under the chairmanship of Lord Curzon, which began work on 27 January.

The Curzon Committee quickly produced a survey indicating a deficit of 3¼ million gross tons of shipping compared to estimated demand in 1916, enough to bring in 13 million tons of goods. They recommended the prohibition of all imports except specified essentials up to that amount. The Board of Trade's response to this suggestion has been harshly criticized. Runciman found Curzon's list of recommended cuts impractical and the outcome was the purposeful elimination of only 1.8 million tons of unnecesarry imports in 1916. The official history of shipping control, however, defends Runciman, pointing out that the information and preparatory work behind the recommendation were insufficient to warrant such drastic action. The total exclusion of certain commodities on that scale could have had an incalculable effect on the economy. Subsequent success in reducing imports was achieved by spreading the cuts between a large number of industries.[11]

This was the sort of work expected of the Shipping Control Committee, but it was not equipped to do it. As with so many other war committees the Curzon Committee had no executive powers to enforce decisions on its own account nor, with only one full-time officer at its disposal, did it have the staff to provide a continuous in-depth analysis of shipping use. The Board of Trade's failure to co-ordinate these civilian agencies into a single unit that could remedy such deficiencies was not as culpable as critics have suggested. Another body was already well-equipped to undertake such a task. This was the Admiralty Transport Department. By the autumn of 1915 demand for shipping from the state trading units was so heavy that the Admiralty set up a separate Requisitioning Branch. It also began to compile data on the world's entire ocean-going transport, the statistics that allowed the controls of the last two years of the war to be effective.

In the absence of priority schedules, decisions taken by the Admiralty Requisitioning Branch occasionally interfered with the importation of food. A particularly annoying example occurred in January 1916. Ships chartered by Ross T. Smythe on behalf of the government were in the process of loading wheat in Argentina when the Admiralty ordered them to take on nitrates for the Ministry of Munitions instead. The result was a loss of profits for the shipowners, who had to carry back a commodity covered by less remunerative Blue Book rates, and a setback to efforts to increase wheat shipments. The event caused an uproar in the wheat trade and an unwelcome reaction by some foreign exporters who instructed their agents in England not to accept British business except on 'free on board' terms, which left all transportation arrangements to the purchaser.[12]

The storm over this incident broke only a few days before the War Committee met to discuss Saltmarsh's admission of failure to acquire the reserve of Australian wheat and to hear Selborne's renewed pleas for the state support of agriculture. Concerned by this combination of events, the War Committee ordered on 10 March that all ships directed into the grain trade by the Requisitioning (Carriage of Foodstuffs) Committee be 'blacklisted'; that is, exempted from requisitioning for naval, military or other purposes except by express authority of the War Committee itself.[13] Further, the Admiralty was requested to pay greater care all round to its civil operations. The Admiralty responded by transferring the responsibility for civil supplies to a new Commercial Branch of the Transport Department. By the time the Ministry of Shipping absorbed it in December 1916, this unit was arranging transport for nearly all of the country's imported supplies in which the government took an interest. Its operations were so efficient that the Ministry made very few changes to the system other than extending control to shipping not yet covered by the regulations. Whether the civil sector would have been better served if the Board of Trade had run the unit instead of the Admiralty, as was implied by the Board's critics, is questionable.

The Admiralty was to assist the flow of imports in another way. In February 1915 congested port facilities had been cited as a major factor in the rise in the cost of food. In December 1915 the docks, their railway connections and their workforce were placed under the authority of a Port and Transit Executive Committee appointed by the Admiralty. This speeded up the rate of discharge at the docks and decreased the turnaround time of unloading vessels, thus increasing the number of voyages that could be made in a given time.

Towards the end of the year the freight shortage gave the British the opportunity to inject fresh life into the Allied co-operative buying programmes, which had begun to languish – to Britain's cost. In November 1915 the authorities were disconcerted to discover that, armed with money recently borrowed from the British Treasury, the Italian government had just bought an entire year's imports of wheat from North America. In the same month actions by the French government similarly strained Allied harmony. During the year France had added to its refrigerated tonnage and, feeling less dependent on Britain, abandoned the Board of Trade's organization and resumed separate purchases of meat. The chance to curb this interallied competition came when both France and Italy submitted greatly increased requests for the use of British shipping in 1916. With the legitimate argument that its own transport problems made it difficult to provide its allies with extra shipping unless attempts were made to effect economies in usage, Britain was able to persuade both countries to sign new agreements to pool acquisitions. A joint committee headed by Lord Crawford began work on 3 January 1916 to obtain wheat for the military forces of Britain, France and Italy. On 31 March, Italy having signed earlier, France and Britain endorsed a contract covering the joint importation of frozen meat for the military for the duration of the war plus three months.[14]

The search for solutions to the shipping problem led the Cabinet Committee on Food Supplies to seriously consider for the first time the possibility of reducing consumption. The subject had come up during the summer of 1915 following the announcement of McKenna's retrenchment campaign. Both Montagu and Hankey suggested ration tickets as a means of enforcing economy. Such stern measures would have been necessary had the government agreed to demands from the Treasury that consumer spending on food and clothing be cut by 20 per cent.[15]

The Prime Minister and the rest of the Cabinet, it seems, were not inclined to go to the extreme of rations. However, they apparently shared Montagu's opinion that 'the working classes must be made to feel the pinch of war',[16] as they revealed later in the year. Asquith, McKenna and Runciman were the main speakers at a conference on the cost of living called by the Parliamentary Committee of the TUC and other labour organizations on 1 December. After the Prime Minister had told the audience that wage earners were substantially better off than before the war and McKenna had blamed the rise in prices on lavish expenditure by the working classes on imported foods, Runciman asked for the reduction of living standards to a level closer to those of the 1870s, when the country consumed on average 12 per cent less meat per head and almost 50 per cent less sugar, tea and tobacco.[17]

A campaign to educate the country in the need for such sacrifices was launched in the spring of 1916. In the Second World War the government had the radio to transmit its messages to the people. Lacking such an entrée into the homes of the masses, the authorities of the First World War had to use the printed word. The public was bombarded with leaflets on the subject of saving food. Some of it offered quite sound advice on food values and the elimination of waste; much offered only amusement or irritation according to the temperament of the reader. One recipient found the widely distributed tract *How To Save And Why*, put out by the Parliamentary War Savings Committee, a perfect gem of absurdity. Among the hints on how the average person could stretch his food budget were to collect acorns, horsechestnuts and beechmast (for the family pig?) and to go gleaning ('some families might well have the benefit of a sack or more of wheat'). An Essex rector, on the other hand, annoyed at receiving bundles of these missives to distribute to his rural parishioners, condemned the pamphlet as typical of the 'total lack of common sense prevailing in London today'.[18]

Other, more promising, methods of effecting economies in imports were also explored. Recognition of the potential value of allotments gained steadily. In January 1916 the Board of Agriculture announced special grants for municipalities providing land for this purpose. At Lord Selborne's urging the Board of Agriculture, the Board of Trade, the Local Government Board and the millers and bakers associations held talks in June 1915 on the closer milling of grain. For the time being this went no further. The difficulties envisaged in March 1916 of maintaining wheat supplies led the Cabinet Committee on Food Supplies to approve an emergency plan to raise the extraction rate from 70 per cent to 80 per cent and an order was drafted, but fearing that the loss of offals for cattle would outweigh the increase in flour for humans, the War Committee deferred the scheme until the stock position worsened.[19] The achievements of the Requisitioning (Carriage of Foodstuffs) Committee made the step unnecessary until later in the year.

Despite the greater care paid by the government to food questions in the winter and spring of 1915–16 problems continued to mount, and in June 1916 supplies and prices became the focus of considerable public discontent and official concern. Satisfactory imports of wheat were reflected in higher stocks than a year previously and a steady price for bread. Supplies of other grains were down, however, and so were stocks of meat, with imports in the second quarter of 1916 running an average of 10,000 tons a month behind those of 1915. Imports of sugar improved slightly towards the middle of the year, but stocks on 1 June 1916 were only about one third as much as on 1 June 1915.

Retail prices, predictably, drifted upward. Government officials estimated that by 1 June the working class cost of living had risen by 45 per cent since the start of the war, with the retail cost of food up 59 per cent. An independent survey suggested that these figures applied only to the more affluent artisan class and put the rise in the cost of food for the average working family at 68 per cent and for the poorest

Table 4.3　　*Stocks of Selected Primary Foodstuffs (000 tons)*

	Wheat	Barley	Oats	Meat	Sugar
1 June 1915	1,185	352	424	63	232
1 June 1916	1,384	321	305	53	87

Source: Ministry of Food, *Monthly Office Reports* (December 1918), Table D.

labouring people at 75 per cent. The cheapest British beef now cost 81 per cent more, the cheapest imported mutton 120 per cent more; sugar had gone up 158 per cent and, due to the failure of the crop after abnormally wet weather, potatoes had more than doubled in price. Average basic wages (without allowing for overtime) increased by only 20 per cent in the same period. An inquiry by the Board of Trade found most working class families cutting back on food purchases. This was primarily in response to price, but some cities were also experiencing distribution problems. In the face of smaller shipments of meat, some wholesalers were reserving supplies for their regular credit customers. This favoured shopkeepers in better-off areas and penalized butchers in poorer neighbourhoods who, in search of bargains, had previously dealt with a variety of wholesalers for cash. In June there were severe shortages of all but the poorest quality meat in several working class districts of London while supplies in nearby middle class communities remained ample. The flow of food to centres of armaments production was meanwhile not keeping pace with the rapid growth of population, and prices were generally higher than in other towns.[20]

Demands for higher pay became more insistent around the country in the spring of 1916, keeping Sir George Askwith, the government's Chief Industrial Commissioner, extremely busy. For the past year the government had stuck to a policy of resisting wage increases. They stood equally firm against constantly reiterated requests by labour representatives for rationing and maximum prices. Apart from the administrative difficulties attached to rationing, it was believed that the political consequences of admitting that the country was in as bad a condition as Germany would be highly damaging to the government's popularity. As far as maximum prices were concerned, government experts agreed that results in 1914 were sufficient reason why they should not be tried again. Competition between traders, not further intervention by the government, was said to offer the public the best protection from exorbitant prices.[21] As before, reports reaching England of the effect of food controls in Germany convinced the Cabinet Committee on Food Supplies that neither rationing nor maximum prices could work. The German press was full of complaints about the way rationing had reduced the urban poor to semi-starvation and how maximum prices had driven up the cost of living and had distorted distribution. After reading one such report, Runciman came to the conclusion that 'artificial cheapness does not produce plenty; it tends to reduce production. High prices stimulate production and importation, and tend to restrict consumption. *Maximum prices* must be accompanied by *compulsory production*'.[22] Since the government could not bring themselves to sanction the latter, they presumably could not proceed with the former.

Press opinion was divided. The Unionist *Morning Post* had backed maximum prices since the beginning of 1915. *The Times* was initially more wary of food regulations, but by the spring of 1916 its editor considered it 'time that people should realise what is happening and be prepared for greater privation and more drastic action on the part of the government', and the paper began featuring articles on the flaws in the current system. Appeals for government intervention appeared as a matter of course in the labour press. The *Spectator* and the voice of radical Liberalism, the *Nation*, struck a different note. The former saw a rise in prices as the only way that consumption could be checked. Reminding the government that 'high prices are . . . , if left alone, their own cure', its editor suggested that the government *increase* prices, rather than lower them, by extra taxes levied on food. The *Nation* saw things only slightly differently. It believed prices should be tackled but only by initiating a drastic reduction in consumption coupled with general monetary controls.[23]

However strong they felt the case against maximum prices to be, the government came to believe in mid–1916 that some concession had to be made to popular feeling. The issue had come to the fore again when Asquith could least afford to take a stand on it. The Prime Minister's acceptance of the Conscription Act and his handling of the Irish question had proved to be the turning point in both his personal career and the viability of his coalition government. Liberal ranks had lost their cohesion during the past few months and the Prime Minister could no longer depend on the support he had once enjoyed from his own party. His gradual abandonment of Liberal principles had left some Liberals disillusioned and resentful of what they regarded as the pusillanimity of the party leadership at the same time that a growing number had become attracted to Lloyd George's more aggressive 'win-the-war' attitude. The granting of Home Rule to Ireland meanwhile lost the coalition the support of several leading Unionists, among them Lord Selborne. Under the circumstances, when the Parliamentary Committee of the TUC announced that a special trades union congress would be held on 30 June to debate the government's food policies, the Cabinet Committee on Food Supplies lost no time in announcing that a departmental committee of the Board of Trade would investigate the principle causes of the rise in the cost of living.

Reaction in labour circles was mixed. 'Just what we asked for,' Harry Gosling, the chairman of the TUC, said on hearing the news. Only a week later, however, the WNC's leadership were worrying that the deliberations of such a committee would prevent any early action on the matter.[24] That the move was indeed just another example of Asquith's 'usual formula of delay' was the opinion of postwar critics. With challenges to the government now occurring constantly, it was claimed, the existence of the committee proved of great value in 'fobbing off' parliamentary questions about the food situation. The government's alleged hypocrisy was blamed on the influence of Runciman, whose 'elaborately sceptical terms of reference' to the committee were said to be eloquent of his attitude to the whole question and to have left no doubts as to his aims.[25]

The government certainly may be forgiven for hoping that debate on this issue could be deferred until the political turbulence caused by conscription and the Irish uprising had died down, but the only motive an employee of the Board of Trade admitted to in a private conversation was the desire to use the committee's report to gain increased powers to break the trade combinations (rings) that were popularly thought to have driven up food prices.[26] Although this may invite scepticism, this was in fact one of the first questions that the committee looked into.

The investigation provided a stage for one of the final confrontations between the defenders of traditional government and the aggressive champions of the new regulatory state. Each side was roughly equal in numbers and the contestants literally faced each other across the debating table from two immovable camps. The chairman, J. M. Robertson, a former Parliamentary Secretary to the Board of Trade, proved helpless in this situation, his own strong commitment to free trade, according to one of those present, rendering him either unable or unwilling to break the deadlock.[27] The result was an enervated compromise report that was not presented until 22 September. Nevertheless, the inquiry hastened the abandonment of peacetime practices and opened the door to full-scale food control.

The committee found no evidence that illegal manipulation of trade was responsible for wartime inflation. The simple laws of supply and demand were enough in themselves. The committee recommended an increase in refrigerated tonnage so as to import more, greater employment of women on the land to produce more at home, and a minimum wage to help lower-paid workers to withstand the rise in prices. More importantly, seven of the twelve members signed a supplementary statement urging the government to extend its powers over the food supply. Besides a number of specific measures, they proposed the general development of state trading in imports and the fixing of 'reasonable prices' for home-produced primary foodstuffs.[28] A second report, issued on 15 November, covered bread, flour and wheat. This contained conflicting suggestions. Some of the committee members wanted to protect the public through low fixed prices for flour and bread; others wanted the government to guarantee a high price for wheat to encourage farmers to produce.[29] By then, however, the authorities had already committed themselves to a number of important food control measures.

Had the government really expected that the Robertson Committee's investigation would allow the subject of prices to be quietly shelved and forgotten, it must have been deeply disappointed. Far from dying down, public interest was stimulated by the inquiry. Labour organizations seized on the chance to pressure the government into amending its policy of wage restraint. The TUC held its conference on 30 June and, with the enthusiastic backing of the delegates, sent a deputation to the Prime Minister on 19 July. This was an abortive affair during which Asquith angered the labour representatives by delivering a lecture on the benefits of free trade. In response, the TUC passed a resolution threatening industrial action unless the government took the problem of food prices seriously. The railwaymen had already declared that they would not wait for the committee's report. On 27 August thousands gathered in the rain in Hyde Park to hear Ben Tillett and other popular speakers inveigh against the government's inaction. Similar meetings were held elsewhere around the country under banners reading 'We Want Cheaper Food' and 'Down With The Food Pirates'.[30]

In parliamentary circles the topic provided the government's critics, both within and without the administration, with fresh ammunition. Lloyd George, who had moved to the War Office on 7 July after Kitchener's death, again tried to use the food question for political ends. A War Office memorandum, issued by the Raw Materials Section of the Contracts Department but bearing all the hallmarks of Lloyd George's personal involvement, declared the widespread popular agitation over inflation prejudicial to the conduct of the war. 'There is a disposition in some quarters', the memorandum read, 'to suggest that it is impossible for the Government to do anything to check the steady inflation of food prices.' Emergency measures already imposed by the War Office and Ministry of Munitions over other commodities showed that it could in fact be done. The writer demanded the complete co-ordination of wheat purchases by the Allied governments and the encouragement of domestic and colonial production by guaranteed prices lasting into the postwar period. The memorandum concluded with the suggestion that these strong war measures would most appropriately be administered by the War Office itself.[31]

After casting around unsuccessfully for a cause that would win him the approval of the Conservative leadership and yet retain for him the good graces of Lloyd George, Churchill too turned to the subject of the cost of living during a parliamentary debate on 22 August. In what has been described as 'the most notable speech' of the sitting, he made an impassioned plea to the government to put the question of food prices 'on a war basis'. What more cruel or unfair way of restricting consumption than by the agency of price, he asked. 'If we are to look upon the whole nation as an army, on our men and women struggling for a common purpose, then they are entitled to their rations and to secure the necessary supplies at prices which their strenuous labour is not incapable of meeting.[32]

Milner was also gathering his forces for an attack on the government, focusing on the agricultural side of the question. The debate on food prices was intensified by depressing reports on the current harvest. Cold wet weather throughout the summer coupled with a general deterioration in the condition of the land due to a reduction in root crops in 1915 had resulted in less than average yields of grain. Production was estimated to be 400,000 tons less than the previous year. The outlook in North America was also poor. The country would have to import more at higher cost. The publication in June of a report by the Board of Agriculture comparing the productivity of British and German farms added to the dismay. Milner led his Unionist sympathizers in the formation of a new organization to promote the state subsidization of agriculture. Through the British Agricultural Section of the British Empire Producers' Organisation, Selborne, Turnor, Prothero, Bathurst and others campaigned for minimum guaranteed prices for grain and potatoes and for a central department to co-ordinate and improve the work of the War Agricultural Committees. Another chance to present their views in an official report came when Selborne persuaded Asquith to appoint him chairman of a committee looking into agriculture as part of a larger study of policy for the reconstruction era after the war.[33]

With the unions up in arms and the matter turned into a political issue, it was virtually incumbent on the government to become more involved. During the second half of 1916 rapid progress was made in the development of food controls. Starting in July, the public got its first taste of 'datum period rationing', which restricted consumption by limiting supplies for sale to a certain percentage of the trade in a more normal year. Finally acknowledging that it could not maintain stocks at their prewar level, the Sugar Commission announced in June that in future distributors would receive only 65 per cent of their sales in 1915. The measure spread the cuts evenly across the board and was clearly designed to protect business interests rather than the public. No attempt was made to eliminate or reduce substantially the use of sugar by the manufacturers of sweets or other non-essential products. The public sometimes found it easier from then on to buy sweets than household sugar. As the Sugar Commission rejected the idea of ration tickets as a 'lighthearted suggestion', shopkeepers introduced their own system to which the government gave its approval.[34] To preserve their stocks for regular customers and discourage hoarders from going from shop to shop, grocers required a minimum purchase of other items (usually 4/- worth) with every pound of sugar bought. Labour representatives complained that this discriminated against poorer consumers, but McKenna defended the practice as beneficial to the working classes. If sugar were sold without other groceries, he claimed, the grocer's supply would run out long before the end of the week when most working class families bought their food. The Robertson Committee also recommended retention of the system as a way of preventing hoarding, although they advised that the minimum purchase be reduced.[35] Another drawback to the datum period arrangement soon emerged. More affluent neighbourhoods, where more sugar had been bought in 1915, got larger 'rations' than poor districts. In munitions centres this inequality was accentuated by the allotment of supplies based on out-of-date population statistics. The unfairness of sugar distribution was to cause a great deal of public dissatisfaction until the introduction of true rationing in 1918.

Also in July, legislation was passed restricting brewing to 85 per cent of output in the year ended 31 March 1916. The trade had already cut back barrelage in 1915, so the new order reduced production to about 73 per cent of prewar. Since all of the sugar and most of the barley used by the brewing industry was imported, this released transport for more essential foodstuffs. Again the measure was too kind to the trade. The brewers accepted the situation gracefully on the understanding that the government would not intervene again for at least a year. No restrictions were placed on exports.[36]

The most radical step was taken on 9 October when, private trading having been suspended for the duration, a Royal Commission headed by Lord Crawford assumed all responsibility for the importation of wheat. Reasons given for this have varied: the prospect of another submarine campaign by Germany, the increasing number of strikes and the government's desire to pacify labour, and the problems that ordinary merchants were having arranging payment for their purchases because of the deficit in foreign exchange.[37] Although these factors no doubt contributed, the main motive cited by the Cabinet Committee on Food Supplies in September was a shortfall in supplies of wheat coming onto the market due to poor harvests around the world. Both France and Italy had announced that they would be importing more, and it was estimated that the requirements of the Allied and neutral countries would exceed available supplies by 20 per cent.[38]

In a situation requiring energetic bargaining to secure the nation the amounts of wheat it needed, it was felt that the private importers could not be relied on. If this were so, it was the fault of the government's own agents. The trade had never recovered its confidence since the state purchasing committees started work in 1914. With government units handling one-seventh of total wheat imports by mid-1916, the potential power of the authorities to use these supplies to force down prices, plus repeated promises that the Dardanelles would be breached, left merchants reluctant to hold more than a minimum amount of stock. Then in the summer of 1916 an error by the Admiralty's requisitioning staff nearly doused all remaining sparks of initiative in the private sector. A large contingent of ships chartered for wheat were sent to the wrong destination. The result was a sudden shortage of freights, considerable anger in trade circles and a heightened aversion by dealers to sign contracts for grain.[39]

Merchants now assumed the less risky occupation of government agent, operating at a fixed percentage under the direction of the Wheat Commission. The latter took over at fair market prices all holdings and existing contracts, negotiated a new freight tariff and established a single purchasing agency in each of the exporting countries. In the United States Samuel Sandays and Company, the largest of the British exporters, was reincorporated as the Wheat Export Company on 20 November. By assuming the operations of a private trader the Wheat Export Company did not need to spend time building a network of agents and contacts. Staffed by men of experience in the trade, it was able to set to work immediately in a businesslike manner. The arrangement also avoided an affront to public opinion in America on the subject of open transactions by foreign governments. The Wheat Commission acted as purchasing agent, placing all orders on behalf of the Allied governments and arranging transportation. A Wheat Executive, a board of representatives of the governments concerned, met from time to time to decide general policy. The British, French, and Italian governments signed a Wheat Executive Agreement pooling orders and shipping on 29 November, and the arrangement was extended during the following year to include Belgium, Portugal and Greece.[40] The establishment of the Wheat Commission meant that the bulk of Britain's food imports were now fully controlled by the state. Between them, the Wheat and Sugar Commissions accounted for three-quarters of the total by calories and for two-thirds by weight. The Board of Trade's meat department and other state trading units were responsible for much of the rest, leaving an insignificant amount uncontrolled at the time of the changeover in government in December 1916.[41]

On 17 October the Board of Trade received powers under the Defence of the Realm Act to make special orders regulating the supply and distribution of food. It announced the existence of a new Food Department, a section of its Employment Department, set up to implement the recommendations of the Robertson Committee. Under the supervision of W. H. Beveridge it had already been at work three weeks, having first met on 26 September to discuss the committee's report. This body was the nucleus of the future Ministry of Food, providing it with both personnel and a folio of legislation in course of preparation. In Beveridge's opinion it was to the first Food Controller's advantage to take over a 'going concern', but it could be said to have been rather the opposite for it laid the Food Controller open to blame for several measures initiated before his appointment. Of these, none would hurt his reputation more than the 'meatless day', the Robertson Committee's answer to the meat shortage. Under this plan restaurants and other public eating places were forbidden to serve meat meals on one specified day a week. Theoretically, this would reduce consumption by the better-off to the benefit of the working classes by releasing extra supplies onto the market and thus lowering prices. In practice, the measure induced people to buy more cereals, the working classes' basic food. Another doubtful step was the resumption of 'maximum prices' lists, with results much as before. Other orders issued by the Board of Trade were less problematic: an increase in the milling standard of grain, stronger regulations against waste and hoarding and a limit on the number of courses that could be served in restaurants.

It has been said that during this period Runciman maintained a dogmatically non-interventionist attitude and that his subordinates in the Food Department despaired of being able to effect any kind of positive action.[42] The records indicate, however, that Runciman showed little or no hesitation in following up the Robertson Committee's proposals. On hearing that the committee favoured a reduction in the price of milk, he immediately ordered an inquiry and had a statement ready for the Cabinet by 27 September. An order checking further increases in the price of milk was among the first issued by the Food Department. Runciman instructed his staff to carry out all of the measures put forward by the committee except one – a proposal for municipal shops to which the Local Government Board in England and the Scottish authorities objected strongly. In a reversal of ideological positions, Runciman ran into strong resistance from the President of the Board of Agriculture, Lord Crawford, when (following up another of the committee's suggestions) he asked for restrictions on prices of domestic agricultural produce. Crawford, a Conservative, believed the public to be well able to withstand the current cost of food and opposed the imposition of price controls on the ground that they would both discourage farmers and reduce output and would invite further intervention by the state in subsidiary areas.[43]

Having gone this far, the government balked at completing the process by appointing a Food Controller to co-ordinate the work in hand. On 17 October Runciman told the Commons that the country did not need one, and it was not until 15 November, apologizing for the drastic nature of the step, that he announced that an appointment would soon be made. Since there was general support in the country for this, his apology was unnecessary. Labour spokesmen had been calling for full control of foodstuffs since the beginning of the war, and as far back as June 1915 the *Morning Post* had proposed a 'Ministry for Munitions of Food' followed only a month later by the *Spectator* with a 'Grand Victualler to the Nation.' *The Times* commented that the only apology necessary was for the new regulations not being drastic enough.[44]

There were several reasons for the delay. Despite all the evidence pointing to the contrary, the government anticipated a negative reaction by the public to such close interference by the state in people's daily lives.[45] There were also fears that overseas suppliers would take advantage of the situation and raise their prices. Particular concern was expressed over possible American responses. A recent survey of trade with the United States had aroused deep dismay. The Treasury was facing a most serious crisis due to the lack of dollar credits and was anxious to avoid any signs of panic that might lead to extra financial pressure. Pierpoint Morgan told Runciman in October that the government's concern was already known in some quarters in the United States and warned that courage by the Wheat Commission in particular was essential if the British were to avoid becoming 'the victims of Chicago'.[46]

After October, however, it became increasingly difficult to justify postponing the appointment of a Food Controller. On 31 October Asquith read to the War Committee a letter from Admiral Sir John Jellicoe advising that the present rate of loss being inflicted on Allied shipping by German submarines would so seriously reduce imports of food and other essential items by the summer of 1917 that the Allies would be forced to accept peace terms unwarranted by the military situation. Germany had intensified its restricted campaign in October, achieving a rate of success unparalleled in the war to date, over 300,000 gross tons of shipping sunk in a month.[47] Around the same time, Crawford circulated a pessimistic memorandum on 'Food

Prospects in 1917'. As head of the Wheat Commission as well as President of the Board of Agriculture he was greatly perturbed by the conjunction of higher shipping losses and the worldwide decline in food output. The British harvest had been 8 per cent smaller in 1916 than the average in the four year period preceding the war. Grain production, which had risen in 1915, had fallen back to the prewar level, while 25 per cent fewer potatoes, 13 per cent less milk and 8 per cent less meat had been produced. Thanks to Admiralty requisitioners who had taken 80 per cent of the country's first-class steam fishing ships, the fish catch had declined by more than one third. With fodder and labour in short supply too, Crawford predicted a decline in herd size during 1917 and the lapse of some farmland into dereliction. He urged the immediate establishment of a central authority to supervise and co-ordinate the import, production and distribution of food.[48]

The outlook had worsened by 10 November when the War Committee met to discuss a report by Runciman on the shipping situation. With destruction far in excess of new shipbuilding for the past two years, the merchant fleet was so diminished that, it was felt, it could no longer be relied on to maintain supplies at even a minimum level of safety. The Admiralty Transport Department could provide only 60 per cent of the carriers presently needed by the Wheat Commission. With the prospect of a more intensive submarine campaign in the spring, a complete breakdown in Allied civilian shipping was likely by June 1917. Runciman had no suggestions to offer other than the release of ships from military use.[49] For Lloyd George, poised for his successful ouster of Asquith from the premiership, the general gloom cast over the War Committee's proceedings by this communication provided a fitting backdrop for his own memorandum, circulated at the same meeting, calling for the immediate appointment of a 'Food Dictator'.[50] This proposal was reportedly greeted by Runciman and McKenna with indignation and disgust, a reception that left Lloyd George 'feeling very sick with everything and talking of resigning and taking on the food job outside the Cabinet'.[51]

The hostile reaction to this apparently reasonable suggestion becomes more understandable when one considers the context in which it was made. McKenna and Runciman were not just stubbornly clutching at the rags of free trade. By that time, the strains within the Cabinet had almost reached breaking point. The depressing setbacks on the military front, the frequent challenges to the government's authority, in the Commons, the almost daily sessions at which nothing was resolved and the perpetual wrangling that occurred at these meetings had so dispirited its members that six ministers were said to be on the brink of resignation. Lloyd George had been in the midst of every dispute in recent months and had now, despite his professed frustration at his colleagues' attitudes, made a suggestion that he must have known would arouse controversy. The difference between a 'Food Controller' and a 'Food Dictator' might appear today to be one of semantics, but to socialist newspapers like the *Clarion* there was a clear distinction.[52] The powers expected to be wielded by a 'Dictator' were far in excess of any that a 'Controller' would have. That Lloyd George was repeating the tactics he used in March during the debate on the Selborne proposals for agricultural development – attempting to win support for a measure by first alarming his colleagues with a more radical proposal – is suggested by the stand he took at the meeting of the War Committee on 13 November. His approach that day was much more circumspect, designed to win over rather than irritate his fellow ministers. He asked for a 'Food Controller' (the term the Prime Minister personally favoured) or even a 'central control authority'. The War Committee, including those who were allegedly so resolutely opposed to the idea only three days earlier, endorsed the suggestion with a minimum of hesitation.[53]

The problem now was to find someone to fill the post. While the government was subjected to the usual charges of procrastination, the refusals piled up. With the administration on the verge of collapse, no-one was willing to take on a job that he might hold for only a few weeks. Among those approached was Milner, who reportedly gave the seventh refusal. It was not that he had changed his mind about the need for food control or that he had any strong objections to joining the government, but he felt he would be wasted in that particular post. 'If they would give me *Food Production*', he told a friend, 'apart from all fiddle-faddle about the control of what people are to eat and drink, I think I could do some good.' What he really wanted, he confided, was a show of his own outside the government.[54]

It was not long before the War Committee was called upon, again by Lloyd George, to make an even more serious decision. On 23 November he proposed rationing. There was good reason by this time at least to prepare the machinery. The basic foodstuff, bread, was likely soon to be in short supply and there would have to be a careful sharing of other commodities if the mass of the population were not to be subjected to serious hardship. The Wheat Commission had advised that stocks were running down dangerously quickly due to the shortage of freight to carry sufficient imports to keep pace with demand. On 22 November London had only two days wheat in store, Bristol two weeks. The War Committee ordered ten of the nineteen ships of the military reserve berthed at Southampton to be dispatched immediately to New York where 700,000 quarters of wheat were held up for lack of transport. Pending the appointment of a Food Controller, it was decided to ask the Medical Department of the Local Government Board to draft a rationing scheme.[55] With shipping in short supply, the quickest way to build up stocks was to concentrate tonnage on the North Atlantic routes, but the problem of exchange also had to be taken into consideration. The American government had just rejected another request by the British and French to float a war loan and the Treasury therefore asked that wheat purchases in the United States cease and those in Canada be limited to $20 million.[56] As before, plenty of credit existed in Australia. Despite the troubles of the Grain Purchasing Committee in the winter of 1915–16, a plea from Runciman that there were not enough ships to transport existing orders from Australia and a warning from the Wheat Commission that the carriage of the Australian crop would tie up one hundred ships for six months, the War Committee decided to channel as much tonnage as possible into the project. It proved impossible to implement. Eight months later the bulk of the Australian crop, already paid for, was still unshipped and Asquith's government was still being faulted for poor judgement. Due partly to this decision, stocks of wheat on 1 January 1917 were the lowest recorded for that time of year during the entire war.

The political crisis meanwhile had come to a head and on 6 December the government was reconstructed as another coalition headed by David Lloyd George. The outgoing government bequeathed its successor a legacy of food problems. A point ignored by its critics is that it also left behind the foundation on which the food controls of the next two years were built. All the arguments about *whether* the government should intervene in the food supply were now over. Imports and shipping had been largely brought under direct regulation. The Wheat Commission, the most efficient and valuable unit of the entire food control system, provided a model for a number of smaller import agencies dealing in other commodities created in 1917. The first concrete steps had been taken to effect economies in the consumption of grain. Some major policy options were on hand: plans for the development of agriculture had been drawn up earlier, proposals for rationing were in course of preparation and other avenues were being explored by the Board of Trade's Food Department, which itself was the core of a future central food authority. These diverse elements had still to be drawn together into a coherent programme of control. To do this and to construct the administrative machinery necessary for the further refinement and application of the system the country needed a Food Controller.

Notes: Chapter 4

1   A. J. P. Taylor, *English History 1914–1945* (Oxford, 1965), p. 34.
2   C. Addison, *Politics From Within 1911–1918*, vol. 2 (London, 1924), pp. 32, 72.
3   Ibid., p. 32.
4   H. M. Hyde, *Lord Reading: The Life of Rufus Isaacs, First Marquess of Reading* (New York, 1967), p. 207; M. P. A. Hankey (Lord Hankey), *The Supreme Command 1914–1918*, vol. 1 (London, 1961), p. 333; E. Grey (Viscount Grey of Fallodon), *Twenty-Five Years 1892–1916*, vol. 2 (New York, 1925), pp. 249–50; M. Bentley, *The Liberal Mind 1914–1929* (Cambridge, 1977), p. 56; Selborne, personal notes, 1916, Box 80/286, Selborne Papers, Bodleian Library, Oxford.
5   Ministry of Food, *Monthly Office Report* (London, December 1918), Table D: Stocks of the principle foods in the United Kingdom.
6   Inter-Departmental Committee on Meat Supplies, *Report*, Cmd 456 (1919), p. 8; High Commissioner, New Zealand to H. W. Macrosty, 22 June 1915, BT 13/63/10, Board of Trade Papers, Public Record Office, London, R. H. R., Note on meat supplies, 14 June 1915, PRO 30/30/4, Milner Papers, Public Record Office, London.
7   Bonar Law to F. C. Gardiner, 8 October 1915, 53/6/43, Bonar Law Papers, House of Lords Record Office.
8   J. A. Salter, *Allied Shipping Control* (London, 1921), p. 50.
9   Ibid., pp. 51–3.
10 Asquith to the King, 18 January 1916, Box 8/133, Asquith Papers, Bodleian Library, Oxford.
11 Addison, *Politics From Within*, vol. 2, p. 333; Salter, *Allied Shipping Control*, pp. 65–6.
12 Salter, *Allied Shipping Control*, pp. 55–6; Runciman to Balfour, 1 March and 4 March 1916, 49716/51 and 54–5, Balfour Papers, British Library, London; R. H. R., Wheat supplies and stocks, 11 April 1916, Box 92, Runciman Papers, University of Newcastle-upon-Tyne.
13 War Committee, Minutes, 10 March 1916, CAB 42/10/9.
14 R. H. R., Purchase of food supplies by the Allies, 6 July 1915, and R. H. R., Joint purchases by the Allies, 28 February 1916, Box 92, Runciman Papers; The Board of Trade and meat supplies, 22 November 1916, MAF 60/434; Report on refrigerated meat purchases undertaken for the British Army and for the French and Italians by the Board of Trade, April 1916, MAF 60/93.
15 Sir G. Paish, The finance of Great Britain, 31 August 1915, D/24/6/76, Lloyd George Papers, House of Lords Record Office, London; M. P. A. Hankey, diary, entry for 23 November 1916, Churchill College, Cambridge.
16 Montagu to Asquith, 3 July 1915, Box 14/88, Asquith Papers.

17   Report of representative conference at Wesleyan Central Hall, *Westminster*, 1
      December 1915, Box 12/4, War Emergency Workers' National Committee
      (WNC) Papers, Transport House, London.
18   C. E. Playne, *Society at War 1914–1916* (London, 1931), pp. 305–6; Clark, diary,
      entry for 21 March 1916, Bodleian Library, Oxford.
19   R. H. R., Scheme for economising wheat, 20 March 1916, and R. H. R., Note on
      war bread, 1 October 1916, Box 92, Runciman Papers; Crawford, Standard bread
      and wheat economy, 5 October 1916, MAF 60/105.
20   Board of Trade, Department of Labour Statistics, Effect of the rise in prices on the
      consumption of food by the working classes, September 1916, Box 103, Runciman
      Papers; F. Wood, 'The increase in the cost of food for different classes of society
      since the outbreak of war', *Journal of the Royal Statistical Society*, vol. 79 (July
      1916), p. 507; Ministry of Food, *Monthly Office Report*, (December, 1918), Table
      F: Percentage increase in retail food prices; A. L. Bowley, *Prices and Wages in the
      United Kingdom, 1914–1920* (Oxford, 1921), p. 106; *The Times*, 13 June 1916 and
      16 September 1916.
21   *Hansard*, vol. 74 HC Deb., 5s., 22 September 1915, cols. 490–1; ibid., 14 October
      1915, col. 1456; *Hansard*, vol. 80 HC Deb., 5s., 21 February 1916, col. 521.
22   H. B., Notes on German food prices, plus Runciman's jotted comments, n.d., Box
      103, Runciman Papers.
23   *Morning Post*, 31 May 1915; W. C. S. Mills to Sir W. Ashley, 8 May 1916, 42247,
      Ashley Papers, British Library, London; *Spectator*, 27 May 1916 and 24 June
      1916; *Nation*, 18 July 1916.
24   *Westminster Gazette*, 17 June 1916; J. S. Middleton to J. Stokes, 24 June 1916,
      9/2/16, WNC Papers.
25   Sir W. H. Beveridge, *British Food Control* (London, 1928), p. 19.
26   W. B. Hardy to Sir J. J. Thomson, 19 June 1916, Box 505, Royal Society Papers,
      Royal Society, London.
27   Ashley, personal notes, n.d., 42247, Ashley Papers.
28   Board of Trade, Departmental Committee on Prices, *Interim Report*, Cd 8358
      (1916).
29   Board of Trade, Departmental Committee on Prices, *Second and Third Reports*, Cd
      8483 (1917–18).
30   Minutes of a deputation to the Rt. Hon. H. H. Asquith, etc., from the Parlia-
      mentary Committee of the TUC at the House of Commons, 19 July 1916, Box
      91/81–104, Asquith Papers; W. Thorne, 'Asquith's cold douche', *Justice*, 10
      August 1916; *The Times*, 28 August 1916 and 7 September 1916.
31   Raw Materials Section of Contracts Department, War Office, Memorandum on
      proposed control of food prices (copy, n.d.), Box 2/9, E. M. H. Lloyd Papers.
      British Library of Political and Economic Science, London.
32   *Hansard*, vol. 85 HC Deb., 5s., 22 August 1916, col. 2514; M. Gilbert, *Winston S.
      Churchill*, vol. 3, *The Challenge of War*, Part 2 (Boston, 1971), pp. 999–1000;
      Beveridge, *British Food Control*, p. 20.
33   T. H. Middleton (Board of Agriculture), *The Recent Development of German
      Agriculture*, Cd 8305 (1916); British Empire Producers' Organisation, British
      Agricultural Section, Interim report, plus Recommendations of Mr Leslie Scott's
      committee referred to in accompanying report, Box 130/263–243, Milner Papers,
      Bodleian Library, Oxford.
34   C. S. Rewcastle, *Sugar Distribution* (London, 19 October 1916), printed copy of
      address to the General Purposes Committee of the Grocers' Federation.
35   The Labour Party Information Bureau, *Bulletin*, number 10 (London, 26 Feb-
      ruary 1917); Board of Trade, Cd 8483, p. 22.
36   H. G. Paul, Provisional proposals in regard to beer and spirits, plus Lord

Devonport to Bonar Law, 5 January 1917, Food Files, Box 2, items 11 and 14, Beveridge Papers, British Library of Political and Economic Science, London.

37   A. Marwick, *The Deluge: British Society and the First World War* (London, 1965), p. 177; T. G. Hall, 'Cheap bread from dear wheat: Herbert Hoover, the Wilson administration, and the management of wheat prices, 1916–1920; PhD thesis, University of California at Davis, 1970, p. 6; K. M. Burk, 'British war missions to the United States 1914–1918', PhD thesis, Oxford University, 1976, p. 93.

38   Alan G. Anderson, Memorandum in answer to the circular of the Committee of Imperial Defence, 25 July 1916, PRO 30/68/2, Anderson Papers, Public Record Office; W. H. Beveridge, personal notes on file of Royal Commission on Wheat Supplies, Food Files, Box 4, Beveridge Papers; Board of Agriculture, Wheat supplies 1916–17, 7 October 1916, Food Files, Box 4, Beveridge Papers.

39   Anderson, Memorandum, 25 July 1916, PRO 30/68/2, Anderson Papers, PRO.

40   Hall, 'Cheap bread from dear wheat', pp. 6–7; J. F. Beale to J. R. Clynes, 15 August 1917, MAF 60/127; Burk, 'British war missions', pp. 95–7.

41   G. Hardach, *The First World War, 1914–1918* (Berkeley, CA, 1977), pp. 124–5.

42   J. Harris, *William Beveridge* (Oxford, 1977), pp. 233–4.

43   Runciman, Milk prices and supplies, 27 September 1916, plus W. H. Beveridge, Notes on action taken on report of committee on food prices. Both in Box 103, Runciman Papers; S. Olivier to Secretary, Board of Trade, 31 October 1916, Food Files, Box 3, Beveridge Papers.

44   *Morning Post*, 2 June 1915; *Spectator*, 10 July 1915; *The Times*, 16 November 1916.

45   War Committee, Minutes, 13 November 1916, CAB 42/24/5.

46   Runciman to Anderson, 26 October 1916, Box 149, Runciman Papers.

47   Jellicoe to Balfour, 29 October 1916, A. T. Patterson (ed.), *The Jellicoe Papers*, vol. 2, p. 88; Hardach, *First World War*, pp. 41–2.

48   Lord Crawford, Food prospects in 1917, 30 October 1916, CAB 42/22/12.

49   Runciman, Merchant shipping, 26 October 1916, CAB 42/22/6.

50   Lloyd George, Food supplies, 10 November 1916, CAB 42/24/3.

51   A. J. P. Taylor (ed.), *Lloyd George: A Diary by Frances Stevenson* (New York, 1971), p. 121, entry for 10 November 1916.

52   *Clarion*, 24 November 1916.

53   War Committee, Minutes, 13 November 1916, CAB 42/24/5; Hankey diary, entry for 13 November 1916.

54   Milner to Lady E. Cecil, 8 December 1916, Box 353/223–4, Milner Papers.

55   War Committee, Minutes, 23 November 1916, CAB 42/25/7.

56   War Committee, 1 December 1916, CAB 42/26/6.

5

The Ministry of Food

'A challenge is music in his ears', one of his contemporaries said of Lloyd George.[1] This was perhaps why Lord Devonport found the Prime Minister 'full of enthusiasm and big ideas for food control' when he visited him on 8 December to accept the invitation to become the country's first Food Controller.[2] One of Lloyd George's ideas was to give the responsibility for the food supply to a new ministry. This, he believed, would free the question from the fetters of past precedent and allow the authorities to go straight to the heart of the matter. Speaking on the food situation a week after he took office, the Prime Minister stressed that 'all prejudices, all predilections must be swept aside'.[3]

These sentiments had a familiar ring to them. The Prime Minister clearly envisaged Devonport doing at the Ministry of Food what he himself had done at the Ministry of Munitions some eighteen months earlier. Lloyd George attributed much of his success with munitions to his appointment of businessmen to executive posts. He admired the enterprise and drive of the entrepreneur and, since many of his recruits offered their services to the government gratis, he found their independence of the bureaucratic pay system useful in circumventing the Treasury's efforts to dampen ministerial enthusiasm for possibly expensive new projects.[4] At their meeting the Prime Minister asked Lord Devonport to bring in as many businessmen as he could at the Ministry of Food.

The new Food Controller himself was certainly qualified to join the ranks of Lloyd George's business experts. A millionaire whose fortune derived from the wholesale grocery firm of Kearley and Tonge, he had the reputation of being an astute businessman. 'As far as food distribution was concerned', Lloyd George reflected later, 'there was no man in the country who had wider experience.' *The Times* declared it 'an appointment of distinction', the *Observer* thought that 'there could hardly be a better choice', even the *Clarion*, although critical of Devonport's stand on labour questions, praised him as 'an energetic and capable organiser'.[5]

Devonport was no stranger to government office. As Sir Hudson Kearley, he had served as Lloyd George's Parliamentary Secretary when the latter headed the Board of Trade in Campbell-Bannerman's administration. He had impressed Lloyd George then by his 'clearheadedness and his businesslike and masterful handling of every problem . . . left to his charge'.[6] Since 1909 Devonport had held the post of Chairman of the Port of London Authority, a position he had filled with admirable firmness in the minds of the ruling classes and with intolerance in the view of the dockers and other workers who came under his jurisdiction. The emotions aroused in labour circles by Devonport's hard-line attitude at the PLA were portentous. General illiberality of mind and a talent for creating resentment among those who had to work under him were to be his downfall at the Ministry of Food.

For the first six months of the ministry's existence its efficiency was greatly impaired by internal disputes. His conversation with the Prime Minister may have left Devonport with the impression that he would be supervising an organization of businessmen. On taking office, however, he found himself the immediate possessor of a civil service staff of seventy-four made up of former employees of the Board of Trade and Board of Agriculture who had been engaged on food questions when the Asquith coalition fell. As with the Ministry of Munitions earlier, a concession to peacetime practices was made by filling the top administrative post at the ministry, that of Permanent Secretary, with a civil servant. This was Sir Henry Rew, the Assistant Secretary of the Board of Agriculture who had handled the state's first purchases of wheat in 1914–15 and who had provided the Cabinet Committee on Food Supplies with data on grain stocks. Other leading civil servants, including W. H. Beveridge, the former head of the Board of Trade's Food Department, found themselves assigned to junior positions in departments run by the ubiquitous business experts.

Some of the businessmen, such as Isidore Salmon who headed Division A of the ministry, had appropriate qualifications and soon established a good working relationship with the permanent officials based on respect. Salmon, a director of Lyons' Corner House, was responsible for sections dealing with hotels and restaurants, sugar products, fruit and vegetables and finance. William P. Burton, a member of the well-known clothing firm was a rather more unusual choice for the helm of Division B, which handled bread, flour and grain, feeding stuffs, fertilizers and export restrictions. The personnel of the dozen or so advisory committees formed by Devonport raised no hackles. Members of the Bakers' Advisory Committee, the Milk Advisory Committee and so on, were selected for their know-how of production and distribution methods in particular trades. By the time the Ministry of Food was created such advisory committees had become a commonplace means of control through co-option of the industry concerned into the administrative system and had produced good results in such instances as the railways and munitions factories.[7] Devonport's appointees to special working committees, on the other hand, were a source of much disharmony. Taking projects away from experienced personnel like Beveridge, whom he threatened to make the office boy, the Food Controller handed them over to favourites like Alfred Butt, a competent and intelligent assistant but one whose past career as the managing director of the Palace Theatre scarcely qualified him to draft a national rationing scheme for sugar.[8]

Devonport carried Lloyd George's dislike of civil service methods to extremes. The Prime Minister believed permanent officials were unsuited to the highly technical problems presented by the war and wanted in charge of key questions men whose minds had not been tainted by years of contact with red tape. He did not intend the bureaucracy to be superannuated, however, merely to be re-utilized in more imaginative ways. Devonport, who described civil servants as 'molluscs', tried to do without them as much as possible.[9] It was not long before the ministry was in upheaval. When Beatrice Webb wrote in her diary that 'the swollen world of Whitehall is seething' with 'the permanent officials, who in pre-war days lived demure and dignified lives . . . now fighting desperately for the control of their departments against invading "interests" and interloping amateurs', she had the Ministry of Food immediately in mind.[10]

Complicating matters was a concurrent attempt by the Royal Society to get itself accepted as the government's official scientific advisor on food policy. The Society had formed a War Committee back in November 1914 to provide assistance on war-related problems, but few assignments connected with food had been forthcoming. The only project of note was an evaluation of the food resources of the United Kingdom commissioned by the Cabinet Committee on Food Supplies in March 1916, which was ready for the new Food Controller's perusal in December.[11] The news that a Food Controller was to be appointed excited the Royal Society, who saw in the event tremendous possibilities for the future of nutritional research. Just as work done by its engineering, physics and chemistry sub-committees had paved the way for the creation in 1915 of Britain's first Department of Scientific and Industrial Research, so, the Royal Society believed, its Food (War) Committee could be a forerunner of a national Food Board of Research. Until this came into being the Royal Society proposed to help the government in two ways: it would superintend experiments to increase the food supply and to find methods of using existing resources more efficiently and members of the Royal Society attached to the Ministry of Food would screen ministerial orders to make sure none were harmful from a physiological or an agricultural point of view.[12] This offer accepted, T. B. Wood, a professor of agronomy at Cambridge, and W. H. Thompson, a noted physiologist, joined the staff of the ministry.

It was only a few weeks before they too were up in arms. Contrary to their expectations they did not become arbiters of food policy. Orders were issued by the ministry about which they had not been consulted and would have opposed if they had. Little was done in the way of research: by February only a few questions about sugar and glucose had been submitted for study. After only one month on the job Wood was on the brink of resignation and by March the Royal Society was considering disassociating itself from the ministry. Devonport's preference for his own point of view was blamed for this contretemps, but in this matter the businessmen and the older civil servants saw eye to eye: Rew told Wood that he could not see how scientific considerations came into the food question at all.[13]

Complaints about the situation at the ministry soon reached Downing Street. News of Beveridge's plight probably filtered back through those members of Lloyd George's personal secretariat who, like Beveridge, formed part of Beatrice Webb's circle. The scientists too gained entrée through the secretariat, aided by its head, Professor W. G. S. Adams, who brought Royal Society memoranda to the attention of the War Cabinet. Other civil servants sought the assistance of Lord Northcliffe, who played a major role in recruiting staff for the new ministry. Charles Bathurst, whom Lloyd George had recommended personally for the post of Parliamentary Secretary, wrote directly to the Prime Minister and Bonar Law about his difficulties with Devonport. Bathurst had been deeply embarrassed by the Food Controller's habit of hugging all important matters to himself. When Devonport had been away from the office ill, as he was on several lengthy occasions, Bathurst had been unable to answer questions on food policy put to him in the Commons.[14]

These conflicts earned Devonport lasting fame as a prime incompetent. Several of his staff got their revenge by ridiculing him in postwar publications, the most influential being Beveridge's official history of food control, which set the tone for all subsequent assessment of this period of food administration.[15] One can appreciate the feelings that went into these books, but it needs to be stressed that they distort the Food Controller's role in events by focusing attention on his personal shortcomings without clearly defining the parameters of his responsibility for policy. The main feature of food policy during this period was the inability of the authorities to come to any settled decision about what line to follow. Time and again measures were taken up for consideration and put aside without any final verdict being made, schemes were continually being drafted that were never used and orders were issued that were rescinded within a few weeks. By the time of Devonport's resignation in May 1917, very little appeared to have been accomplished. The cost of living had continued to soar and people were having even more difficulty getting supplies than before the ministry existed. Devonport left office against a backdrop of popular discontent and labour unrest that forced the government to introduce major policy changes shortly afterwards.

Devonport's critics maintained that this was all his fault. In a letter to Adams written in May 1917, the Royal Society's Secretary, W. B. Hardy, compared the effects of the maladministration of food supply over the past six months with the disasters that preceded the creation of the Ministry of Munitions. Referring to angry demonstrations by working men on May Day just past, Hardy commented that 'the Food Controller must have earned the lasting gratitude of the German Government even if he has failed to merit their esteem'.[16] Devonport had faults enough, but did he deserve remarks of this kind? Were the country's mounting food problems due solely to weak management of the Ministry of Food? Contrary to a recent claim that the Devonport era of food control was 'a standing testimony to the influence of personality in history', the Food Controller exerted less power over the course of events than his critics imagined.[17] As Rew stressed in response to a sally by the Royal Society in April, 'ministerial' food policy during Devonport's term in office was determined primarily by the War Cabinet.[18]

When Lloyd George took over the leadership of the country he planned to eliminate the factors in government that had obstructed speed and efficiency in the decision-making process during the past two years.[19] Asquith had made several attempts at this by creating 'inner cabinets' that theoretically devoted themselves to the central direction of the war effort, but these had always foundered on his desire that important decisions be discussed by the whole cabinet and on the monopolization of the inner cabinets' time by demands for adjudication from the host of feuding committees set up during the war. Lloyd George did away with the larger cabinet, establishing a War Cabinet of five members, which was to determine war policy and settle larger questions. Representing the main political forces in the country the War Cabinet initially consisted of the Prime Minister, Andrew Bonar Law and Lord Curzon, both Conservatives, the leader of the Labour Party, Arthur Henderson, and Lord Milner. Although part of the imperialist movement that swept the Unionist Party earlier in the century, Milner was considered more of an independent in the political spectrum. He had no set role in the War Cabinet and tackled various problems as they arose. One of his more regular duties was to keep an eye on food supply and agriculture.

Lloyd George intended the War Cabinet to remain free from deep involvement in the running of individual departments of state. Germany's resumption of unrestricted submarine attacks on Allied shipping on 1 February 1917, however, triggered a crisis of such proportions that the constant monitoring of the food situation by the War Cabinet was essential. During the submarine campaign it was Professor Adams' job to keep the Prime Minister closely informed of any developments with the food supply. It was for this reason that the Royal Society's criticisms of the Food Controller came so frequently before the War Cabinet. After it was realized in mid-year that the German attacks could be surmounted, Adams moved on to other things and the War Cabinet's attention to food problems became sporadic. The emergency lasted throughout the major part of Devonport's time at the Ministry of Food and during the whole period he did little more than follow the War Cabinet's instructions. Fluctuations of policy followed the ebb and flow of the War Cabinet's fears for the ability of the country to survive the enemy's campaign.

Inconsistency of policy was also reflective of the confusion that reigned within the central government itself during the first six months of Lloyd George's term, notwithstanding later claims that the change of government had effected an immediate transformation in administrative efficiency. The new system proved unable to cope with the demands put on it and there was a period of readjustment while some of the War Cabinet's responsibilities were gradually delegated to yet more *ad hoc* and standing sub-committees. Managed by a new cabinet secretariat run by Maurice Hankey, the system began to operate smoothly only in mid–1917, by which time problems with the new ministries created in December 1916 had also come to a head and had begun to be ironed out. As with the war effort in general, the turning point in food control came in June 1917.

Among the matters that needed to be settled during the first part of 1917 was clarification of the Ministry of Food's responsibilities. As with the other new ministries these had not been fully thought out at the beginning. Devonport was much troubled by the vagueness of Lloyd George's instructions to him in December 1916, but lacking the imagination and ability to concentrate on essentials he never pressed for a clearer mandate.[20] His successor, Lord Rhondda, made it a priority and was ultimately able to create the great administrative unit the Prime Minster had envisaged. Devonport's critics did not take into account the constraints on his freedom of activity imposed by deficiencies in the ministry's construction. Not only were the main points of policy not his to decide, but the legal powers conferred on the Food Controller were insufficient. Until 10 January 1917 he worked through the authority vested in the Board of Trade by the Defence of the Realm Act in November 1916. In January the Food Controller was assigned the duty of regulating the supply and consumption of food 'as he saw fit'. He was not given the authority, on the other hand, to requisition supplies at contract prices like the Minister of Munitions or the head of the Army Contracts Department. This meant that the Ministry of Food could not introduce effective price controls, since prices could only be set if the Food Controller became the titular owner of the supplies in question. Moreover, existing state trading units handling food supplies were not put under the Ministry of Food's jurisdiction. Devonport and Rew exerted a certain influence over the Wheat and Sugar Commissions through membership on their boards. The Food Controller had no authority at all, however, over the departments of the Board of Trade, War Office and Ministry of Munitions that were importing meat, cheese, oats and various oils and fats for the armed forces. Devonport also lacked the specialized knowledge that was needed to organize a large-scale state trading venture. Rhondda and his second-in-command, in contrast, were able to adapt the techniques they had learned in the Army Contracts Department.

Though hindered by a vacillating War Cabinet and an unsuitable chief at the Ministry of Food some progress was made towards full control. The most successful work was done in conjunction with the Wheat Commission, to which the Food Controller gave valuable support. Competent handling of grain imports helped the country survive the worst challenge to its survival to date. Devonport also effected economies in grain usage that have been assessed as the most important factor in the nation's victory over food shortages.[21] A countrywide campaign to make food economy part of everyday life similarly had successful results, though ridiculed by the Food Controller's critics. As part of this campaign Devonport prepared the way for the administrative system established under his successor – decentralized control under the direction of a central authority – by the formation of local food control committees. Finally, although not put into effect in this period, rationing schemes for sugar and other foodstuffs were prepared.

The prime task facing the food authorities in December 1916 was that of importing enough cereals. The situation was already most serious when the Asquith coalition was dissolved and the resumption by Germany of unrestricted sinkings on 1 February 1917 compounded the problem. Devonport acquitted himself well in the face of this challenge. Although not directly involved with the day-to-day working of the Wheat Commission, the Food Controller acted as a link between the War Cabinet and the Commission and was generally held responsible for the Commission's efforts to keep up imports. Devonport's constant support of the Commission's work and his active intervention on its behalf with the War Cabinet earned general approval.

The financial crisis gave the Food Controller his first chance to show what he was made of. Lloyd George's Chancellor of the Exchequer, Bonar Law, was just as concerned by the trade deficit with North America as McKenna and upheld the embargo imposed by the Asquith coalition on the purchase of wheat from the United States. The Treasury told the Wheat Commission early in December that after the 22nd of the month it would have only £6·4 million left to buy wheat in both North and South America. Sir Alan Anderson, the vice-chairman of the Wheat Commission, and Sir John Beale, the chairman of the Wheat Executive, appealed to the Food Controller for help. Because of the cessation of buying in North America and the impossibility of transporting the Australian crop, stocks were falling rapidly. The Commission considered it imperative that the embargo be lifted immediately. Proving that he was capable of cutting corners and acting in the decisive manner expected of one of Lloyd George's experts, Devonport went straight to Bonar Law and was able to persuade him the same day to lift the Treasury restrictions. The incident reflected a considerable loss of authority by the Treasury over spending and although it was to state its views to greater purpose on at least one occasion in the near future, its ability to affect food policy was to all events over. Heavy buying in the United States followed Devonport's intervention and in January sixty-three of the seventy-five ships previously ordered to carry Australian grain were diverted to the North Atlantic routes.[22] Had this decision not been taken, the country would have been even more ill-prepared than it was to survive the attempt by Germany to starve it into surrender.

Because of the temporary suspension in buying and the lag between order and shipment, however, the position declined further in January. Imports during the first two weeks of 1917 were half of those a year previously and stocks consequently fell faster than usual. Germany was well aware of the possibilities of the situation. It had been keeping a close watch on Britain's burgeoning difficulties with food supply for some time and was exceptionally well-informed about its store of wheat. In December 1916 German statisticians accurately predicted the rapid decline in stocks in the new year. The enemy also noted with satisfaction the growing truculence of the unions and other labour groups over food problems in the second half of 1916. They believed that resistance from labour would prevent the British government from applying adequate remedial controls in a sudden emergency. Runciman's frequent complaints in Parliament about the adverse effect of military requisitioning on civilian transport similarly bolstered the Germans' confidence that they could defeat Britain at sea. As Admiral von Holtzendorff, Germany's Chief of the Naval Staff, pointed out to Marshal von Hindenburg on 22 December, an unrestricted submarine campaign would force Britain to withdraw even more ships from the mercantile marine for military purposes.[23] Under the circumstances, the temptation to deal Britain a knock-out blow was overwhelming.

The German naval staff calculated that the destruction of 600,000 gross tons of British, Allied and neutral shipping a month would force Britain out of the war within five months. Their near success needs little retelling. Between the start of the campaign on 1 February and September, when a convoy system introduced in May finally brought Allied losses back to the level of January, German submarines sunk an average of 630,000 tons of shipping a month. In April alone the Allies lost 866,610 tons of shipping, 60 per cent of it British or Empire-owned. One quarter of the vessels sailing from Britain that month went down.[24] Survival was made all the more questionable by the withdrawal of neutral shipping from the more dangerous routes. That Britain was able to overcome the crisis was due in large part to the psychological and practical boost given to the Allied cause by the entry of the United States into the war in April. Also contributing significantly was the fact that Britain proved better able to manage its food supplies, particularly wheat, than the enemy expected.

Wheat stocks continued to fall quickly during February and March. By mid-February less than eleven weeks' supply remained, a position normally reached some two months later in the cereal year. At that point, the Wheat Commission censored out wheat statistics from the monthly trade returns.[25] Concern mounted at the end of March when the Argentinian government – persuaded, the British believed, by Germany – banned exports of grain to the United Kingdom.[26] As the Wheat Commission had by then given up trying to ship the Australian crop and India was exporting less than usual due to a poor harvest, the Allies had become almost exclusively dependent on supplies from the United States and Canada.

Unrealistic demands by the War Cabinet increased the pressure under which the Wheat Commission was working. On 2 February the Prime Minister instructed Devonport to double wheat stocks over the next three to four months, an order he amended to two months later the same day. With rather less than twelve weeks supply on hand at that date, this would mean the accumulation of a twenty-three week stock by the end of April. As Devonport replied, it was an impossible task under the present conditions. To do it in four months would mean importing double the amount currently being shipped in each week, and this at a time when transport and dollar credits were in short supply, when requests for assistance from France and Italy were becoming more frequent and when the world supply of wheat was running short. Towards the end of March, the Food Controller was able to persuade the War Cabinet to accept the more practical aim of a thirteen-week reserve. Even this seemed unattainable in April, when the losses of shipping to enemy attack soared. The British authorities estimated that if the trend continued, the country would have only a four-week supply left at the end of August, at which stage the position would be untenable.[27] Although not immediately apparent, however, early May proved to be the turning point in the campaign.

Improvements in shipping control since December 1916 helped bring this about. Under Sir Joseph Maclay, another of Lloyd George's business experts, the new Ministry of Shipping extended existing requisitioning legislation to all British vessels and brought home the ships that had evaded Runciman's earlier order limiting the overseas use of tonnage. Great efforts were also made to replace lost shipping by new construction in yards in the United Kingdom and by purchase abroad. During 1917 over 1,300,000 tons of shipping were returned to the register, double that of the previous year.[28] Even with the greatly stepped-up production of the American yards this did not compensate for tonnage being sunk, but it did help narrow the gap and bolster confidence. Meanwhile, the government took steps to ensure that the very best use was made of shipping still in service. In February 1917 a Tonnage Priority Committee, made up of representatives of the importing ministries, began to allot freight space on the basis of importance of the commodity to the war effort.

The bulk of the country's imports fell into two categories, munitions material and foodstuffs. At the end of March the War Cabinet put food, primarily wheat, first on the list of priorities. Milner was deputed to confer with heads of departments to redraft import programmes for other commodities so as to divert as much transport as possible to food. In June the entire (increased) demands of the Ministry of Food for shipping were met. Developments on the western front minimized the adverse effect that the reduction of imports of munitions could have had on the military effort. For some months past, the German army had been busy constructing the 'Hindenburg Line', a string of trenches and gun emplacements that would enable it to defend its positions with fewer men. As a result, the Allied troops had been drawing less heavily on stocks of ammunition than previously anticipated.[29]

In mid-April the import drive threatened to founder on the type of inter-departmental inefficiency and lack of co-operation supposedly banished with the Asquith coalition. Nineteen British ships were reported lying idle in New York harbour for want of cargoes of wheat to load. The Ministry of Shipping blamed the food authorities for not ordering enough grain. In defence of the Wheat Commission, the Food Controller countered that they had bought enough to fill the ships in question a dozen times over. The supplies could not be brought to port in time to coincide with the ships' arrival because of a back-up on the American railways, which were straining under an unprecedented amount of traffic flowing to the eastern seaboard. The true culprit, Devonport suggested, was the Ministry of Shipping itself, which had given the Commission only one day's notice that the transport was available.[30]

Despite these problems the tide began to turn after the first week in May, when stock levels of wheat dipped below the danger limit of seven weeks' supply, the lowest figure of the war. From then on the position improved steadily. By 1 July stocks were back to normal, by 1 August the thirteen-week reserve had been built and by 1 September the combination of heavier imports plus a good domestic harvest allowed Britain to enter the new cereal year with a six-month supply of wheat on hand, 650,000 tons more than in September 1916.[31]

With imports in constant danger of being cut off, it was obviously essential that the most efficient use be made of existing supplies. Stocks of grain had to be stretched as far as possible whether by increasing the amount of flour taken from the kernel, eliminating non-food uses of cereals, getting people to eat less if they could or readjusting the amounts of grain consumed by humans and animals to give preference to the former. There was no problem with the first of these. The extraction rate had been increased for the first time in the war by the Board of Trade in November 1916 from 70 per cent to 76 per cent. The Ministry of Food ordered further increases and the gradual admixture of flours from barley, oats, rice, pulses and potatoes on 11 January, 24 February and 14 April 1917. As of 10 April 81 per cent of the wheat grain had to be used for flour, of which at least 10 per cent used in bread had to come from sources other than wheat. Millers were allowed to add a further 15 per cent dilutents if they wished.

The Food Controller ran into some difficulty with the second objective. The obvious focus of attack was the brewing industry, which used hundreds of tons of barley each year, most of which was imported. Devonport asked the War Cabinet on 5 January for a reduction in the output of beer to a maximum 50 per cent of that produced in 1915 and for a ban on exports.[32] It was not until 29 March, however, that he was permitted to announce that new restrictions would come into force on 1 April. The delay made it look as if the Food Controller was dragging his feet. It was not he who had been procrastinating, however, but the War Cabinet. At the time of Devonport's request for a cutback the War Cabinet was already in a wrangle with the Central Control Board (Liquor Traffic) and the brewers over the future of the industry. At issue was first whether the state should nationalize the industry or merely subject it to strict control during the war, and second whether brewing should be banned entirely or merely restricted severely and the beverage diluted. The brewers had some strong supporters; the Asquith government had been forced to give way earlier in face of stormy opposition to full state control from the Conservative back benches. The authorities also had to weigh the possibility, of course, of angry protests from the drinking public, an important consideration because of growing industrial unrest. In the face of this controversy, the War Cabinet kept putting off a decision. Only on 14 February did it appoint a committee headed by the Home Secretary, Sir George Cave, to investigate the financial effects of further curbs on brewing. The Food Controller then had to wait until 21 March before the committee reported an agreement with the brewers on a cessation of exports and a reduction in output to one third of the 1915–16 barrelage. This brought production down to 28 per cent of prewar. An order of 20 February had already regulated malting by allowing it to proceed only under licence, and on 16 April the Ministry of Food took possession of all stocks of barley remaining in the country.[33]

It was over the question of limiting consumption of cereals in the form of bread that Devonport's troubles began. There were two ways in which the public could be got to eat less: compulsory rationing and an appeal to people to cut back voluntarily. At the time of the Food Controller's appointment the Medical Department of the Local Government Board was already looking into rationing. A summary of projects in hand at the Ministry of Food at the end of December included the LGB's proposals for weekly per capita rations of four pounds of bread (or equivalent in flour), three-quarters of a pound of sugar and two pounds of meat.[34]

Devonport himself did not approve of compulsory rationing 'with its tickets, its officials, its vast expense, and so un-English in character'. For a man in his position he held unsuitable views on the subject of mandatory controls imposed on food trades by the government. He believed the control of the food industries by a department of state to be wrong and maintained that the only people who could be depended on to improve the food position were the merchants, whose historic function it had been to provide the country with the commodities it needed.[35] At the beginning of January the Food Controller received a letter from the Royal Society's Food (War) Committee expressing their opposition to the compulsory rationing of bread and meat. Pointing out that bread provided the greater part of the population with its major source of energy, they urged the authorities to make every effort to maintain the bread supply by whatever means it could, even if the wheat supply fell. They stressed that since the consumption of bread increased with the poverty of the family, equitable distribution was out of the question. They also advised that meat, which played a small part in the diets of the poor, should be left to the 'natural control' of price.[36]

Although the Royal Society was soon to complain loudly that the Food Controller was ignoring them, two steps taken by Devonport in January reveal that he had read the Committee's letter and had appreciated what it had to say. A departmental committee that took over the question of rationing from the LGB on 10 January was told to concentrate on sugar. Other commodities were to be merely 'kept in mind'.[37] Then at a meeting with the War Cabinet on 23 January the Food Controller, citing the dependence of the working classes on cereals and the abundance of herd animals in the country, argued against the adoption of compulsory rationing of bread and meat.[38] It was the War Cabinet that insisted on the full rationing scheme being pursued. Despite the unsatisfactory level of wheat supplies it was considered unavoidable that the Ministry of Food share in cuts in imports designed to overcome the crisis in shipping. Devonport was requested to proceed with the drafting of rationing plans for sugar and to calculate how much tonnage could be saved if the other items were rationed too. He was ordered in the meantime to advise the public of the level to which they should reduce their food consumption voluntarily. A week later, the Prime Minister's order that wheat stocks were to be greatly increased conflicted with this decision to reduce food imports, but did not rescind the order that the Ministry of Food should go ahead with preparations for rationing.

The beginning of February found the Food (War) Committee, whom Devonport had not deigned to inform about the stand he had

taken on 23 January, up in arms about the Food Controller's apparent
disregard of their advice. 'Voluntary rations' had just been announced
by the press. The public were asked to eat no more than four pounds
of breadstuffs, three-quarters of a pound of sugar and two and
one-half pounds of meat each a week. Did the authorities realize, the
Committee asked, that the average prewar consumption of bread was
five and one-quarter pounds, that it had risen during the war to six
pounds, that the poorest working class families ate ten pounds a head
and that some male labourers consumed as much as fourteen pounds?
The reduction of even one pound a week by these individuals would
result in a noticeable loss of physical energy. With the poor unable to
afford substitutes, it was impossible to ration bread without the
gravest danger to health and national efficiency. Further detailed
memoranda followed in the same vein later in February and early
March.[39]

Devonport foolishly held himself aloof from the Royal Society. He
neither acknowledged their letters nor met their representatives. As a
result they took their complaints to Professor Adams. By mid-March
he was most unhappy with the government's continued interest in
bread rationing, both compulsory and voluntary, and with the general
state of affairs at the Ministry of Food. On 17 March he asked the
Food (War) Committee for copies of their latest memorandum to
Lord Devonport, 'The Primary Importance of Bread' issued on 16
March, for distribution at the next meeting of the War Cabinet.[40] It
seemed probable at that time that once the Ministry had produced a
viable scheme the War Cabinet would order bread tickets. Requests
for this had come from a number of sources. Following the advice of
the Food (War) Committee Devonport had suggested that the import
restrictions proposed on 23 January be confined to feed for animals,
but on 21 February the Inter-Departmental Committee on Restriction of Imports recommended a reduction in shipping carrying food
for humans, a step that could only be taken, the Committee felt, under
compulsory rationing.[41] The subject came up again on 2 March, when
the War Cabinet met to consider an appeal from the Pope to the
warring nations for an international agreement to outlaw 'warfare by
starvation.' Believing that Germany would only use a respite in the
blockade to rebuild its own food stocks before resuming attacks on
Allied shipping, the War Cabinet rejected the Pope's proposal. But
this left the question of how much longer Britain could hold out. The
Admiralty felt that the possibility of continuing the war into 1918

depended mainly on the extent to which the food supply could be guaranteed. It was suggested that if the consumption of cereals could be reduced by one half, the country could survive another year.[42] Shortly after this the French representative on the Wheat Executive, M. Vilgrain, begged the Royal Society for help in combating pressure on the British and French governments from Italy, which due to its own difficulty in maintaining supplies wanted bread rationing introduced in all three countries. Some labour groups were also calling for bread rationing because they believed that the recent increase in the price of the quartern (4 pound) loaf from 10d to 1/- (the result of heavy trading by the Wheat Commission in the expensive North American market) was taking bread away from the poorest classes.[43]

On 17 and 24 March Adams prepared two statements on the wheat supply for the War Cabinet based on the Royal Society's argument that the right policy for cereals was not to limit consumption to fit a reduced supply but to procure whatever amount was necessary to fill the demand. Since shortly after reading these the War Cabinet decided to give priority to the import of foodstuffs, especially wheat, the Royal Society assumed that the authorities had seen the wisdom of their advice and had given up the idea of rationing bread. The Secretary of the Food (War) Committee elatedly commented that the Committee was obviously now recognized as the government's advisory body by everyone except the Food Controller.[44] But despite the Royal Society's jubilation, the spectre of compulsory bread rationing had not been banished for good; it raised its head again only a few weeks later. The enormity of shipping losses in April and the inexorably downward trend of wheat stocks alarmed the authorities considerably. Severe local food shortages had developed, especially in the East End of London and in Ireland, where two districts were said to be within measurable distance of famine.[45] On 16 April Jellicoe, now First Sea Lord, appealed in person to Devonport to intervene with the Prime Minister and on the 22nd himself submitted a memorandum to the War Cabinet recommending all food stocks be conserved immediately before the submarine attacks became worse.[46] Despite his own dislike of compulsion, the Food Controller could not but agree, and the same day that Jellicoe spoke to him he appointed a new committee under Beveridge to draft a comprehensive scheme for the rationing of bread and meat, the plans for sugar being almost complete. As an initial step, the Ministry of Food took control of the flour mills on 20 April. With the full approval of the Prime Minister, the Food

Controller announced these preparations in the House of Lords on 25 April.

The various schemes considered by Beveridge's committee in the course of the next few weeks indicate that it had taken serious note of the variation in importance of bread in the diet by occupation, if not altogether by income. The most elaborate plan called for a five-tier system that allotted a maximum eleven pounds of bread a week to men in heavy manual work and four pounds to those in sedentary occupations. The more affluent were to be allowed to substitute meat for their cereal ration on a pound for pound basis. Whether an agricultural labourer could have afforded the minimum three pounds of meat he was awarded to supplement his maximum eleven pounds of bread was questionable, but at least the committee had tried to base their system on reality.[47]

The final stages of the debate on bread rationing illustrate how quickly Lloyd George could abandon both colleagues and principles when they no longer suited his purpose. On 2 May, a breakfast session with the Prime Minister and Devonport left C. P. Scott, the editor of the *Manchester Guardian*, with the understanding that the only problem holding up compulsory rationing was the difficulty of adjusting it to suit the varying methods of the population. The Prime Minister told him specifically that compulsory rationing was inevitable.[48] By the 7th, Lloyd George had changed his ground, leaving Devonport out on a limb. At a meeting with the War Cabinet that day, Devonport asked for formal permission to establish the machinery for compulsory rationing and to print the necessary documents. This would take two and a half months, so that the ministry needed to begin the process well in advance of the projected date of introduction. He told the War Cabinet that the country could get by for food until the next harvest but that the statistics predicted problems in the autumn. The War Cabinet refused to give their permission without more information which they asked Milner, Henderson and Devonport to gather as a small committee.[49] This was an embarrassing snub for the Food Controller, who only a few days before had been assured of the Prime Minister's backing.

A few days later, on 10 May, Lloyd George cheerfully disassociated himself from the idea of bread rationing altogether. The occasion was a secret session of the House of Commons. The Prime Minister told the Members of Parliament that he had no anxiety about the food supply at all. Claiming, with wild exaggeration, that by 1 September the country would possess a forty-five week supply of cereals, he asserted that bread rationing could be forgotten. Asked why he had told the House in January that the country was approaching a famine, the Prime Minister replied to laughter that he had wanted to encourage cultivation at home. His secretary, Frances Stevenson, recorded in her diary that Lloyd George was very pleased with his performance that day.[50]

Again the Royal Society believed itself responsible for this latest turnabout. Congratulating the Food (War) Committee, Professor Sir William Ashley wrote that in preventing rationing 'the Royal Society has performed a service to the country that can hardly be exaggerated'. The idea that the 'breadstuffs policy' (as the decision to leave bread unrationed became referred to) was based on advice by the scientists was perpetuated in the official history of wartime food control.[51] In fact, although they coincided with the War Cabinet's decision, scientific principles had nothing to do with the matter. Nor did confidence about supplies. Wheat stocks in the first week of May were the lowest of the war and although the safe arrival of large shipments during the month improved the outlook considerably by 1 June, it was not yet evident at the time of the secret session that the crisis had been passed. One influential opponent was the Treasury. Devonport had estimated that rationing would cost £760,000 during the first year of operations, an expenditure that the Treasury condemned as 'very substantial'.[52] The main reason why the project was dropped, however, was because the leader of the Labour Party, Arthur Henderson, had warned that it would cause the swelling labour unrest to escalate out of control.[53]

Henderson was not the only Labour representative in Parliament to believe that the mass of working people would violently resist compulsory rationing of bread or of any other foodstuff. The future Food Controller J. R. Clynes denounced the 'detestable food tickets' that would allegedly add to the hardships of the poor and inflame tempers. George Roberts, another Labour MP who became Food Controller after the war, later revealed that the government feared riots if the rations left the public hungry but unable to buy more while bread was still available in the shops. Recent events in Russia had shown how far things could go when people could not obtain bread.[54] On what they based their views of how the average working person felt is a mystery. Organized labour had been agitating for the control of food distribution since the beginning of the war and had not excluded bread.

The *Herald* carried an appeal in March 1917 for bread rationing and that same month H. H. Hyndman's National Socialist Party proposed that municipal and district food stores be opened to distribute bread, flour and other necessities. In May, the War Emergency Workers' National Committee asked for 'the rationing of food in short supply', and the Miners' Federation requested the government to take over the entire supply of food to secure equitable distribution. Except for the Parliamentary Labour Party no-one seemed to find the proposition alarming. One suspects that Lord Lansdowne interpreted the popular mind correctly when he told the Lords on 8 May that there was nothing in the country that could be called a general reluctance to submit to a system of rationing if it became necessary. 'To some people', he observed, 'I think it would come as a positive relief'.[55]

However true this may have been, the decision not to ration bread proved to be a wise one. The free availability of bread as a cheap source of calories became all-important as other foodstuffs became more difficult to obtain later in 1917 and 1918, especially when meat became scarce at the turn of the year. It was also good psychology, offering the British public the reassurance that however bad things were in other countries a certain amount of normality still prevailed in Britain. The 'breadstuffs policy' worked so well that it was to become the fundamental axiom of food control during the Second World War as well.

Because of the primary importance of breadstuffs in the diet, careful consideration had to be given to the potential effect on supply and demand of wheat before decisions were taken that might alter the availability or use of major substitutes – other grains and pulses, potatoes and meat. That Britain imported such a large proportion of its wheat also had to be kept in mind. If the food authorities restricted the consumption of a home-produced substitute, this could both increase the demand for wheat and place further strain on transport and on the funding for imports. Conversely, greater consumption of home-produced substitutes could be expected to reduce the demand for bread and relieve pressure on imports.

This reasoning was the basis of the opposition to mandatory 'meatless days' and to the rationing of meat. The Royal Society believed that the government should not restrict the consumption of meat but should encourage the public to eat more. They proposed a drastic culling of the nation's herds of cattle through the slaughter of all animals over 17 months old instead of at 2½ years as was the practice.[56] This would bring more meat onto the market and would also divert to human consumption the grain used as animal fodder. A similar suggestion to cut back herds by age to a number that could be maintained on grass, wastage from flour mills and roots unfit for human consumption was made during the Second World War. It was rejected for reasons that should have made the authorities in the First World War pause for thought too. After the slaughter of all the mature beasts, the animals coming onto the market would be carrying more bone and skin and less meat than usual. After an initial glut of meat, there would be less for sale than before, causing people to depend even more heavily on breadstuffs. A forceful illustration of this occurred in Germany in April 1917 when the government attempted to solve the bread shortage by a massive compulsory slaughter of cattle, including milch cows. They only succeeded in deepening the crisis by destroying within a few weeks food reserves that could have been drawn on gradually over a long period of time.[57]

Since herds of beef cattle had been well maintained in Britain since 1914, however, some reduction in their numbers could have been sustained in 1917 without damage to the farming industry. It could have been achieved without threatening future meat supplies unduly by ordering farmers to slaughter a certain percentage of animals in each age group, thus maintaining a steady flow of mature high-yielding animals to market. To do this by administrative order, however, would be an arduous task that would involve the ministry's representatives making decisions on individual cases that might be deeply resented by the farmers concerned. The results probably would not justify the upheaval in farming circles. A more practical proposition was to let the farmer himself make the decision to reduce his livestock through indirect pressure, such as the rationing of feed. This method was to be applied in the closing months of the war.[58]

The proposal to ration meat had the same fate as that for bread: its popularity with the War Cabinet depended on the trend of the submarine campaign and it was rejected along with bread rationing in May. 'Meatless days' were tried very briefly, however, to the detriment of the Food Controller's reputation. Holding that they were 'ineffective, wasteful, and likely to cause abnormal demands for substitutes', Devonport consistently opposed them during his first three months in office. He nevertheless agreed to a limited trial of them after the War Office announced it wanted to draw on civilian supplies in order to stockpile a reserve from imports. At a meeting on 19 March the Food Controller, representatives of the War Office, Board of Trade and Board of Agriculture, and Professor Adams and Tom Jones of the Prime Minister's personal secretariat decided not to apply the measure to the population as a whole but to confine it to diners in restaurants and hotels. As this would only affect the more affluent, who could afford to eat less, the Food Controller suggested it could serve a 'moral' purpose by reducing over-consumption by the few while helping to maintain supplies for the many.[59]

The 'Hotels Order' was in effect only one month before it was revoked at the beginning of May, a development that made Devonport look foolishly inconsistent. The Royal Society was responsible for the withdrawal of the measure. The fuss they made about an order of such limited scope makes one suspect that there was some truth in Rew's counterblast that the foundation of their attack was their anger that they had not yet been accepted by the Ministry of Food as the dictators of food policy.[60] 'Meatless days' ran counter to the Royal Society's suggestion that people be encouraged to eat more meat and it also increased the pressure on cereals. Adams agreed and outlined the Royal Society's arguments in several memoranda he prepared for the War Cabinet. Encouraged by his attitude the Secretary of the Food (War) Committee met Adams on 4 April and gave him a copy of the Committee's latest paper, 'The Danger of Restricting the Consumption of Meat'. So amicable was this meeting that the Royal Society began to send their communications to Downing Street the day before they went to the Ministry of Food. Finally, on 24 April the Royal Society submitted a thorough denunciation of the Food Controller and all his works, charging him with ignorance of elementary and fundamental physiological considerations and with following an erratic and contradictory course that had 'paved the way to disaster'.[61]

While the War Cabinet wavered back and forth on the subject of compulsory rationing, the Ministry of Food went ahead, as instructed on 23 January, with the attempt to persuade the public to reduce consumption voluntarily. 'Exhortation tempered with thunderbolts', one contemporary called it – the thunderbolts being the threat of compulsion if the voluntary campaign did not have the required results.[62] For two months the programme was supervised by Rew aided by the members of the National War Savings Committee, which amalgamated with the Ministry of Food, and some newly hired female staff who gave demonstrations of 'war cookery' and promoted the use of unpopular but available foodstuffs. It was a low-keyed affair until 26 March when a Director-General of Food Economy was appointed to run a more intensive drive.

Kennedy Jones, the joint founder of the *Daily Mail* and a former editor of the *Evening News*, organized a lively publicity campaign. Among his promotion was an updated version of George III's Proclamation of 1800, used to exhort the population to eat less bread during the Napoleonic Wars. The reason given for economy in 1800 was 'fear of starvation', but so as not to encourage the enemy the 1917 version read 'determination to win the war at all costs'. This was ordered to be read at services on four consecutive weeks starting on 2 May in every church, chapel, synagogue and Salvation Army barracks in the country. It was also published in 1,600 newspapers and posters went up in every Post Office. Millions of pledge cards were sent to local war savings committees to distribute to those willing to earn the right to wear a purple ribbon by reducing their food purchases. Cinemas were asked to screen a specially produced film on the food crisis (shown, according to the Ministry of Food, to 'hearty and sustained applause'). A large number of speakers, including the comedian Harry Lauder, toured the lecture halls. Convictions under the new laws banning waste were printed in all the papers. A Food Economy Handbook was published containing nutritional advice and directions on stretching one's food budget. And raising vegetables became patriotic. In 1916 Bradford could rent out only six hundred allotments; by May 1917 over 1,700 were under cultivation. As part of the campaign nearly 1,000 local food control committees were established around the country to execute the orders issued by the ministry, powers being conferred on the local authorities by the Defence of the Realm Act in May.[63]

The Food Controller's critics found several things wrong with all this. First, although it involved a good deal of noise and activity, the economy campaign was felt to have left the deeper question of food policy untouched. On the surface, nothing much else seemed to be happening at the Ministry of Food. Ironically, at the same time that Devonport was being attacked for promoting compulsory rationing, his name became synonymous with voluntarism. The scientific experts meanwhile easily demolished statements made in the Food Economy Handbook, some of which, they claimed, could have emanated from the pages of *Punch*. Others, including some of the ministry's lecturers themselves, complained that the appeals were badly tailored to their audiences. There was certainly something farcical in telling agricultural workers, the lowest paid in the land, to give up meat and eat pulses, cereals and cream instead.[64]

One question not raised during the campaign was whether the overall consumption of food in the country could be reduced by any substantial amount. In the study of the United Kingdom's food resources that they had prepared for the Cabinet Committee on Food Supplies in 1916, the Royal Society estimated that total supplies were normally only 5 per cent above the minimum necessary for proper nutrition. Net imports of foodstuffs fell in 1917. In the first quarter of the year 15 per cent less food was shipped in than during the corresponding period in 1916. Total imports for the year fell 6 per cent compared to 1916. This was offset somewhat by more food raised at home and by economies such as the higher extraction rate of grain and the compulsory admixture of other flours with wheat flour in bread. Potential demand for food rose slightly, however. Population growth kept civilian numbers steady despite heavy recruiting by the army, whose rations were about one-third higher in calories than the average diet in civilian life. All in all, it has been estimated that potential demand outstripped supplies from all sources by about 3 per cent in 1917, the deficit being overcome by drawing on stocks carried forward from previous years.[65] Calculations of potential civilian demand were based on prewar average consumption of calories, which hid a great variation in the amounts of food consumed by different classes. There were those who could have cut back as the economy campaigners asked, but for the great majority there was no leeway in their diets. They already ate less than they should for optimum physical efficiency. The only change their consumption patterns would allow was the substitution of one foodstuff for another. National rationing policy in 1918 reflected this: it effected not an overall reduction in food consumption but a rough levelling of consumption patterns in the country as a whole.

Although the economy campaign could not live up fully to expectations and despite the merriment it caused among the experts, it did have results. The consumption of cereals fell by about 10 per cent between February and June, even though there was a shortage of potatoes. In addition its educative value was significant, if not for the public then for the Ministry of Food, which discovered how little of its work was understood or appreciated by the country at large. The ministry's lecturers found that many people still did not know, after nearly three years, why a war should affect the food supply at all.[66]

One place that published an account of its part in the economy campaign was King's Lynn, where an exhaustive door-to-door survey was made.[67] This was a country town of about 20,000 people and the experiences of its inhabitants were necessarily somewhat different to those of people living in the munitions centres or other large urban areas. Nevertheless, the survey does provide a glimpse of what the man in the street thought about it all. In contrast to the more affluent Worthing where, according to the Ministry of Food, a 'typical' 92 per cent of the households approached signed the pledge, only 55 per cent promised to practice food economy in King's Lynn. Fully 43 per cent refused point blank. The canvassers met with widespread confusion about what they were doing. Large numbers of people thought the drive was a ruse to find out something else: a means test or a census for military purposes to search out boys of sixteen. The fulminations of the scientific experts on the damage the campaign was wreaking on national patterns of consumption were much less pertinent when one considers how little of the ministry's advice had filtered into the awareness of the ordinary working person. A researcher in Glasgow during this period found the same lack of information there among the poorer people. Of ten families visited in one street at the end of February, only two had even heard of 'voluntary rations' and neither thought they had anything to do with them.[68]

Those in King's Lynn who knew what the economy drive was about but refused to sign anyway gave a variety of reasons. Some thought it unnecessary to eat less, that there was plenty of food in the country. Others said they were earning good money for the first time in their lives and were going to spend it on more food not less. Also cited was the waste of food by the army, the feeding of steak and milk to pets, the 'pampering' of German prisoners-of-war, food hoarding by the rich and delay in starting food controls by the government. Although by the time the survey was taken Devonport had resigned, a number objected on the grounds that the Food Controller should not be a person with a business interest in the things he had to control. Surprisingly few said the voluntary rations were not large enough. The two main groups of objections numerically were the cost of living (especially the price of bread) and the problem of obtaining sugar.

As far as the first of these was concerned, people complained that they had already cut back their purchases of food because of high prices and resented being asked to give up more, especially when the government had not checked 'profiteering'. This was something Devonport was not well-equipped to tackle, lacking both a sympathetic attitude and the knowledge of how to go about it. Questioned by reporters about 'profiteering' on 2 May, he replied that if by that was meant making the best of opportunity, he thought a number of people had done that during the war.[69] This was not a wise comment from a man with his business interests. The few attempts the Food Controller made to peg prices were not successful. He brought to the administration of 'maximum prices' no new technique of making them work. His methods were similar to those of the Board of Trade. After consultations with delegates from all over the United Kingdom, the Home and Foreign Produce Exchange fixed fortnightly maximum prices. As before, these drifted steadily upwards. On 1 January 1917 the retail cost of food stood at 87 per cent above the prewar level; by 1 June it had risen to 102 per cent.[70]

Three examples of 'price control' in this period illustrate what was wrong with the ministry's approach. In the case of potatoes, the problem was a compound of the lack of accountancy staff, of local enforcement and of control over distribution. The first half of 1917 found the country with a failed potato crop, soaring prices and a good deal of popular dissatisfaction. Housewives in Maryport, Cumberland, ransacked the farmers' carts in mid-January when the latter refused to sell potatoes at a 'fair' price. In retaliation the farmers declared a 'blockade' of the town, leaving it virtually without potatoes and butter. With incidents like this occurring, the ministry had to step in. Some of the pressure was relieved by diverting supplies from the army to civilians. The ministry also took the bold step of fixing a maximum retail price, to satisfy the public, and a maximum price that farmers could charge customers, which had been requested by the military victualling authorities. In the absence of enforceable penalties, farmers flagrantly evaded the maximum prices order by charging up to £2 per ton for 'carting'. Where maximum prices were complied with, the situation was not improved. Wholesale prices and distribution had not been regulated and supplies were soon monopolized by buyers close to the growing areas who did not have to watch transportation costs. This left industrial towns at a distance from farming regions with both shorter supplies and higher prices than before.[71] To bring this system into working order proved beyond the capacity and the authority of the ministry's staff.

Equally instructive was the Food Controller's intervention to curb the rise in the cost of imported Burmah beans. As wheat supplies fell during the spring, the value of the beans as grain substitutes increased and they became lucrative objects of speculation. Instead of passing in one stage from importer to wholesaler, consignments were passed from hand to hand. One lot of beans sold in November 1916 for £36 a ton was eventually resold in March for £90 a ton. The Food Controller ordered the entire stock in the country on 1 May to be requisitioned from the original consignees at £37 a ton, as if no other transactions had taken place. It worked, but because the Food Controller had been given no authority to requisition supplies, it was illegal and had to be retroactively sanctioned by a special Act of Parliament, not a method that could be used often.[72]

The experience showed that to control foodstuffs effectively the state had to be the nominal trader, something the Ministry of Food could not become by law. It could get round this only with the co-operation of existing state trading units. For example, contracts signed by the Board of Trade with the governments of Canada and New Zealand in March for the purchase of cheese at specified prices for an agreed period allowed the ministry to fix a firm retail price in Britain for as long as the shipments lasted. Although cheese cost considerably more on 1 July than it had on 1 January, it was the only important foodstuff to decline in price between 1 April and 1 July. The greater availability of milk in the summer months at home accounted for part of this, but a steady price for imports proved undeniably helpful.

The other major complaint of the inhabitants of King's Lynn, that sugar was often so hard to come by, was one heard all over the country. Devonport removed one grievance when he outlawed the conditional sales of other items that grocers had imposed on their customers buying sugar. This was welcomed by the public but condemned by the Food Controller's critics who charged that he had removed the one method by which the shops could reserve their supplies for regular customers. The datum period scheme had been continued. In November 1916 quotas were again reduced by the Sugar Commission, this time to 60 per cent of consumption in 1915. Supplies sent to rural districts containing large numbers of low-paid agricultural workers, whose purchases had been below average in 1915, and to urban centres of rapid population growth were even more insufficient in the spring of 1917 than previously. In March people in parts of Ireland could not even depend on obtaining one-quarter of a pound of sugar a week, while to provide Newcastle with the three-quarters of a pound a head suggested in the voluntary rationing scheme the Sugar Commission would have had to send to the city an extra ten tons of sugar a week. Even when the weekly voluntary ration was reduced to half a pound on 25 April, many could not buy so much.[73]

Several municipalities and co-operative societies started to ration the sugar supplies allotted to them. Bradford and Nottingham both had a municipal system, the former rationing potatoes as well. That no national plan came into effect while Devonport was in charge was not his fault. With a sugar card scheme drafted by Beveridge earlier before it, the Butt Committee produced firm proposals by the end of January. Several alternative schemes were also drawn up in the months that followed. The War Cabinet's hesitation delayed action until June. On receiving permission from the Prime Minister at the end of April to prepare concrete plans for compulsory rationing, the Food Controller presented the War Cabinet at the beginning of May with two proposals for sugar: one a true rationing plan based on tickets issued to individuals, which he himself preferred, the other a system of family registration with retailers that would allow an improvement in distribution. The War Cabinet unwisely chose the second.

Professor Adams had a role in this, his last major involvement in food policy. Adams had been complaining about the unsatisfactory handling of sugar supplies for some two months, telling the War Cabinet on 17 and 24 March that the voluntary ration was too high and that greater restrictions were needed on industrial uses of sugar. When Devonport submitted his rationing proposals, however, Adams energetically opposed them. Being one who considered sugar of great nutritional importance, he pressed the War Cabinet to give it import priority over wheat. He also argued that stocks were too low to ration. The sugar supply had indeed been hard hit by the submarine campaign. Cargoes lost in April represented 29 per cent of the toal shipped and at one point, on 27 April, the country had only a four day stock in hand. Fearing angry protests from the public if the authorities failed to have the supplies to cover the ration tickets, Adams advised that reserves be built up before the government commit itself on this score.[74]

The public was protesting anyway. By May the level of labour unrest, much of it stemming from the failure of the government to solve the country's food problems, had prompted the War Cabinet to consider far-reaching changes in food policy. But if labour and the country at large were to be convinced of the government's sincerity in tackling the issue, there had to be a change of leadership at the Ministry of Food. Devonport, the ostensible author of the erratic policies of the last six months, was firmly associated in the popular mind with half-measures and delay. His departure would also satisfy one of the most vocal of the ministry's critics, the Royal Society. Moreover, a 'sounding out' of the Food Controller's views by Milner and Henderson early in May convinced the War Cabinet that Devonport would not undertake a great expansion of the state's responsibilities for food supply in the right spirit. Following a meeting with the Prime Minister at which Lloyd George 'spoke his mind very strongly', Devonport resigned, officially for reasons of health, on 28 May.[75]

Notes: Chapter 5

1 A. G. Gardiner, *Pillars of Society* (London, 1916), pp. 296–7.
2 H. E. Kearley (Lord Devonport), *The Travelled Road: Some Memoirs of a Busy Life* (Rochester, Kent, 1935), p. 206.
3 Lloyd George, *The Great Crusade*, arranged by F. L. Stevenson (New York, 1918), p. 248; Speech at Gray's Inn, 14 December 1916.
4 C. Wrigley, 'The Ministry of Munitions: an innovatory department', in Burk (ed.), *War and the State: The Transformation of British Government 1914–1919* (London, 1982), pp. 40–1.
5 Lloyd George, *War Memoirs*, vol. 3 (London, 1933–6), p. 1078; Sir N. Curtis-Bennett, *The Food of the People: being the History of Industrial Feeding* (London, 1949), p. 232; *The Times*, 9 December 1916; *Observer*, 10 December 1916; *Clarion*, 15 December 1916.
6 Lloyd George, ibid.
7 List of committees formed in connection with the work of the Ministry of Food at Grosvenor House, W1, June 1917, Food Files, Box 12, Beveridge Papers, British Library of Political and Economic Science; D. French, 'The rise and fall of "business as usual"', in Burk (ed.), *War and the State*, p. 15.
8 Beveridge, personal notes, n.d., Main Series, item 4, file 25, Beveridge Papers.
9 F. H. Coller, *A State Trading Adventure* (London, 1925), p. 37.
10 B. P. Webb, *Diaries, 1873–1943* (microfiche edition, Cambridge, 1978), f. 3492, entry for 22 February 1917.
11 Board of Trade, *Report of the Physiology (War) Committee of the Royal Society on the Food Supply of the United Kingdom*, Cd 8421 (1916).
12 Physiology (War) Committee: Food Sub-Committee, A proposal to constitute a board of research to deal with food problems, 30 November 1916, and Food (War) Committee, Memorandum to Lord Devonport, 18 December 1916. Report 28a. Both in Royal Society Papers, Reports, London.
13 W. B. Hardy to F. G. Hopkins, 7 February 1917. D. Noël Paton to Hardy, 13 March 1917. Hardy to Ashley, 11 April 1917. All in Box 530, Royal Society Papers.

14 Bathurst to Prime Minister, 28 April 1917, F/15/2/10a, Lloyd George Papers, House of Lords Record Office, London.
15 Sir W. H. Beveridge, *British Food Control* (London, 1928), Chapter 4; Sir S. Tallents, *Man and Boy* (London, 1943).
16 Hardy to W. G. S. Adams, 4 May 1917, Box 527, Royal Society Papers.
17 A. Marwick, *The Deluge: British Society and the First World War* (London, 1965), p. 192.
18 R. H. Rew, The national food policy, 26 April 1917, CAB 24/12.
19 For more detail see J. Turner, 'Cabinets, committees and secretariats: the higher direction of war', in Burke (ed.), *War and the State*, pp. 57–83.
20 Kearley (Lord Devonport), *The Travelled Road*, p. 204.
21 P. E. Dewey, 'Food production and policy in the United Kingdom, 1914–1918', *Transactions of the Royal Historical Society*, No. 30 (1980), p. 86.
22 A. G. Anderson, Memorandum, 17 January 1917, PRO 30/68/3 Anderson Papers, Public Record Office, London; Wheat Commission to Food Controller, 28 December 1916, Main Series, item 4, file 20, Beveridge Papers; Kearley (Lord Devonport), *The Travelled Road*, p. 207.
23 V. R. Easterling, 'Great Britain's peril and the convoy controversy: a study of the intended effects of unrestricted U-boat warfare and the convoy system as a countermeasure, World War One', PhD thesis, University of Colorado, 1951, pp. 124, 138, 311.
24 J. A. Salter, *Allied Shipping Control* (London, 1921), p. 358; D. A. E. Hardach, *The First World War 1914–1918* (Berkely, CA, 1977), pp. 42–3.
25 Wheat Commission, Minutes, 16 February 1917, Food Files, Box 4, Beveridge Papers.
26 Imperial War Cabinet, Minutes, 29 March 1917, CAB 23/40.
27 Hankey to Devenport, 2 February 1917. Devonport to Hankey, 5 February 1917. Both in Food Files, Box 4, Beveridge Papers; G. E. Underhill, 'History of the Ministry of Food', chapter 4, Food Files, Box 22, Beveridge Papers.
28 Salter, *Allied Shipping Control*, pp. 81–2.
29 M. P. A. Hankey, *The Supreme Command 1914–1918*, vol. 2 (London 1961), pp. 643–4; Hankey to Prime Minister, 29 March 1917, CAB 21/95.
30 War Cabinet, Minutes, 13 April 1917, CAB 23/2/110; Prime Minister to Devonport, 13 April 1917. Devonport to Prime Minister, 14 April 1917. Both in F/15/2/7 and 8, Lloyd George Papers.
31 Ministry of Food, *Monthly Office Report* (London, December 1948), Table D: Stocks of the principle foods in the United Kingdom.
32 H. G. Paul, Provisional proposals in regard to beer and spirits; Devonport to Bonar Law, 5 January 1917, Food Files, Box 2, Items 1 and 14, Beveridge Papers.
33 Beveridge, *British Food Control*, p. 101.
34 Beveridge, Memorandum as to the work of the Ministry of Food, 28 December 1916, Food Files, Box 12, Beveridge Papers.
35 *Hansard*, vol. 24 HL Deb., 5s., 25 April 1917, col. 948; Ministry of Food, *Weekly Bulletin*, 2 May 1917.
36 Royal Society Food (War) Committee, The question of bread and meat, 4 January 1917, Report 8, Royal Society Papers.
37 Rationing Advisory Committee, Minutes, 2–30 January 1917. A. Butt to Devonport, 31 January 1917. Both in Food Files, Box 8, Beveridge Papers; Kearley (Lord Devonport), *The Travelled Road*, p. 209.
38 War Cabinet, Minutes, 23 January 1917, CAB 23/1/136–7.
39 Food (War) Committee, The national food policy. The primary importance of bread stuffs, 2 February 1917, Report 28b; Supplement to memorandum of 2 February 1917, 10 February 1917, Report 28c; The primary importance of bread,

16 March 1917, Report 28d; The danger of restricting the consumption of meat, 30 March 1917, Report 28e; Paton, Memorandum on the dietary requirement of the civil population of the United Kingdom, February 1917. Reports, Royal Society Papers.

40 Hardy to Ashley, 17 March 1917, 42244B, Ashley Papers, British Library, London; Royal Society Food (War) Committee, Report 28d, Royal Society Papers.

41 War Cabinet, Minutes, 21 February 1917, Appendix 1: Inter-departmental Committee on Restriction of Imports, Report, CAB 23/1/257.

42 War Cabinet, Minutes, 2 March 1917, CAB 23/3/7.

43 Hardy to W. M. Fletcher, 3 March 1917, Box 527, Royal Society Papers.

44 W. G. S. Adams, Papers sent to Prime Minister for Cabinet discussion of food situation, March 1917, 17 March 1917, F/232, Lloyd George Papers; Adams to Prime Minister, 24 March 1917, F/15/2/5, Lloyd George Papers; War Cabinet, Minutes, 15 March 1917, Appendix 2: W. G. S. Adams, The food question, CAB 23/2/38; Hardy to Ashley, 5 April 1917, 42244B, Ashley Papers.

45 War Cabinet, Minutes, 7 May 1917, CAB 23/2/154–5.

46 Kearley (Lord Devonport), *The Travelled Road*, pp. 213–14; First Sea Lord, The submarine menace and food supply, 22 April, 1917, CAB 24/11.

47 Beveridge, Report of committee on scale of bread rations, May 1917, Main Series, item 4, file 21, Beveridge Papers; Beveridge, Scale of combined bread and meat rations, Food files, Box 8, Beveridge Papers.

48 T. Wilson (ed.), *The Political Diaries of C. P. Scott 1911–1928* (London, 1970), p. 283.

49 War Cabinet, Minutes, 7 May 1917, CAB 23/2/155.

50 A. J. P. Taylor (ed.), *Lloyd George: A Diary by Francis Stevenson* (New York, 1971), p. 157, entry for 12 May 1917; Runciman, personal note, 10 May 1917, Box 161, Runciman Papers, University of Newcastle-upon-Tyne.

51 Ashley to Hardy, 11 May 1917, Box 527, Royal Society Papers; Beveridge, *British Food Control*, p. 83.

52 Rew to Hankey, 28 April 1917, CAB 21/84; Underhill, 'History', Food Files, Box 22, Beveridge Papers.

53 Kearley (Lord Devonport), *The Travelled Road*, p. 215; Lloyd George, *War Memoirs*, vol. 4, p. 1955.

54 G. H. Roberts, Re: imposition of war-time rationing, 5 October 1919, MAF 60/128; *Hansard*, vol. 87 HC Deb., 5s., 16 November 1916, col. 1123.

55 H. M. Hyndman to J. S. Middleton, 24 March 1917, 12/44/1–2, War Emergency Workers' National Committee (WNC) Papers, Transport House, London; J. S. Middleton, *The National Food Supply* (circular, London, May 1917), 9/2/52, WNC Papers; Miners' Federation of Great Britain to Prime Minister (enclosing copy of resolution, 17 May 1917), 18 May 1917, CAB 24/13; *Hansard*, vol. 24 HL Deb., 5s., 8 May 1917, col. 1112.

56 Board of Trade, Cd 8421; Hardy, A tragic muddle, May 1917, Box 527, Royal Society Papers.

57 J. Williams, *The Other Battleground: the Home Fronts – Britain, France and Germany 1914–18* (Chicago, 1972), p. 225.

58 R. J. Hammond, *Food and Agriculture in Britain 1939–45: Aspects of Wartime Control* (Stanford, CA, 1954), vol. 1, pp. 173–9

59 H. E. D., Conference on food supplies, 19 March 1917, CAB 24/8; Rew, The national food policy, 26 April 1917, CAB 24/12; Devenport to Prime Minister, 1 May 1917, F/15/2/13, Lloyd George Papers.

60 Rew, The national food policy, 26 April 1917, CAB 24/12.

61 Royal Society Food (War) Committee, Report 28e; The national food policy,

Report 28h. Both in Reports, Royal Society Papers; Hardy to Sir A. Kempe, 4 April 1917. Hardy to Rew, 24 April 1917. Both in Box 530, Royal Society Papers.

62 Coller, *State Trading*, p. 31.

63 Ministry of Food, *Weekly Bulletin*, 20 June 1917.

64 E. I. Spriggs, *Food and How to Save It* (London, 1917); Hardy, A tragic muddle, Box 527, Royal Society Papers; C. S. Peel, *How We Lived Then 1914–1918* (London, 1929), p. 27.

65 Board of Trade, Cd 8421, p. 18; Beveridge, *British Food Control*, p. 354; Dewey, 'Food production and policy', passim.

66 C. S. Peel, *A Year in Public Life* (London, 1919), pp. 43–4.

67 King's Lynn and District Central War Savings Committee, Food Economy Section, *The Voice of King's Lynn on the Subject of the Food Economy Campaign* (September 1917).

68 M. Ferguson, 'The family budgets and dietaries of forty labouring class families in Glasgow in war time', *Proceedings of the Royal Society of Edinburgh*, vol. 37 (November 1916–July 1917), p. 132.

69 Ministry of Food, *Weekly Bulletin*, 2 May 1917.

70 A. L. Bowley, *Prices and Wages in the United Kingdom 1914–1920* (Oxford, 1921), p. 70.

71 Clark, diaries, entry for 20 January 1917, Bodleian Library, Oxford; Beveridge, *British Food Control*, p. 42; G. Frances (St. Helen's Trades and Labour Council) to J. S. Middleton, 19 February 1917, 10/2/14, WNC Papers.

72 Beveridge, *British Food Control*, p. 37.

73 *Hansard*, vol. 91 HC Deb., 5s., 8 March 1917, col. 574: List of districts to receive additional supplies, Food Files, Box 7, Beveridge Papers.

74 Adams to Prime Minister, 17 and 24 March 1917, F/232 and F15/2/5, Lloyd George Papers; J. Turner, *Lloyd George's Secretariat* (Cambridge, 1980), pp. 54, 57.

75 Hardy to Paton, 21 May 1917, Box 530, Royal Society Papers; Underhill, 'History', Food Files, Box 22, Beveridge Papers.

6

Labour and the New Consumerism

June 1917 marked the beginning of what has been called the 'heroic age of food control'.[1] Under Devonport's successor Lord Rhondda (the former D. A. Thomas) the scope of the Ministry of Food's activities expanded dramatically. Most foodstuffs were brought under regulation, food prices were stabilized and what to the ordinary person was the epitome of food control – rationing – was finally put into effect. This could not have been done without a similarly great expansion of staff. Lord Devonport had considered the ministry to be growing by leaps and bounds, but at the time of his resignation it was still a relatively small unit of about 400 people. In a surge of activity reminiscent of Lloyd George's development of the Ministry of Munitions, Rhondda added 3,000 people to the staff of the central office in the last six months of 1917 and another 1,000 in the first half of 1918. Including divisional employees and members of 1,900 local food committees, about 26,000 men and women were involved in food administration by the end of the war.[2]

A business expert himself, Rhondda continued the policy of hiring businessmen to fill the executive posts at the ministry. In February 1918 recruits from the business world and the professions held all but 12 per cent of the executive level jobs. With rationing just going into effect, Rhondda then turned to increasing the numbers of civil servants at the ministry, not wishing, as he said, to waste his experts' time on administrative detail with which they were unfamiliar.[3] As before, the post of Permanent Secretary went to a civil servant. Ulick Wintour, a former employee of the Board of Trade and since October 1914 Director of Army Contracts at the War Office, took over from Sir Henry Rew on 25 June.

Rhondda's relationship with his civil service staff was as euphoric as Devonport's had been stormy. Lacking the physical energy and the interest to concern himself with day-to-day affairs, he depended heavily on Wintour, who in turn made sure that the senior permanent officials did not lack assignments as they had under Devonport. Rhondda's readiness to delegate and to back up his staff whenever called upon earned him the gratitude and loyalty of all. In addition, he possessed the gift of great personal popularity. After his death, any criticism of him was buried under an avalanche of eulogies from family and friends. Among these must be included the official history of food control written by Beveridge, who had good personal reasons to be grateful for Rhondda's protection of those who worked for him. Another who posthumously bolstered the Food Controller's reputation was Lloyd George: Lord Beaverbrook observed in 1928 that since the war Rhondda had been 'so canonised by Lloyd George that no praise of him *can* be too high'.[4] During Rhondda's term in office, however, the Prime Minister had at times felt quite differently, as this chapter will describe.

Under Wintour's guidance the ministry was reorganized along administratively more logical lines. In May 1917 there were more than sixteen separate boards and committees reporting directly to the Permanent Secretary, a cumbersome system with little co-operation between the units. By the end of the year this had been streamlined into a Secretary's Department and eight sections: cereals; sugar; meat, milk and fats; fish, fruits and vegetables; provisions and miscellaneous foods; finance; food economy; and local authorities. The cereal and sugar sections were in effect the Wheat and Sugar Commissions, still independent of the ministry but brought into closer co-operation with it. In addition to its responsibilities for imports, the Wheat Commission was put in charge of the mills and generally delegated to act as the ministry's agent with respect to domestic grain supplies. Sir John Beale, the chairman of the Wheat Executive, joined the Ministry of Food as an Assistant Secretary. A senior member of the Sugar Commission took a similar post. One of the most important innovations occurred in the finance section, where Rhondda established a costing department staffed with trained accountants to evaluate current costs of production and estimate fair profit margins. Together with an amendment of the Food Controller's powers under the Defence of the Realm Act, which gave the Food Controller the authority to requisition goods and determine the prices paid for them, this allowed the formulation of a workable system of fixed prices. Partly through Rhondda's own efforts and partly as a result of outside pressure the Food Controller's responsibility for food imports was made more complete. The Ministry of Munitions, for instance, relinquished control over oils and fats to the Ministry of Food and the War Office transferred the task of importing oats to the Wheat Commission. The co-ordination of food control would have been complete had the ministry's takeover of the Board of Trade's meat department not been prevented by strong resistance from the War Office. The ministry assumed responsibility for purchases in North America, but the Board of Trade continued to import supplies from Australasia.

The key to such a rapid development of a far-ranging government department was decentralization. The system introduced under Rhondda's and Wintour's aegis was not new. It was basically the same as that used by the Army Contracts Department, with which they had both been associated, and by the Ministry of Munitions: the division of the country into a number of districts each supervised by an area officer who was allowed to show a good deal of initiative in applying centrally formulated policy to local conditions. In August 1917 the United Kingdom was divided into seventeen regional units headed by Divisional Food Commissioners with their own administrative and legal staffs.[5] There were eleven divisions in England (two – Home Counties North and Home Counties South – under one commissioner), two in Wales, three in Scotland and one in Ireland (which had a Food Board). Assisting the divisional commissioners in enforcing and administering ministerial orders, but controlled not by them but by the local authorities section of the ministry, were approximately 1,900 local food control committees, originally set up in May by Lord Devonport and reconstituted in August to obtain a more representative cross-section of the community in their membership. Trade unionists had been much annoyed by the monopolization of the committees by farmers and tradesmen; Rhondda ordered that at least one labour representative and one woman be among the committee's dozen members. This was later amended in the case of large urban areas to two labour representatives, and by the end of the war women and labour accounted for about one quarter of the membership.[6] An important administrative function of these local food committees was licensing. Controls over prices and distribution were made effective by requiring all dealers to register either with the local authorities, as in the case of retailers, or with the central office, as with wholesalers. Evasion of food control laws could be punished by withdrawal of a dealer's licence to trade.

Detailed descriptions of the methods used by the Ministry of Food to handle specific foodstuffs and of the machinery of price control and rationing are contained in several studies published shortly after the war.[7] Concerned as these are with commodities and costs, they offer few insights into other factors that shaped food policy. Two major sources of influence are evident in 1917–18: labour speaking in the name of the consumer and the United States Food Administration acting through the inter-allied trading system. The former will be examined in the following pages, the latter in chapter 7.

The organization of the food supply during the war required various adjustments in the traditional relationship between state and people. Most of these were only temporary diversions from the norm and vanished along with the food control apparatus after the war. Others left a more lasting impression on the national lifestyle. Among the latter was one that, it has been said, typified the period of maximum control – the unprecedented care taken by the government of the consumer.[8] Official policy towards the consumer in the past, whether during the last great national emergency, the Napoleonic Wars, or the century of peace that followed, had been one of neglect. The law provided some protection against commercial fraud and, to a limited degree, the adulteration of food, but in general the consumer was expected to look after his own interests. Prevailing *laissez-faire* principles supported this attitude as did the fact that although every individual in the land consumed goods and services, 'the consumer' as a social force simply did not exist. The novelty of the situation during the First World War lay as much in the development of a cohesive consumer consciousness and the emergence of recognized spokesmen and women who campaigned for consumer rights, as it did in the modification of the national philosophy of government.

The War Cabinet embarked on its consumer-oriented course of action in June 1917. Providing a philosophical underpinning for this was a change that was taking place in public opinion about the obligations of the state to the people. The past year had witnessed the emergence of a serious public debate about the effect that the war was having on the social and political foundations of national life. The collective nature of the prolonged war effort, the sacrifices demanded of every citizen, led to a re-evaluation of what a just and democratic

Table 6.1   *Trade Union Membership (thousands)*

Year	Male	Female	Total
1914	3,707	436	4,143
1915	3,865	491	4,356
1916	4,014	626	4,640
1917	4,618	878	5,496
1918	5,324	1,209	6,533

Source: N. B. Dearle, *An Economic Chronicle of the Great War for Great Britain and Ireland 1914–1919* (New Haven, CT, 1929), passim.

society entailed. To translate this debate into concrete action the War Cabinet formed in mid–1917 a Ministry of Reconstruction, whose task it was to prepare a blueprint for a better life for all after the war. Among its goals were the upgrading of national health care, wider opportunities for education, better housing and nationwide unemployment insurance – an agenda, one historian has observed, that sketched a Fabian form of 'socialism for consumers if not yet for producers'.[9] The willingness of the authorities to revamp their thinking on food supply and its associated problem, the cost of living, both of which closely affected the well-being of the mass of the population, can also be interpreted as a facet of this transformation of social thought.

Practical considerations provided the sharpest spur for a change in food policy, however. The government had come under considerable pressure from labour. The labour movement had developed tremendously since the start of the war, in both the political and organizational senses. The growth of the war industries had brought about a great expansion of union membership, while the dependence of the war effort on the productivity of the domestic workforce had enhanced the status of both national and local labour leaders. A number of labour men had been given responsible posts in government. It was not the parliamentary contingent that prodded the War Cabinet to do something about the food supply, however, but the rank and file of the movement.

The industrial unrest that had simmered throughout 1916 spread by the spring of 1917 to every district in the country, culminating in May in the most extensive strikes of the war. Unofficial walkouts in the engineering industry idled some 200,000 men and cost the country 1½ million working days. Unwelcome as this development was in itself in the midst of a national emergency, its occurrence in conjunction with recent events abroad caused the authorities great concern. The Russian Revolution had provided a vision of a new social order that tempted Britain's traditionally trade unionist labourers to look to the left. The May Day march was a celebration of the overthrow of the tsarist regime, as was a special conference of delegates from trades councils and labour parties held in Leeds on 3 June. Interest in the International revived. Arthur Henderson and other, usually more moderate, labour leaders were openly speculating whether political pressure brought to bear by the international labour movement on the belligerent governments could be used to end the war 'democratically'. In addition, most local trades councils were now calling on the government to issue a statement of war aims and to negotiate an end to the war.[10] With British society as a whole in the grips of a deep war weariness by 1917, the government feared that the airing of such pacifist sentiments might cause the industrial unrest to escalate into widespread civil disorder and this in turn disaffect the troops at the front.

Much of the tension within the country arose from dissatisfaction with the food supply. Despite rumours that the trouble in the factories had been engineered by German agents and pacifists trying to corrupt the workers, eight regional commissions set up at the end of May to investigate the reasons for the industrial unrest all found food to be at the root of the discontent.[11] Food problems not only caused specific complaints, the commissioners noted, but aggravated other issues, raising them in people's minds to intolerable proportions. The less difficulty a people experienced in satisfying its food wants, the better prepared it was psychologically to withstand other stresses. All agreed that a change of approach was essential. The commissioners for the northwestern district, which included the munitions town of Barrow-in-Furness, where emotions were running particularly high, warned the government that if it did not undertake immediately 'to control the supply and deliver the goods . . . there [would] not only be unrest before the winter but something much worse'.[12]

Guidance for the authorities on how to mollify the industrial temper was available in the manifestos of a recently emerged phenomenon, Britain's first consumer advocates. In several respects the labour movement and the consumer movement overlapped. The latter originated from the former and drew its leadership and main strength from the same sources. But the consumer movement was the more com-

prehensive of the two. The self-appointed champion on the consuming public, the War Emergency Workers' National Committee
(WNC), claimed to speak on behalf of the entire working class, not
just the unionized part of it and included in its definition of 'the
public' the lower middle class as well, which brought some 90 per cent
of the population under its aegis.[13] At the time of its formation in
August 1914 the WNC had expected to concentrate on industrial
relations, but as a secondary function this 'Committee of Public
Safety', as H. M. Hyndman liked to call it, decided to campaign for
legislation that would enable consumers to withstand the effects of
war more easily.[14] Food, coal and rent all drew its attention. Among
the measures promoted by the WNC from very early on were the
assumption by the state of responsibility for the purchase, storage and
distribution of food, maximum prices, encouragement to farmers to
grow more grain, vegetable allotments, the state control of shipping, a
bread subsidy and special nutritional programmes for mothers and
children – all of which, to one degree or another, were ultimately
adopted.[15] The wider scope of the WNC's interests in comparison
with those of the traditional trades organizations, it might be suggested, contributed to labour's wartime development into a broad-based
political movement of national appeal.

The WNC had little influence over food policy until June 1917. The
Liberal government did, it is true, try maximum prices, but the
Cabinet Committee on Food Supplies had not invited consumer
representatives to join the trade advisory panels which set them, nor
were voluntary price curbs what the WNC had in mind. Deprived of
the opportunity to participate directly in policy-making, the WNC
turned to indirect methods. They formed their own food committees
to investigate the rising cost of living and inequitable distribution
patterns, they publicized their findings in the press and at skilfully
promoted mammoth meetings and demonstrations and they sent
reports regularly to the appropriate government departments. Even if
one discounts the concurrent agitation in the factories as a protest
against food problems, the WNC's activity alone belied a claim made
by the official history of food control and too often repeated, that the
food supply aroused no interest among the public during the first two
years of the war.[16]

The controls instituted by Asquith's coalition and by Lloyd
George's new government between mid–1916 and mid–1917 did not
satisfy the WNC that the food supply was being dealt with adequately.

Protests from labour groups around the country became progressively
more angry. Indeed, Lloyd George's coming to power made no
immediate difference to policy as far as the consumer was concerned.
The Prime Minister promised dynamic action in areas hitherto neglected by Asquith, and in an interview with Labour leaders the day
after he took office Lloyd George outlined a programme that purpor-
tedly would give greater weight to the labour point of view. The
majority of those present came away heartened. Ramsay MacDonald
and Sidney Webb, the main theorist of the WNC, were dismayed by
the whole affair. MacDonald found Lloyd George's performance
'remarkable', a three-quarter of an hour display of 'blarney &
promises of the vaguest kind'. 'It was humiliating to see the sub-
servience of most of our men', MacDonald recorded in his diary,
'their anxiety to please Ll.G. & protect him from a close examination.
They swallowed everything & were glad to do so'.[17]

By early May, however, even before the industrial commissioners
had issued their warnings, the government was ready to take labour's
views more seriously. The War Cabinet had decided to reorient food
policy to include several measures advocated by the WNC. Extensive
action on the food question was being delayed only until a
replacement for Lord Devonport could be found.[18] This was more
difficult than anticipated. On 26 May the Prime Minister told Frances
Stevenson that he wanted to place a labour man in the post to show the
working classes that the government was sincere in its attempts to
redress popular grievances.[19] Several labour representatives were
approached at the end of the month. Robert Smillie, the president of
the Miners' Federation of Great Britain and a prominent member of
the WNC, refused to serve in any government headed by Lloyd
George. Harry May, the leader of the Co-operative Wholesale Society,
similarly declined the honour on the grounds that it would be 'the
cemetery of the CWS'. There was also some talk of a Food Board
which would include representatives of the WNC and other labour
organizations, but this was not a serious proposition.[20]

Despite these appearances to the contrary, there are indications
that Lloyd George was not entirely honest in his search for a labour
appointee. He does not seem to have looked too hard in these circles
and none of the Labour Members of Parliament seem to have been
considered for the post. The Prime Minister was soon casting around
openly among the traditional holders of government office. He considered several possible candidates before returning to his very first

choice, Lord Rhondda, whom he had approached some time *before* his conversation with Miss Stevenson. Rhondda, then President of the Local Government Board, was a sick man and had been advised by his doctors not to undertake any very demanding war work, but he promised Lloyd George on 26 May to accept the Ministry of Food if no-one else was found. He became Food Controller on 14 June.[21] This meant, of course, as a newspaper placard announced at the time, 'another lord appointed as Food Controller'.[22] Lloyd George salved his conscience as far as the working man was concerned by choosing the Labour MP J. R. Clynes as the ministry's new Parliamentary Secretary.

In retrospect, there is little doubt that Rhondda's appointment was influenced strongly by Lloyd George's urgent need to find someone who could cope with the increasingly sensitive issues arising from Britain's trade with the United States (see chapter 7). Lloyd George had been extremely impressed by Rhondda's masterly reorganization of the Ministry of Munitions' purchasing system in North America in 1915. Moreover, the excellent rapport Rhondda enjoyed with American officials and businessmen rendered his appointment to the Ministry of Food acceptable to the United States government. The selection of a labour representative for the post, on the other hand, may have alarmed the rather conservative American authorities and could have prejudiced unfavourably the progress of the delicate financial negotiations then under way. Whatever Rhondda's knowledge of American affairs, his background may well have led some to question whether he was the right man to handle the domestic situation. He was not only a large-scale employer but a strong defender of employers' rights who had sat on the opposite side of the bargaining table to Smillie during a colliery dispute in the autumn of 1916. Rhondda was also a lifelong supporter of free trade and 'individualism' who openly admitted his dislike of government interference in civil affairs.[23] His assets offset these drawbacks, however. Like Lloyd George and Churchill, he considered that the exigencies of war justified the temporary suspension of personal beliefs. He was also a man who, once his mind was made up, followed his convictions through to the end, there were no half measures for him. The success of his commercial ventures had given Rhondda the reputation of a thoroughly capable administrator. He owed his achievements to a penchant for hard work, an open mind and the loyalty he inspired in his subordinates. Most importantly, he brought to his new position a

grim determination to make a success of it. Passed over for high office
by the Liberal leadership before the war, he had confided to several
associates in recent months his dogged resolve to gain some personal
credit before the war was over.[24] Now deprived by his transfer from
the Local Government Board of the chance to be in the vanguard of
the future Ministry of Health, he threw all his energies into the
Ministry of Food.

One of his first aims was to establish himself in the good graces of
labour spokesmen. Rhondda was an adept at public relations, but his
approach to labour issues was by no means a superficial display of
bonhomie. Despite Rhondda's status as an employer, Smillie admired
him for his willingness to listen seriously to what the working man had
to say, and delegates from the WNC were similarly impressed with
this side of the Food Controller's character when they visited him on
22 June to discuss the government's intentions. At this and several
subsequent meetings in the next few months Rhondda was at pains to
make clear that he came to the ministry as a consumer advocate. 'I
don't care a hang who suffers, whose interests go under', he
reportedly told a private session of heads of government, 'if I can
make this job of the Ministry of Food a success for the consumer.'[25]

Although Rhondda appeared responsible for the change in food
policy that followed his appointment, he fulfilled a programme
drafted before his arrival at the ministry. This included a state subsidy
that reduced the price of the quartern loaf to 9d, price control in
general, a special scheme for meat that was meant to increase supplies
as prices fell, sugar rationing and a relaxation of the recent restrictions
on brewing. In several respects, the introduction of such a programme
could not have been more ill-timed. The submarine campaign was at
its height, the ministry was in the midst of concerted efforts to build
up grain stocks and the country's financial problems were moving to a
crescendo in the United States. The seemingly most sensible thing to
do would have been to avoid for the time being any action that would
place further pressure on shipping, supplies or international
exchange. Most of the new programme did just that. The bread
subsidy and the retreat on brewing would encourage the consumption
of cereals, endangering stockpiling efforts and increasing the need for
imports and dollar credits. Lower food prices in general would
stimulate demand and make it more difficult to maintain supplies.
Only sugar rationing would have no adverse consequences. That the
government could not only contemplate such a programme but put it

into force was an indication of how dangerous they considered the social currents to be.

The bread subsidy was the key element in the programme. It was introduced in the face of strenuous objections from most of the ministry's staff, leading Liberals and the Chancellor of the Exchequer. For those who had just spent six months feverishly working to conserve grain supplies at the War Cabinet's request, the about-face was too much to accept. None of Devonport's old staff approved of the subsidy and several resignations followed.[26] In Parliament, McKenna and Runciman, who had shown great forebearance in face of the state's growing involvement with food supply since the end of 1916, expressed deep consternation at what this 'dangerous policy' of selling food below cost might do to the shipping industry, freight rates and domestic farming.[27] Bonar Law, enmeshed in an acute financial crisis was appalled by the prospect of having to find extra dollar credits for higher imports of wheat and was only persuaded to sanction the scheme by fear of the social consequences if it did not go through.[28]

The subsidised loaf had long featured among the WNC's proposals. It had first been suggested in March 1915, although it was only when Hyndman took up the cause of the '6d loaf' in January 1916 that the WNC began to pursue the matter vigorously. The authorities were not receptive to the idea then, but after a summer of industrial disturbances and a recommendation for cheaper cereal products from the Robertson Committee on prices, they at least agreed to discuss it. It came up on the War Committee's agenda on 13 November 1916 but a bread subsidy was far too controversial a question to elicit a decision from an Asquithian cabinet. Devonport took up the proposal again in February 1917 but was forced to set it aside temporarily in view of the War Cabinet's order to conserve supplies.[29] By April the 6d loaf had become something of a 'King Charles' head' at labour meetings. The government's policy of building up stocks using expensive American wheat had resulted in the rapid increase in the cost of the loaf from 10d in December to the 'crowning infamy' of 1/- in March.[30] Paradoxically, it was not the price of bread that rekindled the interest of the government but the fear of the social repercussions of scarcity. It was thought there would be riots if bread was rationed while it was so dear, and a subsidy was proposed as an answer. The possibility of using a subsidized loaf as a pacifying agent not surprisingly retained its attraction as the industrial unrest spread, even though plans to ration bread were dropped. The War Cabinet asked Devonport to assess the viability of the scheme. A statistical report was ready by 5 June and formed the basis of Rhondda's legislation, which went into effect on 17 September.[31]

The bread subsidy was the central feature of a wider plan to stem the inflation in food costs in general. In May the Miners' Federation threatened to engage in further industrial action unless steps to fix prices were taken within a month. The War Cabinet wanted the Food Controller to give the matter his first attention and consequently raised no objections when Rhondda made his acceptance of the post contingent upon receiving a free hand in dealing with prices.[32] The amendment of the Defence of the Realm Act on 29 June, which gave the Food Controller the power to requisition goods from suppliers, and the introduction of proper cost accounting at the ministry were followed by the issue of a long string of maximum prices orders, starting on 3 September with limits on the wholesale prices of butter and cheese and on butchers' profits. Except for some fruits, for which only maximum wholesale prices were set, and a few minor foodstuffs such as rice, oatmeal and lentils, for which only maximum retail prices were announced, most foodstuffs had maximum prices imposed at both the wholesale and retail levels. Imported commodities handled by state trading units and some domestic products that could now be requisitioned at source by the ministry were controlled at every stage from market to the corner shop and a ladder of prices set accordingly. This group included such major foodstuffs as cereals, sugar, meat, cheese, margarine, condensed milk and imported bacon. Ultimately, 90 per cent of all food sold fell into one of the categories of control.[33]

The regulations applying to meat are illustrative of the extensive authority now possessed by the Food Controller to intervene in the marketing process. The War Cabinet had decided that the domestic meat supply warranted special attention. Allegations by labour that lower income families had borne the brunt of price increases were sustained by statistics. Between July 1914 and June 1917 the average price of meat sold by shops classified by the Ministry of Food as 'low class' rose at a much higher rate than that of meat sold by 'middle class' and 'high class' shops, by 215 per cent compared to 107 per cent and 79 per cent respectively. Sales dropped in a similarly uneven manner, by 43 per cent, 39 per cent and 24 per cent respectively.[34] The decline in purchases by the working classes was all the more significant in view of the very great disparity that existed in consumption patterns before the war. The problem was the loss of cheap imports. Before the war imports accounted for 40 per cent of the meat in the shops; in 1917 only 12½ per cent of the country's total supply came from abroad and most of this was taken by the armed forces.[35] The scheme that had prompted the meatless day experiment earlier in the year, the Army's plan to stockpile a reserve by drawing on domestic, civilian supplies, was due to go into effect on 1 August. Given the level of social unrest in the country the War Cabinet believed it unwise to proceed unless efforts were made at the same time to improve the supply and price of meat for the ordinary consumer.[36]

Rhondda was therefore encouraged to embark on a complex and controversial series of controls aimed at regulating the meat supply from the farmer's barn to the butcher's slab. Again, the model was the Army Contracts system. Britain was divided into fourteen livestock areas each with its own commissioner. All dealers, auctioneers and slaughterhouse employees were designated agents of the state. Wholesalers registered with their regional offices; retailers registered with one wholesaler only. The system was co-ordinated by officials at the Ministry of Food. A Central Livestock and Meat Trade Advisory Committee reviewed the ministry's orders and kept an eye on the flow of supplies around the country. Local committees of farmers, auctioneers and butchers were responsible for conformity to the rules in their areas. A census of livestock (taken on 2 December) and the correlation of these figures with the population statistics rounded out the system.[37] When these arrangements were complete the Ministry of Food, as the titular owner of all supplies in the country, could determine the amount of meat that could be bought by any one consumer each week and fix prices for every type of meat sold, thus ensuring a much more equal distribution of supplies among the population. Until this system went into operation, piecemeal regulations were in effect. Retail prices were curbed by an order of 3 September restricting butchers' profits to a maximum aggregate of 2½d per pound of all meat sold or 20 per cent, whichever was less. Local food committees could set maximum prices for specific cuts if they wished. To limit farm prices and to encourage breeders to send more beasts to the slaughter, thereby increasing the meat supply, the ministry set a descending scale of prices for cattle at market between September and the following January.

Sugar rationing completed the main elements in the government's programme of consumer policies. Despite its high cost, it was not the price of sugar that upset working people so much as its scarcity. The War Cabinet intended to set matters right. The scheme they selected on 28 May was not a true rationing plan based on coupons that guaranteed a fixed amount to the bearer but a system of local registration that would theoretically allow the distribution pattern to be rectified. Families were asked to register as a unit with one local retailer who in turn would draw his supplies from one wholesale outlet. The wholesalers would then transmit their needs to the Sugar Commission which, armed with up-to-date information on the country's demographic pattern, would share out available supplies fairly. The scheme was similar to one submitted to the ministry by the WNC.[38]

Devonport had objected to this plan on the grounds that it would be cumbersome and inefficient. War had created a mobile society. If people had *individual* registration cards, he argued, they could transfer their rations to another retailer with a minimum of fuss when they left home to work in the new war industries. The scheme would also be easy to extend to other foods. Rhondda agreed, and he was able to persuade the War Cabinet to switch plans in September.[39] By then, most people had already registered as families and all the paperwork now had to be done again. According to the official history, the public bore this 'with exemplary goodwill', but other sources recorded sharp criticism of the ministry around the country.[40] To those lacking education and an understanding of official jargon, the new application forms were difficult to complete. The ministry received thousands of forms listing the fictitious name and address used in the explanatory leaflet. Many in all walks of life objected to the government's apparently senseless prying into personal affairs. Applicants were asked to provide not only their ages and occupations but the name of the schools their children attended. A good number did not even realize they had to reapply, with the consequence that when the scheme finally went into force, hundreds of thousands of people were temporarily cut off from their supplies – among them, reportedly, the Prime Minister himself.[41] The leisurely pace of the administrators in setting up this scheme irritated everyone. The plan was not due to go into effect until 1 January and preparations were hopelessly behind schedule. The main problem was an attempt to prepare by hand a master card index of every individual in the country. The project collapsed under the sheer magnitude of the task and was abandoned the following spring. the local authorities meanwhile assumed responsibility for registration.

The sugar scheme was only one disappointment that autumn. With the exception of the bread subsidy, which worked so well that it inspired a whole series of similar subsidies in the Second World War, and the relatively unimportant change in the brewing regulations, the government's programme failed to give satisfaction. Far from improving the social climate in the second half of 1917, the new measures made matters worse. The maximum prices orders proved particularly troublesome. Their effect was felt remarkably soon. Between July 1914 and June 1917 the retail price of food had advanced 104 per cent compared to an increase in the overall cost of living of 75 per cent. Thanks mainly to the bread subsidy, the food price index rose only two points in September. There was a temporary drop in October when the effects of the meat regulations were first felt, but increases in as yet uncontrolled items brought the level back up to 106 per cent above prewar in November. Prices then stayed stable until the end of the following summer.[42] However, Rhondda's tremendous administrative accomplishment of designing fixed prices that actually worked was offset almost completely by initial side effects. Moreover, it did not immediately stop charges of profiteering. Pay scales in a number of industries were revised during the winter and spring of 1917–18, raising average basic wages from an estimated 40 per cent above prewar in July 1917 to 80 per cent a year later. Regular overtime compensated further.[43] Until wages began to overtake the wartime increase in the cost of food, however, the prices set by the ministry were considered by labour to be too high. In December both a deputation from the Parliamentary Committee of the TUC to the Prime Minister and speakers at a National Convention on the Food Supply, held by the WNC and other labour organizations, cited the price of food as one of the most pressing issues still facing both government and labour.[44]

The complaints were not unjustified. Poorer families could not afford much milk when the maximum price was set at 8d a quart. Local food committees were astonished by the order and many initiated schemes to control wholesale operations and distribution in their areas and thus ensure a lower retail cost. Their actions kept the average price of milk down to 7d during the winter of 1917–18.[45] Despite his promise to consumers, Rhondda was forced by falling yields to offer support to producers. Bacon, an important item in working class diets, was another food set at a price many found prohibitive. This was done in an attempt to recoup some of the expenses incurred by the ministry in importing large quantities of bacon from the United States.[46] In many cases, the profit margins allowed by the costing departments were too generous. The 2½d per pound profit allowed to butchers compared very unfavourably with the ½d to 1d prewar average. The ministry based its calculations on the operating expenses of the least efficient unit. The better run the business, the more money it therefore made. The food authorities of the Second World War did not copy Rhondda's general pricing methods. They preferred the system used by his meat department – when it got itself fully organized early in 1918 – whereby prices were set at the level of the average producer and the less efficient were subsidized from a pool of profits recovered from the more efficient.[47] In defence of Rhondda's approach in the autumn of 1917, it should be pointed out that the pooling method required a far more extensive costing staff than he was able to assemble in haste in June.

The most unfortunate effect of price control was its disruption of distribution patterns. This had been predicted in 1914 and since then lessons had been given by the fiasco that followed Devonport's fixing of potato prices in February and by the breakdown of Germany's supply system. Unless accompanied by the simultaneous regulation of the supply flow, fixed prices had a tendency either to cause produce to be withdrawn from the market entirely, as was the case with the notorious 'disappearing rabbit', or to channel supplies to fewer outlets.[48] Once limited by what they could charge, retailers at a distance from wholesale distribution centres could not bid competitively against those with lower transportation costs to consider. Imports as well as domestic goods were affected. When Rhondda fixed the price of butter, Danish and Dutch traders took their produce to other countries. Supplies of margarine, bacon, tea and cheese similarly followed the path of greatest profitability during the autumn and winter of 1917–18.

The meat orders had such a devastating impact that Rhondda had to defend his actions and his powers at a special hearing in the House of Lords. The source of the trouble was the descending scale of prices for cattle at market. On taking office, Rhondda rejected an agreement worked out earlier by Devonport and the military authorities and insisted on much lower fixed prices from start to finish. After strong protests from the Board of Agriculture, Milner stepped in to arbitrate and foolishly compromised by starting the scale at a very high rate to satisfy the Board of Agriculture and ending it at a very low rate to satisfy the Ministry of Food. Farmers naturally rushed to unload their livestock while the higher prices were still in effect, causing a glut of animals on the market in September and October and a dearth afterwards. The administrative machinery to regulate distribution was not yet ready. As the unrestricted wholesale price rose rapidly, butchers in towns far from the market centres had difficulty finding supplies they could afford. This hurt the smaller retailer most. Grocery chains and the large West End stores could operate their meat departments at a loss, subsidized by the sale of other merchandise. The prospect of a widespread butchers' strike and an almost meatless Christmas in the capital prompted emergency action by the ministry to get some meat into the shops by 24 December, but not before the situation had caused widespread consternation. In January 1918 the shortage was so bad that Rhondda was forced to order not one but two meatless days a week in public eating places. The Royal Society not only had no objection to this, they also supported the introduction of meat rationing. The empty shops bore little relation to the number of animals on the farm. Herds of cattle remained at much the same size as prewar. Having learned a lesson, the Ministry of Food announced a price scale for the 1918–19 season that would encourage steady marketing by rising as winter set in instead of falling.[49]

The breakdown in distribution caused severe local shortages, especially in rural areas and munitions centres. Unable to depend on regular shipments, shops kept running out of basic items. On 18 October, for instance, the village shopkeeper of Great Leighs in Essex had no tea or butter and only eleven pounds of very fat bacon for sale. He had received from the wholesaler only one quarter of his orders of groceries that week.[50] The shortages bore most heavily on the working classes. To give two examples: although nutritionally worthless at that time, margarine was a commodity that most families could not do without, especially when butter was in short supply too. It made bread palatable, and 'bread and a scrape' formed the entire breakfast and tea of millions of women and children every day of their lives. A lack of cheese similarly meant loss of a meal, this time for miners and agricultural workers who traditionally depended on it for their mid-day break.[51]

With the shortages came the queues. These had been a common

sight during the potato shortage earlier in the year, scandalizing labour spokesmen, but they were nothing to what they became later.[52] Towards the end of 1917, lines outside grocery stores were forming as early as 5 a.m., and often swelled into huge crowds. On 17 December over 3,000 people were reported waiting for margarine outside a shop in southeast London, some 1,000 of whom were sent away empty-handed.[53] Keynes had some fun calculating the theoretical length of a queue if q equalled wages divided by prices times supply – the answer: infinity![54] Most contemporaries found the phenomenon both disagreeable and threatening. The mood of the queues was often angry. Inspectors from the Ministry of Labour took serious note of threats by women in Sheffield late in November to raid the stores unless provided with tea and sugar. When their menfolk began downing tools to take their places in the queues, the potential for trouble increased. The miners' leader, Bob Smillie, warned the government that working men simply would not put up with 'having their wives and children waiting outside shop doors almost begging for food to be sold to them'. And in January newspapers reported 'wild scenes' around the country as people rushed shops and stalls to buy provisions.[55]

Popular resentment over the queues was intensified by the conviction of the working classes that they alone were affected by the food shortages. Allegations of class discrimination, 'one law for the rich, another for the poor', multiplied. Rumours (spread by 'pacifists and socialists' according to the Ministry of Labour) charging that the wealthier members of society had brought on the present crisis by hoarding, led to rowdy demonstrations in the West Riding of Yorkshire at the beginning of December. An article in the *Herald* describing 'How They Starve At The Ritz' caused a sensation when it appeared on 24 November. Reprinted in leaflet form and distributed by the thousand in factories and yards around the country, it fanned the flames for weeks. Although theoretically restricted by voluntary rationing scales and by orders governing sales in restaurants, a *Herald* reporter had been able to buy a six course meal that included four rolls, hors d'oeuvre, smoked salmon, a wide choice of soups, fish, meat entrees and desserts and unlimited servings of cream, cheese and other savories. One of the Ritz's more usual patrons, W. Ormsby Gore, admitted privately to Hankey a few weeks later that having dined there recently himself he was not surprised that the restaurant was being used as a rock of offense by the labour press. Referring to the same article, a report on the situation commissioned by the Prime Minister warned that if further trouble was to be avoided, the government simply had to treat all alike.[56]

The coincidence of the queues and these revelations with a singularly ill-timed economy campaign run by Sir Arthur Yapp of the YMCA added fuel to the fire. The voluntary rations so derisorily associated with Devonport were revived by Rhondda in November, prodding the Royal Society, who learned from the press that these rations had been 'carefully considered by scientific people and food experts', into indignant remonstrances.[57] Labour groups charged that while the poor were restricted to the 'Yapp scale' by the impossibility of buying more, the rich were flagrantly disregarding the appeal to eat less. On a return visit to the Ritz in December, the *Herald*'s reporter found the menu much as before.[58] Yapp's statements on the food situation were often inane. He told one public meeting that the government had purposely allowed prices to rise before fixing maximums so that the Ministry of Food could be seen to cheapen food. Feelings ran so high wherever he appeared that the authorities warned him not to attempt to address meetings in the great industrial centres.[59]

Despite the government's hopes, labour disputes continued at a high level after June. Over 3 million working days were lost in the last six months of the year, 1 million of them in November alone. Only one week after Rhondda's public announcement of the full programme of food controls on 26 July 50,000 Lanarkshire miners downed tools in protest against food prices. The introduction of the bread subsidy in September was followed almost at once by threats to call a general strike from the Shipbuilding Engineering and Allied Trades Federation. The union agreed to hold off after the Ministry of Food promised firm action over the next few months, but talks soon resumed when the food situation deteriorated. By January 1918 a general strike seemed imminent. Industrial disputes that month cost the nation 533,000 working days and the unions were debating whether to ask the Labour Members of Parliament to withdraw in protest from the government.[60]

With the spectre of Russia to haunt imaginations, it was not long before the thoughts of the government and the ruling classes turned to the subject of revolution. Was it not true, as the *Herald* pointed out, that 'almost all revolutions start because people wait in crowds for food?'[61] Rumours were circulating as early as August. Towards the end of September, *The Times* ran a series of articles under the general heading 'The Ferment of Revolution', which purported to reveal 'the conscious revolutionary movement aimed at complete overthrow of the existing economic and social order' that lay behind the façade of labour unrest. Although it did not accuse individual union members of being unpatriotic, it questioned the loyalty of organized labour as a whole. Much to Smillie's indignation, it was whispered in November that German gold was behind recent demonstrations by Welsh miners, who were singled out in *The Times*' series as 'exploiters' of the nation. The accusations were considered serious enough to warrant an official statement in the Lords by Milner asserting the government's confidence in the unanimity of the nation's stand towards the war.[62]

Throughout these incidents, the War Cabinet presented an out-wardly calm front, but in private they were reportedly 'much perturbed at these rumours of revolutionary feeling among the working class'. Milner, then contemplating the advantages of a negotiated peace, was one of the most alarmed, according to Beatrice Webb, 'hankering after peace by agreement with the Hohenzolerns lest worse befall the British and German Junker class alike'.[63] The parliamentary Labour leadership was also said to be unhappy that the social upheaval they desired in theory seemed to be getting under way before the Germans had been defeated.[64] Another source of concern was the effect these domestic upheavals were having on the armed forces. In the winter of 1917–18 large numbers of men on leave were seen attending meetings organized by labour groups in protest against the food situation. The reports these men carried back to the front combined with a stream of complaints in letters written by relatives at home were affecting morale badly. The head censor at Calais informed the government that the question loomed 'larger in the minds of the mass of the men than any other.' On 22 February the Prime Minister, Bonar Law and General H. Bonham Carter of G. S. Training, GHQ, visited the Ministry of Food to express their displeasure with events, a meeting, one member of the ministry recorded, that left the Food Controller looking like 'a bullied schoolboy'.[65]

This was a critical period for Rhondda. Far from being the success he had dreamed of, he was in danger of ending his government career as an even greater failure than Devonport. He was under attack from all sides. The labour press had been demanding his dismissal for some time: 'Please – no more millionare controllers', the *Herald* begged in

November. The Prime Minister was disposed by February to grant this request, confiding to Hankey on the 24th that he was thinking of sacking Rhondda. Both Lloyd George and Bonar Law considered food administration the weakest element in the war effort at that time and the general concensus of opinion in leading parliamentary circles was that there should be a severe restriction of the ministry's powers to interefere in the economy, especially in the areas of domestic production and price fixing. There was talk of restructuring the food control system along lines suggested by Milner, with three main units – Home Production, Foreign Purchase, and Distribution and Control of Prices – headed by separate ministers who would meet as a board under the chairmanship of a member of the War Cabinet. Rather than be demoted to a Director-General of Distribution, Rhondda was rumoured to be thinking of resigning.[66]

The chaos in food administration was generally blamed on senior employees of the ministry rather than on Rhondda personally. The Prime Minister considered 'the present staff . . . totally inadequate to the gigantic and difficult task'.[67] The Food Controller's illness had advanced by February 1918 to the point where he was leaving even large questions of policy to his subordinates, expecting them to make definite recommendations, not to present balanced alternatives for his decision. His methods have been described as a 'gambler's technique' of appointing men to various jobs, leaving them entirely on their own to get on with it, and rating his action a success if two out of three chances came off.[68] Some of the ministry's critics felt that Rhondda's luck had deserted him in the cases of Wintour and Beveridge. Both George Barnes and Austen Chamberlain conducted discreet investigations into affairs at the Ministry of Food for the Prime Minister around this time. Barnes reported too much left to the Permanent Secretary's discretion with the result that he and his protégé, Beveridge, had created a bottleneck in administration through which everything had to pass. Chamberlain considered Wintour a very able administrator, but he agreed with Barnes that Wintour's abrasive personality was causing problems both within the ministry and with other government departments and with foreign governments too.[69] Beveridge, another difficult character, was simply not thought up to the job of under-secretary. Lloyd George repeatedly asked Rhondda to replace him, suggesting either Max Aitken (soon to become Lord Beaverbrook) or Lord Morant as a replacement. Morant did in fact visit the Ministry of Food in February in connection with this, but felt himself too old for the challenge, 'an extinct volcano'.[70] Much to Lloyd George's annoyance the Food Controller was 'unfortunately' out of town when the Prime Minister called to discuss the subject of new staff in February, and Beveridge and his co-workers, in the former's own words, were left 'to save their reputations' and that of Rhondda himself by their association with the new food controls that were just about to come into force.[71]

The food authorities took two unprecedented courses of action early in 1918: the introduction of compulsory rationing and the co-option of the consumer into the policy-making process. The former completely salvaged Rhondda's sinking reputation. In the few months of life left to him before his death in July, he gained all the laurels he had hoped for. After Rhondda's funeral Beveridge wrote in a private letter: 'we were burying a popular idol who had achieved something like a miraculous success in every home in the country'. Compulsory rationing, which began on a local basis for a few basic foods in November 1917 and developed by July 1918 into a national system covering a variety of foodstuffs, ironed out the defects in the distribution flow, got rid of the queues and banished along with them most of the labour unrest associated with food problems. For these services, *The Times* later declared, Rhondda should be remembered as 'the greatest of food controllers'.[72]

Whether this epitaph is deserved is another question. Although rationing would have been impossible without the development of the huge bureaucratic machine that monitored it, Rhondda received credit for a development that he personally tried to defer and that was set in motion by people outside the ministry responding to problems caused at least partially by orders issued by the ministry. The popularity of compulsory rationing depended to a very great extent on the inordinately long resistance to it by the government in the face of clamorous appeals from all over the country. The WNC and other labour groups had been calling for the equal distribution of essential foodstuffs since the earliest months of the war. They had amply demonstrated their support for this during the Devonport era and had stepped up their campaign as problems with distribution grew in the second half of 1917. It was the subject of numerous articles in the press, the object of deputations to the Prime Minister and officials of the Ministry of Food and the repetitive theme of public meetings. It was made a condition of industrial peace: the Labour Conference on

29 December promised the government more strikes if the authorities did not act soon, and in February, just before the London scheme went into effect, railway workers in Barrow-in-Furness voted to stop work every Saturday until compulsory rationing was promised for the whole country.[73]

With what appeared to be an acute food shortage looming, some saw compulsory rationing as a way to protect the consumer against rapacious businessmen. 'A stand has to be made for the consumers' interests against the traders' interests,' a member of a deputation from the co-operative movement told Rhondda and Lloyd George on 31 October. 'We ask for an effective rationing of essential foodstuffs.'[74] The Food Controller's ambivalence on this almost certainly delayed its introduction. Until 10 December Rhondda did not press the War Cabinet to agree to rationing *per se* but only to grant permission for the preparation of plans, which he said would take four months. It is hardly surprising that the War Cabinet hesitated to commit themselves when they read in the Food Controller's memoranda of 28 November and 4 December that he was 'strongly opposed' to rationing.[75] Clynes' views probably reinforced doubts. He advised that rationing would worsen industrial relations rather than improve them and he publicly expressed his opposition to food tickets on a number of occasions in December and January.[76]

The Ministry of Food was prodded into action by the appearance around the country of municipal rationing schemes devised by local food control committees who could wait no longer for the central government to come to a decision. Gravesend was the first, with rationing of sugar early in November, of butter, tea and margarine on 8 December, and of meat on 5 January. That small town's plan was based on individual ration cards. Birmingham's plan, serving a population of 1 million, used family cards. In both cases customers had to register for their groceries with one retailer. By the time the ministry was ready to act, the country would have been covered by a myriad of independent programmes that would have been difficult to supersede. The Food Controller had two choices: to concentrate on the preparation of the centralized, uniform national plan he preferred and to ignore the activities of the local authorities, or to accept the fact of municipal initiative and co-ordinate the work in progress by insisting on similar schemes containing certain standard allowances. The second was by far the best alternative. On 22 December, therefore, Rhondda issued a Food Control Committees (Local Distribution) Order, which confirmed the power of the local authorities to enforce food control in their districts, and a week later he distributed a leaflet describing various model schemes. Only a few restrictions were placed on the local food control committees: they had to get prior approval of their plans from the ministry, their weekly allowances of certain foods could not exceed maximums prescribed by the Food Controller and distribution had to be controlled by the customer/ retailer registration technique. By 22 January 1918, 170 local plans had been submitted for approval, the majority of them coming from communities in the industrial north and Midlands.[77]

It was not until 30 January that the War Cabinet gave the order for national compulsory rationing. A week earlier Rhondda had submitted, along with a formal request to introduce rationing 'at the most convenient date', a 'scale of rations' drafted in December by a committee chaired by Beveridge.[78] The scheme was a five-class system covering bread and flour, meat, fats (butter, margarine and lard) and sugar. The Food Controller had diplomatically invited the Royal Society to participate in the preparation of this plan and their representative, Dr D. Noël Paton, a staunch opponent of compulsory rationing, had fought the bureaucrats successfully for a high level of rationed calories for those who most needed them. The scale ran from 2,660 rationed calories for men on heavy industrial work to 1,110 for children under 6 years of age; weekly rations of bread ranged from 9 pounds to 3 pounds, meat from 3 pounds to 1 pound and fats from ¾ pound to ½ pound; ½ pound of sugar was allotted each week to everyone. It was suggested that the central index of the population, at that date still under construction by the sugar rationing staff, could be used as a basis for the issue of the appropriate ration cards.

Sugar rationing had meanwhile gone into effect nationwide on 1 January and, since the War Cabinet wanted to review the political situation when Rhondda had perfected his plans for cereals before it introduced that programme, the ministry's immediate concern was the rationing of meat and fats. Again, they were hurried along by the local authorities. The local food committees in London had already decided on 4 January to establish a unified scheme for butter and margarine, and the chaotic shortage of meat brought about by the ministry's pricing policy persuaded them to incorporate meat rationing into these arrangements a little later. The complexity of the undertaking, arising from the very great number of people who would be affected, prompted the London committees to ask the Ministry of

Food to run the project. The London and Home Counties Scheme for meat and fats went into effect on 25 February and was extended to the rest of the nation on 7 April. On 14 July the local rationing of certain other foodstuffs was incorporated into a uniform national plan. Every person in Britain now had a ration book issued by the Ministry of Food containing detachable coupons for sugar, table fats (butter and margarine), lard and meat, plus spare coupons that could be used if the need arose. Local rationing of tea, cheese, jam and miscellaneous items continued wherever the local food control committees thought it necessary. In Ireland, an agricultural country with many 'self-producers', only sugar was rationed.

In practice, rationing bore little resemblance to the proposals that had been drafted by the various committees in 1917. Only the sugar allowance remained the same. Bread rationing was never introduced, although preparations were made for the contingency. The fats coupons provided 4 ounces of butter or margarine a week to start (5 ounces from 15 June) plus 2 ounces of lard. The meat coupons, which had a cash not weight value, bought about 1 pound of meat a week plus 4 to 8 ounces of bacon. Supplementary rations of bacon were issued to men on heavy industrial work and to others as supplies warranted. The rationing of meat by value was greeted by the public as a particularly fair move. The value of the coupons, and hence what one customer could spend on meat each week, fluctuated with supplies. It was 1/3 in February, 10d in May and 1/9 in July. People could choose between buying a larger quantity of cheaper meat each week or squandering one month's coupons on a choice cut. This had little effect on working class consumption but brought a noticeable difference to the homes of the better off. One member of the upper-middle class writing to his brother in Canada in June 1918 divulged that his family now ate butcher's meat (meat other than bacon) only once a week, and very little of it then. But he made no complaint: 'We all feel the pinch of the regulations', he wrote, 'but at the same time we realise their rough justice.'[79]

Among the WNC's demands earlier in the war was the establishment of special nutritional programmes for nursing mothers and young children. By the end of 1917 a number of local authorities were running such programmes, and with the machinery for rationing being set up around the country Rhondda took the opportunity to try to expand these schemes into a nationwide system. His main aim was to channel the country's dwindling supplies of fresh milk to those who would most benefit from them. Production of milk fell by more than one quarter during the war, from a total of 1,008 million gallons in 1914 to 728 million gallons in 1918.[80] The Food Controller did not ration milk, but he curtailed sales in restaurants and, through the Milk (Mothers and Children) Order of 8 February 1918, empowered local authorities in England and Wales to arrange for special supplies of food and milk for expectant and nursing mothers and milk for children under five. A similar order for Scotland was issued on 4 September. To encourage communities to go ahead, those who wished to provide free or cheaper food and milk in necessitous cases were allowed to charge the expense to the rates. This was Rhondda's way of avoiding another subsidy like that for bread, but, as a Ministry of Food official noted, 'most of the local authorities were shy of helping the Ministry in this manner'.[81] By April two whole counties, twenty-six metropolitan boroughs, fifty-one county boroughs and eighty-seven other communities in England and Wales were providing some kind of benefit.[82] In most cases, however, this was no more than the issue of priority tickets that gave the holders first call on supplies in the area, the customer paying the full retail price. Priority tickets for nursing mothers, infants, invalids and those in special institutions became mandatory nationwide on 5 October 1918, when the Milk (Local Distribution) Order required retailers to supply the needs of these groups before selling supplies to other customers. Through poverty and ignorance many of those who needed the milk did not get it. The high price of milk, sustained by the ministry's generous maximum prices order, kept consumption low in most families. In addition, not everyone appreciated the programme. Health workers in Woolwich, for instance, found it impossible to impress on the local women – most of whom could not afford to use their priority tickets – the value of milk as a food for themselves and their young children.[83]

A change in the dietary habits of the working classes was something that Rhondda would very much have liked to see. The narrow and monotonous nature of most people's diets enhanced the impact of the food shortages by restricting flexibility in using substitutes. The adamant conservatism of working people led them during the potato shortage to reject rice, cornmeal and dried beans as alternatives and at the height of the meat crisis to object to fish as a main meal.[84] Rhondda hoped that people could be persuaded to widen their culinary horizons in national restaurants, which he also favoured for their economy value (ministry experts estimated that widespread patronage might save 10 to 25 per cent of the food normally consumed in the country) and for their potential use as 'feeding stations' in the event that another submarine campaign cut off imported supplies.

National restaurants, first called 'communal kitchens', were already in existence when Rhondda took office. The first government-sponsored restaurant was opened in May 1917. They were cost-priced or subsidized enterprises, some merely selling ready-cooked food to take away, others providing cafeteria-type service. In the first two years of the war, private voluntary organizations opened a number of communal kitchens around the country with the intention of helping the respectable poor combat the rise in food prices. These were charitable undertakings along traditional lines. In early 1917 the philosophical reappraisal of society that was taking place brought a new idealism to the venture. One enthusiast held that the new communal kitchens were born from 'the breath of reconstruction' that was infusing fresh life into the social organism, the kitchens were said to epitomize democracy, a symbol of the shared war experience. They were to be clean, bright and readily accessible to all classes.[85] The reality was harshly disillusioning. The communal kitchen, its name so disagreeably reminiscent of the old soup kitchen, remained a stolidly lower-class institution located in a dingy back street or public baths and presided over by the familiar Lady Bountiful. Despite nominal support for the kitchens by the WNC and Sylvia Pankhurst, the average working person shunned them. 'It was thought that Public Kitchens were to be inflicted upon the poor as some kind of punishment for a crime unstated', one ministry official commented.[86] The more affluent members of society did not patronize the kitchens either, allegedly uneasy at the aura of social levelling that hung over the undertaking. According to the *New Statesman*, 'communal suggested communism, Socialism, fair dealing for all, consideration for the poor, abolition of distinctions of rank and money'.[87] One could think of less esoteric reasons why those who could afford to do so would prefer to dine elsewhere.

While egalitarianism in public dining held no appeal for the British people, it was the egalitarian aspects of compulsory rationing that contributed most to its popularity. To the modern mind, rationing suggests an across-the-board reduction of consumption; during the First World War what was achieved was a levelling of consumption of essential foodstuffs by the various classes in society. The wealthy still

Table 6.2 *Weekly Per Capita Consumption of Essential Foodstuffs in the Average Workingclass Family*

	lbs 1914	lbs 1918	Change in per cent
Bread and flour	7.33	7.55	+3
Meat	1.49	.96	−36
Bacon	.26	.56	+115
Lard	.22	.17	−23
Butter	.37	.17	−54
Margarine	.09	.20	+122
Potatoes	3.41	4.38	+28
Cheese	.18	.09	−50
Sugar	1.29	.62	−52

Source: Report of the Working Classes Cost of Living Committee, Cd 8980 (1918).

enjoyed a better diet, being able to afford to supplement their basic rations with whatever unrationed goods they could find in the shops. These supplementary purchases were of little or no concern to the average person, however. Except for sugar, most people were not allotted substantially less rationed foods than they bought in peacetime. Price was still the main limiting factor in working class consumption. When the meat allowance rose, poorer people could not afford to take up the full ration. There was some substitution of one food for another in short supply: bacon for other meat, margarine for butter, bread and potatoes for meat and cheese. The decline in nutritional standards that this represented was not noted by contemporaries, who judged the adequacy of a diet primarily in terms of calories. On this basis, prewar standards were roughly maintained, consumption of the average working person falling by only 3 per cent during the war.[88]

The fact that 'the food coupon was honoured like a bank-note' was, according to the official history, another source of public approval.[89] There was always sufficient food in the country to cover the rations. From mid–1917 on the Ministry of Food maintained a policy of building up emergency reserves in case Germany succeeded in cutting off imports. Rationing, in its turn, helped in the implementation of this policy. While weekly allowances of sugar remained at 8 ounces, for instance, stocks rose swiftly from the nadir of 18,000 tons on 1 May 1917 to 209,000 tons on 1 January 1918 and to 414,000 tons on 1 November 1918.[90] Reserves of meat, bacon, tea, cheese, butter and lard were also accumulated, providing the country with a valuable cushion against the effects of the import restrictions imposed during the final campaign of the war.

The creation of a Consumers' Council in January 1918 was intended as convincing proof that the authorities had indeed fundamentally altered their approach to the food question. In terms of practical impact on the everyday lives of the people, other of the ministry's actions were much stronger indicators of policy change than was the Council. The latter had no legal power to enforce the passage of measures favouring the consumer. It was merely an advisory body. Its symbolic value, however, far outweighed this drawback. It was a visible proof that consumers had finally achieved a say in the development of legislation affecting them.

Rhondda and Clynes, who suggested the move to the Food Controller, were both well aware of the publicity value of a Consumers' Council. To be represented on the official food advisory committee was one of labour's earliest and most persistent requests since the war began. Rhondda had no intention of allowing interference in the running of the ministry, but he believed the Consumers' Council would be a useful tool for making food legislation palatable to the mass of the population. Convinced, wrongly of course, that rationing would cause an outcry, he hoped that its impact would be sweetened by a Consumers' Council that shared the responsibility for such a measure by discussing and approving the necessary orders before they were put into force. Creation of the Council was thus a fundamental corollary to the introduction of rationing and a subtle method of containing labour unrest by allowing its representatives to give vent to their feelings within the confines of government circles rather than outside them.

Ministry officials were careful not to mention this aspect of the matter in public but labour leaders astutely guessed the reasons for the Council's birth. They themselves felt that the government's procrastination had resulted in problems so serious that no measures could prevent distress due to dire shortages, and they feared that a Consumers' Council would be used as a screen to hide the ministry's past mistakes.[91] Due to these reservations and the fact that Clynes, a *government* official, was to be chairman of the *Consumers'* Council, several prominent socialists and union officials, including Sidney Webb and H. M. Hyndman, refused Rhondda's invitation to participate. Hyndman soon reconsidered and joined the Council as a representative of the WNC. Despite his reputation for being difficult, the ministry was relieved to have him with them. Hyndman was known throughout the world as a Socialist agitator, lecturer and propagandist and was regarded by many in labour circles, abroad as well as at home, as a prophet. His participation would be an endorsement of the Council, while to leave him challenging the system from without might defeat the whole conciliatory purpose of the exercise. Hyndman's widow later revealed that he derived a good deal of pleasure from the fact that in the early days of the Council the more conservative elements on it regarded him with 'curiosity, hostility and fear'.[92]

The Council consisted originally of six delegates from the WNC and the Parliamentary Committee of the TUC combined; six from the co-operative movement, which like the WNC but less flamboyantly had long campaigned for consumers' rights on behalf of its 15 million members; three from the Standing Joint Committee of Industrial Women's Organisations; four members of the Ministry of Food; and three individuals appointed by the ministry to represent the 'unorganized consumer'. On seeing the names of the latter, Hyndman incredulously demanded to be informed whether 'our precious profiteer rulers have all gone mad', for the chosen three were Lord Rathcreedan, a wealthy landowner, the Countess of Selborne, wife of the former President of the Board of Agriculture, and Sir William Ashley.[93] Ashley was in fact a good choice due to his knowledge of statistics and economics and his experience on several war committees, but he too doubted the wisdom of appointing three titled people to a body that was designed to soothe working class resentment at being previously 'left out'.[94] These three were Rhondda's personal choice, selected by him for the express purpose of ensuring that the Consumer's Council would not develop into a true pressure group capable of real influence over food policies. Before the first meeting on 1 February he took Lady Selborne and Ashley aside and told them that their duty would be to moderate the zeal of the labour members, especially Hyndman.[95] Presumably, Lord Rathcreedan was treated to similar confidences. Ashley was the only one of the three not to disappoint Rhondda's hopes. Although far from unsympathetic to the ordinary consumer's concerns, he applied a firm brake to any attempt to spur the ministry into radical action. Rathcreedan was a sensible man but not strong enough to play other than a minor role, while Lady Selborne irritated everyone but Hyndman by her constant, ineffective interruptions. The main clashes were fought out by Ashley and Hyndman, who gradually developed considerable mutual respect.

What was the outcome of these exercises? Did either side achieve any of the goals they had aimed for? The labour contingent's hopes were none too high to start with. After the first meeting Hyndman wrote to the Secretary of the WNC, J. S. Middleton, that 'we can do little, if any, good on the Food Consumers' Council,' but, he added, 'it puts a few determined persons inside the enemy's entrenchments' which might, he believed, be useful at a critical moment.[96] The most that could be done now, it was felt, was to make sure that the ministry's legislation was subjected to thorough criticism before being loosed on the public. The Ministry of Food did seem to do its best in this respect. At its weekly meetings the Council was presented with batches of orders to debate and listened to reports on the food situation given by government spokesmen. On 5 February, for example, Sir Leo Chiozza Money, Parliamentary Secretary to the Ministry of Shipping, provided the Council with the latest figures on shipping losses, and on 24 July Herbert Hoover, the Food Administrator of the United States, outlined his food policies. The Council was certainly kept informed of the ministry's actions. As Hyndman complained, however, the decision to issue an order was arrived at independently of the Consumers' Council and it reached them only for debate. The most the members could do was to delay its implementation. In fact, the Council was felt to have rather too much power here by some of the ministry's staff. Beveridge, defending himself against charges that *he* was holding up the passage of certain legislation affecting the sale of sweets, could point to the strong opposition to the order that had blocked its approval by the Council. The order had to go back for further discussion in the department concerned before it was finally presented in acceptable form some time later.[97] This sort of scrutiny at least ensured that hastily conceived and ambivalently phrased measures were weeded out for reappraisal and redrafting.

One major frustration was the inability of the Council members to introduce legislation themselves. To produce anything really effective needed considerable personal experience or a prolonged investigation. Some effort was made to give the members the working knowledge they lacked by appointing them to one of the ministry's standing advisory committees – finance, storage, transport and so on – where they were supposed to ensure that the rights of the consumer were clearly stated. Their presence was resented by the ministry's regular staff, however. Even Ashley, a trained statistician, found his services unwanted by the head of the statistics department. E. C. K. Gonner.[98] Hyndman nevertheless made at least one effort to initiate legislation despite the difficulties. This was an attempt in March to persuade the government to impose bread rationing. The War Cabinet was still determined to avoid this until all else failed and Rhondda had told the Council at its very first meeting that the authorities would not consider bread rationing. It is debatable whether Hyndman really believed the measure essential to the well-being of the average person or whether he merely wanted to frighten the government with talk of 'anarchical queues of hungry folk' in the hope of prodding them into accepting some less radical measure. Judging by his tactics in the WNC, it was probably the latter; and after Ashley rushed to the rescue with statistical proof that the country could survive unrationed until at least the next harvest, Hyndman never mentioned the subject again.[99]

In retrospect, the Consumers' Council did achieve something for the ordinary person. It established the principle of consumer representation. The Council proved to be a serious consultative body that, although temporarily disbanded with the Ministry of Food in 1921, was found worthy of revival as a permanent unit at a later date. It also scored victories in several, not-insignificant instances. The Council was responsible for the enforcement in 1918 of legislation covering pure food and accurate weights and measures, notably in the dairy industry and in jam-making plants, and was able to get several inferior items taken off the market. Moreover, both government and WNC spokesmen attributed the slowing of price increases towards the end of the war to the efforts of the Council to get subsidies and controls extended.[100]

For its part, the government was satisfied that it had achieved its goals. Labour unrest connected with food policies subsided remarkably in 1918. The elimination of most of the distribution problems together with rising incomes accounted for a large part of this, but the fact that the Council provided, in Mrs Hyndman's words, 'a lightning conductor' for complaints contributed not a little to the easing of social tensions. Above all, the authorities felt that the Consumers' Council 'had done great things in educating Labour generally (and in particular the most vocal and unbalanced part of Labour) in the difficulties of administering (and even of understanding) problems so complex and far-reaching'.[101]

Labour could have replied to this patronizing statement that the very fact of the Council's existence, together with the rest of the government's consumer-oriented policies, proved that the authorities too had received an education. Just as the witness warned the Royal Commission in 1905: the twentieth-century workman had indeed proved to be a far different fellow from the unorganized labourer the authorities had had to deal with a century earlier.

Notes: Chapter 6

1 Sir W. H. Beveridge, *British Food Control* (London, 1928), p. 51.
2 Statement of staff at Ministry of Food, 31 December 1917, R. E. Thornley to Mrs Mair, June 1919. Both in Food Files, Box 12 Beveridge Papers, British Library of Political and Economic Science, London.
3 Rhondda to Bonar Law, 14 February 1918, T172/796, Treasury Papers, Public Record Office.
4 Lord Beaverbrook, *Politicians and the War* (London, 1960), p. 77.
5 For a description of work at one of these see H. W. Clemesha, *Food Control in the North-Western Division* (Manchester, 1922).
6 For more details see A. Clinton, *The Trade Union Rank and File: Trades Councils in Britain 1900–40* (Manchester, 1977), pp. 68–71.
7 For example, Beveridge, *British Food Control*; F. H. Coller, *A State Trading Adventure* (London, 1925); E. M. H. Lloyd, *Experiments in State Control at the War Office and the Ministry of Food* (Oxford, 1924).
8 R. E. Prothero (Lord Ernle), *English Farming, Past and Present* (Revised edition, London, 1961), p. 400.
9 K. O. Morgan, *Consensus and Disunity: The Lloyd George Coalition Government 1918–1922* (Oxford, 1979), p. 24.
10 C. Wrigley, *David Lloyd George, and the British Labour Movement* (Brighton, 1976), p. 191; C. F. Brand, 'British labor and the International during the great war', *Journal of Modern History*, vol. 8, no. 1 (March 1936), passim; Clinton, *Trade Union Rank and File*, pp. 76–7.
11 A. J. P. Taylor (ed.), *Lloyd George: A Diary by Francis Stevenson* (New York, 1971), p. 159, entry for 26 May 1917.
12 Commission of Enquiry into Industrial Unrest, G. N. Barnes (Chairman), *Summary*, Cd 8696 (1917–18), p. 5. Number 2 Division, North Western Area, *Report*, Cd 8663 (1917–18), p. 14.
13 War Emergency Workers National Committee (WNC), *Report on the Workers' National Committee Proposals on Military Pensions, Etc.* (leaflet, 1915), Transport House, London.
14 R. T. Hyndman, *The Last Years of H. M. Hyndman* (London, 1923), pp. 85–6.
15 J. M. Winter, *Socialism and The Challenge of War: Ideas and Politics in Britain 1912–18* (London, 1974), pp. 199–206; Various WNC leaflets, including: *Report, August 1914 to March 1916* (1916), p. 3, *Summary of Minutes of Executive Committee Meetings* (28 September 1914 and 2 December 1914), *Memoranda and Recommendations on the Increased Prices of Wheat and Coal* (1916), p. 5, British Library, London.
16 Beveridge, *British Food Control*, 9.
17 Ramsay MacDonald, diary. Entry for 7 December 1916, PRO 30/69/1753, MacDonald Papers, Public Record Office, London.

18 Hardy to Ashley, 9 May 1917, 42244B, Ashley Papers, British Library, London.
19 Taylor (ed.), *Lloyd George: A Diary*, p. 159, entry for 26 May 1917.
20 R. Smillie, *My Life for Labour* (London, 1924), pp. 176–7; K. Middlemas (ed.), *Thomas Jones' Whitehall Diary* (London, 1969), p. 36, entry for 29 August 1917; Milner, Memorandum on possible organisation of Ministry of Food, 12 June 1917, Box 162/18–35, Milner Papers, Bodleian Library, Oxford; J. S. Middleton to M. Crossley, 14 June 1917, 9/2/67, WNC Papers.
21 Rhondda to Prime Minister, 26 May 1917 and 14 June 1917, F/43/5/10 and 21. Lloyd George Papers, House of Lords Record Office, London.
22 Quoted by Sir T. G. Jones, *The Unbroken Front: Ministry of Food, 1916–1944* (London, 1944), p. 8.
23 *Hansard*, vol. 25 HL Deb., 5s., 11 July 1917, col. 908.
24 Sir G. Newman, diary, entry for 16 January 1917, Newman Papers, Ministry of Health Library, London; Middlemas, *Thomas Jones' Whitehall Diary*, p. 27, entry for 6 April 1917.
25 G. E. Underhill, 'History of the Ministry of Food', chapter 4, Food Files, Box 22, Beveridge Papers.
26 Rew, letter to Editor, *The Times*, 22 October 1921.
27 *Hansard*, vol. 96 HC Deb., 5s., 24 July 1917, cols. 1133–4, 1136.
28 *Hansard*, vol. 96 HC Deb., 5s., 30 July 1917, col. 1868; Extract from War Cabinet Minutes, 19 July 1917, MAF 60/54.
29 J. S. Middleton to Asquith, 5 February 1916, 11/274, WNC Papers; Middleton to Runciman, 5 February 1916, 11/275, WNC Papers; Middleton to Editor, *Star*, 23 July 1917, 29/2/1, WNC Papers; War Committee, Minutes, 13 November 1916, CAB 42/24/5.
30 Hyndman, The six-penny quartern loaf, March 1917, 12/44/3, WNC Papers: Transcript of meeting with Lord Rhondda, 22 June 1917, 12/145, WNC Papers; *The Times*, 4 and 8 December 1916; *Herald*, 31 March 1917; *Hansard*, vol. 90 HC Deb., 5s., 15 February 1917, col. 783; *Hansard*, vol. 94 HC Deb., 5s., 20 June 1917, cols. 1800–1.
31 Milner, Memorandum on food rationing and the discouragement of the enemy, 28 April 1917, Box 161/129–133, Milner Papers, Bodleian Library, Oxford; Report by non-milling members of the Flour Mills Control Committee to Lord Devonport, 5 June 1917, Food Files, Box 5, Beveridge Papers.
32 Miners' Federation of Great Britain to Prime Minister (enclosing copy of resolution, 17 May 1917), 18 May 1917, CAB 24/13; Rhondda to Prime Minister, 14 June 1917, F/43/5/21, Lloyd George Papers.
33 Beveridge, *British Food Control*, pp. 163–4.
34 Ministry of Food, Costings Department, Costs and profits of retail butchers [late 1917], Food Files, Box 10, Beveridge Papers.
35 Jones, *Unbroken Front*, p. 10.
36 War Cabinet, Minutes, 19 March 1917, CAB 23/2/49.
37 For more details see Lloyd, *Experiments in State Control*, pp. 177–184.
38 W. Barber, Bradford and District Trades and Labour Council, Suggested scheme for rationing the public with sugar, 5 April 1917, 12/53/2, WNC Papers; Middleton to Devonport, 14 May 1917, 10/2/18, WNC Papers; Underhill, 'History', Food Files, Box 22, Beveridge Papers.
39 C. J. H., Sugar distribution scheme, 21 September 1917, Food Files, Box 7, Beveridge Papers.
40 Beveridge, *British Food Control*, p. 192; *The Times History of the War*, vol. 15 (London, 1918), p. 267; Ministry of Labour, The labour situation. Report for week ending 5 December 1917, CAB 24/34.

41 E. R. Simmons to Middleton, 21 September 1917, 10/3/58, WNC Papers; J. R. Clynes, *Memoirs*, vol. 1 (London, 1937), p. 225.

42 A. L. Bowley, *Prices and Wages in the United Kingdom 1914–1920* (Oxford, 1921), p. 70.

43 Ibid., pp. 105–6; Working Classes Cost of Living Committee, *Report*, Cd 8980 (1918), p. 9.

44 Minutes of deputation from Parliamentary Committee of the TUC to the Prime Minister, 12 December 1917, F/222/1, Lloyd George Papers; *National Convention on the National Food Supply* (circular, 29 December 1917), 9/2/96, WNC Papers.

45 Clemesha, *Food Control in the North-Western Division*, pp. 92, 96.

46 Bowley, *Prices and Wages*, pp. 50, 53; *National Convention*, 9/2/96, WNC Papers.

47 Bowley, ibid., pp. 84–5; E. J. Foley, Food [1928], MAF 60/523.

48 Beveridge, *British Food Control*, p. 166.

49 Report of the committee to consider the supply of home-killed beef for army purposes, 9 July 1917, MAF 60/59; Minutes of meeting July 17 on food prices, F/71/11/1, Lloyd George Papers; W. H. Wills, Fixing of cattle prices during period of control [1919], Food Files, Box 20, Beveridge Papers; R. E. Prothero to Prime Minister, 28 February 1918 (enclosing copy of letter to Rhondda), F/15/8/30 and 30b, Lloyd George Papers.

50 Clark, diaries, Bodleian Library, Oxford, entry for 18 October 1917.

51 Minutes of deputation from Parliamentary Committee of the TUC, 12 December 1917, F/221/1, Lloyd George Papers; Jones *Unbroken Front*, p. 42.

52 Clinton, *Trade Union Rank and File*, p. 68.

53 Beveridge, *British Food Control*, pp. 195–6.

54 J. M. Keynes, *The Collected Writings of John Maynard Keynes*, E. Johnson (ed.), vol. 16 (Cambridge, 1971–1980), p. 266, letter to his mother, 24 December 1917.

55 Ministry of Labour, The labour situation, CAB 24/34; *National Convention*, 9/2/96, WNC Papers; *Observer*, 20 January 1918.

56 *Herald*, 24 November 1917; Dr Macnamara to Prime Minister, The civil population and the war, 27 November 1917, F/6/49, Lloyd George Papers; Gore to Hankey, 1 January 1918, F/23/2/1, Lloyd George Papers.

57 Hardy to Rhondda, 12 November 1917, Box 530, Royal Society Papers, Royal Society, London.

58 *Herald*, 22 December 1917.

59 C. S. Peel, *A Year in Public Life* (London, 1919), pp. 167–8; *Hansard*, vol. 100 HC Deb., 5s., 17 December 1917, col. 1712.

60 Clynes, *Memoirs*, p. 226; Ministry of Labour, The labour situation, Report for week ending 9 January 1918, CAB 24/38; Resolutions on the relations of the Labour Party and the government to be discussed at the Nottingham conference, January 1918, F/1/4/8, Lloyd George Papers.

61 *Herald*, 21 February 1918.

62 Lord Stamfordham to Prime Minister, 9 August 1917 (enclosing extract of letter from Bishop of Chelmsford), F/29/1/47, Lloyd George Papers; *The Times*, 25–28 September 1917, 7 November 1917; *Hansard*, vol. 26 HL Deb., 5s., 7 November 1917, col. 934.

63 B. P. Webb, *Diaries 1873–1943* (microfiche edition, Cambridge, 1978), ff. 3542–3, entry for 5 October 1917.

64 W. W. Astor to Prime Minister, 9 February 1918, 1066/1/767, Astor Papers, Reading University.

65 S. Walton, The effect of food queues at home on men at the Front, 16 April 1918, MAF 60/243; Sir S. Tallents, *Man and Boy* (London, 1943), p. 243.

66 *Herald*, 3 November 1917; Hankey, diary, entry for 24 February 1918, Churchill College, Cambridge; Bonar Law to Lord Derby, 4 February 1918, T172/796; A.

Chamberlain to Prime Minister, 28 May 1918, AC 15/1/15, Chamberlain Papers, University of Birmingham; Middlemas, *Thomas Jones' Whitehall Diary*, p. 54. Entry for 20 March 1918; C. A. Repington, *The First World War 1914–1918*, vol. 2 (London, 1920), p. 240.

67   Prime Minister to Rhondda, 8 February 1918, F/43/5/55, Lloyd George Papers; Bonar Law to Derby, 4 February 1918, T172/796.

68   W. H. Beveridge, *Power and Influence* (London, 1953), p. 165.

69   Barnes to Prime Minister, 11 March 1918, F/4/2/25, Lloyd George Papers; Chamberlain to Prime Minister, 28 May 1918. AC 15/1/15, Chamberlain Papers.

70   Beveridge, personal notes, Main Series, item 4, file 25, Beveridge Papers.

71   Prime Minister to Rhondda, 8 February 1918, F/43/5/55, Lloyd George Papers; Beveridge, *Power and Influence*, p. 166.

72   Beveridge, personal notes (extract from letter to his mother), Main Series, item 4, file 25, Beveridge Papers; *The Times*, 16 March 1921.

73   Requests for rationing are too numerous to quote comprehensively. Labour's demands were passed on in many of the official documents and reports cited in this chapter, including the Ministry of Labour weekly reports and Macnamara's report. See also articles in the *Herald*, *Clarion*, *Morning Post* and *Spectator*, in particular.

74   The Co-operative Union Ltd, *Co-operative National Emergency Conference, October 17 and 18, 1917* and *Report of the Deputation to the Prime Minister, October 31, 1917* (printed together) (London, 1917), p. 123.

75   Report by Lord Rhondda on compulsory rationing and distribution of essential foods, 28 November 1917, MAF 60/108; Rhondda to Prime Minister, 4 December 1917, F/43/5/44, Lloyd George Papers; Rhondda, The food situation, 10 December 1917, MAF 60/56; Rhondda, Compulsory rationing, 24 January 1918 (enclosing Scale of rations), MAF 60/108; War Cabinet, Minutes, 30 January, 1918, CAB 23/5/73–4.

76   *Morning Post*, 3 December 1917; *Observer*, 13 January 1918.

77   Beveridge, *British Food Control*, p. 200.

78   War Cabinet, Minutes, 30 January 1918, CAB 23/5/73–4; Rhondda, Compulsory rationing, 24 January 1918, MAF 60/108.

79   S. Gwynn (ed.), *The Anvil of War: Letters between F. S. Oliver and his Brother 1914–1918* (London, 1936), pp. 329, 331.

80   Ministry of Food, Memorandum on the permanent control of the milk trade, 14 May 1919, Food Files, Box 20, Beveridge Papers.

81   Beveridge, *British Food Control*, pp. 262–3.

82   *Hansard*, vol. 104 HC Deb., 5s., 9 April 1918, col. 1332.

83   A. Robinson to M. Phillips, 23 April 1918, Consumers' Council Papers, CCC.1/39, Transport House, London.

84   Peel, *A Year in Public Life*, 172; C. S. Peel, *How We Lived Then 1914–1918* (London, 1929), pp. 90–1.

85   F. L. Turner, *National Kitchens and National Health: A Great Public Work* (leaflet, London, 1917).

86   Peel, *A Year in Public Life*, p. 189.

87   *New Statesman*, 27 April 1918, vol. 11, p. 68.

88   Board of Trade, Cd 8980, p. 17.

89   Beveridge, *British Food Control*, p. 231.

90   Ministry of Food, *Monthly Office Report* (London, December 1918), Table D: Stocks of the principle foods in the United Kingdom.

91   Consumers' Council, Memorandum, n.d., 5/4/21, WNC Papers.

92   Clynes, *Memoirs*, p. 237; Hyndman, *The Last Years of H. M. Hyndman*, p. 170.

93   Hyndman to Middleton, 20 February 1918, 10/1/121, WNC Papers.

94 Ashley, personal notes, 42249, Ashley Papers.
95 Ibid.
96 Hyndman to Middleton, 2 February 1918, 5/4/20, WNC Papers.
97 Beveridge to C. Bathurst, 4 April 1918, Main Series, item 4, file 27i, Beveridge Papers.
98 Hyndman, Report on orders given to the Consumers' Council, n.d. and Ashley, personal notes, 42249, Ashley Papers.
99 Hyndman, Bread rationing, n.d., 42249, Ashley Papers; Hyndman, notes on bread rationing, CC/GEN.23, Consumers' Council Papers.
100 Coller, *State Trading*, p. 184; Assistant Secretary of the WNC to J. Hall, 14 September 1918, 10/1/186, WNC Papers; Clynes, Food prices and subsidies, 24 September 1918, CAB 23/7/123.
101 S. Walton to Ashley, 21 July 1918, 42249, Ashley Papers.

7

American Influence on British Food Policy: Herbert Hoover and the Inter-Allied Trading System

The opening of British Treasury files of the First World War era to research in the 1970s led to a revival of interest in the part played by economics in the wartime relationship between the British and American governments. Earlier, attention had concentrated on the American side of the question, especially during the interwar years when Senator George Norris's contention, voiced in April 1917, that the United States had entered the war 'upon command of gold' was widely accepted as a valid interpretation of events. Scholars had traced significant links between the huge volume of trade and loans to the European Allies and the wartime attitudes and decisions of President Wilson and his advisors. The newly-opened British archives widened the scope of the inquiry. 'Economic influence,' one researcher found, 'was a two-way street, and commercial and financial ties formed critical aspects of diplomacy on both sides of the Atlantic.' By the beginning of 1917, he continued, the United States government was in a strong position to influence British war policy, so dependent had Britain become on the United States for supplies and credit. The moderate reception of Wilson's peace initiative in December 1916 was cited as evidence of this. Yet, the study concluded, the United States could make no effective use of its financial might once it had entered the war on the Allied side.[1]

Whatever the truth of this conclusion for war policy as a whole, there is ample evidence to show that it did not hold for food policy. The participation of the United States in the war gave the Americans an opportunity to use the weapon of finances and supply to bring about a total reorganization of the Allied trading arrangements with

North America and to influence food policy within individual Allied countries. A series of inter-allied councils took over from the mass of rival, national units the responsibility for financing, purchasing and shipping to Europe such essential products as munitions materiel, oil, steel and food. The creation of this system had a great impact on the food control mechanisms of the European nations. It entailed the imposition of complementary regulations over the domestic ends of the trade, an increase in the number of personnel working on food questions and the transference of a certain degree of control over import policy from the individual countries to an outside entity. In theory, this entity consisted of the Allies in equal partnership; in practice, because of the United States' economic power and role as major supplier, the American authorities – especially the energetic head of the American Food Administration, Herbert Hoover – had the predominant voice in the decision-making process.

As the country with the greatest proportion of imports in its food supply, Britain felt the pressure exerted by the United States more than did the other European Allies. Little indication of this is to be found in the official history of wartime food control. There it was stated that the inter-allied system influenced British policy only towards the very end of the war, after July 1918, the co-ordination of international marketing and the spread of controls being portrayed as products of pre-existing domestic trends and the personal desire of Rhondda to bring the country's entire food supply under regulation. These factors certainly played a part. The new arrangements were a logical extension of such international trading units as the CIR and the Wheat Commission and Rhondda's commitment to organization cannot be denied. A further challenge to the suggestion that policy was shaped from outside rests on the fact that it was Lloyd George who pressed at Rapallo for the full co-ordination of the Allied military effort through the means of a Supreme Inter-Allied War Council. Moreover, after the military setbacks of 1917, the spirit of international co-operation was in the air: 'One Front, One Army, One Nation,' to quote the French Premier, Paul Painlevé.[2] Receptive as they may have been to the idea of co-ordination of resources in the military sphere, however, the Europeans were ambivalent about collaboration in the civilian sphere. The Americans, on the other hand, while also interested in military co-operation, had a veritable 'passion' for inter-allied civilian war agencies.[3] Fresh from his visit to Italy in November 1917, Lloyd George was persuaded only very reluctantly to endorse a proposed inter-allied conference in Paris later that same month to debate improved liaison in such areas as man-power, tonnage, finance, food supplies and war industries. Significantly, the Prime Minister agreed to attend the conference after a hint from President Wilson's personal envoy, Colonel House, that the United States would cease to back the British government in financial matters unless he did so. 'It is planned to urge Lloyd George to help bring about co-ordination in our working forces,' House recorded in his diary, 'and we have picked Lord Reading [Britain's financial representative in Washington] to see that it is properly done ... I called Reading's attention to the importance of Lloyd George working cordially with me. If he did, I thought his Government could not be overthrown. In saying this I intended a covert threat which I think Reading caught.'[4]

Both the British and the French conceded after the war that the inter-allied system had worked well, especially during the last four months of the war. The waste and expense stemming from competition among the Allies for the same goods and services had been virtually eliminated, and it was agreed that stock levels had been higher than they would have been if the inter-allied organization had not existed. Yet, as the French High Commissioner to the United States observed, 'the weight of the international arrangements was not always borne gladly by the Europeans'. The cause of this, as of official reticence on the subject, was resentment that the system had brought the European Allies, in at least one important area of war policy, too much under the control of the Americans.[5]

Rhondda came to the Ministry of Food in the midst of a grave crisis in the dollar exchange. This was the culmination of a series of events dating back to the previous September. Exasperated by the British blockade of the Continent and the blacklisting of American companies that were trading with the Central Powers, the United States Congress empowered President Wilson on 5 September 1916 to retaliate against countries discriminating against American trade. Although energetic protests from Britain and France and lack of support from the other nations soon deflected the United States from this purpose, the British government decided it would be wise to evaluate just how significant the closure of the American market would be for Britain's war effort. The committee appointed to look into the question was appalled by what it found. In food, raw

Table 7.1 *Imports of Principal Foodstuffs from the United States. Per cent of Total Food Imports.*

	1913	1915	1918
Wheat and flour	34.7	49.0	52.3
Meat	1.6	8.3	31.2
Bacon and ham	44.9	60.9	83.7
Oats	7.0	52.0	n.a.
Rye	10.0	93.0	n.a.
Barley	13.0	47.0	n.a.
Dairy produce	0.2	n.a.	37.8

Source: R. H. Rew, Report by the Food Controller on the dependence of the United Kingdom on supplies of foodstuffs from the United States, 21 December 1916, CAB 37/162/1 and CAB 1/21/6 (Tables); Sources of imported supply, 1913 and 1918 (certain principal foodstuffs), MAF 60/445.

materials and steel, its chairman, Lord Eustace Percy, reported, 'American supplies are so necessary to us that reprisals, while they would produce tremendous distress in America, would also practically stop the war'. Britain was by then placing fully 40 per cent of its war orders in North America.[6] The report fed already pessimistic attitudes within the Asquith government. 'If things go on as at present,' McKenna told the Cabinet, 'I venture to say with certainty that by next June or earlier the President of the American Republic will be in a position, if he wishes, to dictate his own terms to us.'[7] The main fear was that Wilson, then campaigning for re-election on a neutrality ticket, might use his country's economic power to stop the war at a point disadvantageous to the Allies. The change of government in Britain that December brought to office men less ready to submit to such pressure. Under Lloyd George's aegis the new Ministry of Food made its own analysis of the supply position in the event of a rupture with the United States. This served only to underscore the warnings of the Percy Committee. In the case of food alone, it was found that the United States had become Britain's single most important supplier.

Although disconcerted by the country's material dependence on the United States, the statesmen were primarily worried by the financial implications. Wrongly, they assumed that if they had the funds, they could continue to buy as much as was needed. The negotiations that culminated in the formation of the inter-allied system therefore revolved around the matter of dollar credits. Despite earlier fears, J. P. Morgan and Company had little difficulty assisting the Allied governments to transact business in the United States until September 1916. The Percy Committee's investigation that month revealed that fresh arrangements would soon have to be made. Of the £5 million a day currently being spent on the war, the Treasury had to find the equivalent of £2 million in dollars, three-fifths of the expenditure being met by the sale of gold and securities, two-fifths by credits arranged by Morgan's using government holdings as collateral. The government's reserves were now so depleted that from the beginning of 1917, five-sixths of the trade would have to be financed by loans.[8] To raise money on this scale, bonds would have to be sold on the open market, and if this were to be done successfully, the rapport between the two countries would have to show a marked improvement.

There was little chance of this in the winter of 1916–17. Anglo-American relations were at their lowest ebb of the war. On 27 November, a month after the British and French governments floated a joint bond issue of $300 million, the Federal Reserve Board advised American banks to restrict their overseas lending on the grounds that long-term loans to the European Allies were a poor risk. Several factors contributed to this action: concern over the effect that the influx of gold from abroad and the huge debits run up by foreign governments was having on the American money market; political antagonism between the Democratic Wilson administration and the Republican J. P. Morgan and Company, which was proving prejudicial to Britain's interests; and, as McKenna had feared, the belief shared by the Board's governor, W. P. G. Harding, and President Wilson, who intervened to get the Board's statement worded more strongly, that America's financial influence could be exerted to end the war.[9]

The Federal Reserve Board's warning had drastic consequences. Strong reactions shook the money markets in London and New York. In the first week of December alone the Treasury had to pay out $76 million to support the sterling exchange. 'Another ten days of this,' Keynes is quoted as saying, 'and we should have been finished.' Similar views were expressed by Morgan's, which itself bought $80 million of exchange in one week.[10] Britain and France were forced to give up plans to float an (unsecured) joint loan of $500 million in January. All British purchasing in the United States was suspended. Arrangements made privately by the Wheat Export Company tided the Allies over the emergency as far as cereal needs were concerned. A

$30 million loan from a group of banks in New York allowed the Wheat Commission to continue buying until the end of February, when trading temporarily ceased.[11] Alarmed that Morgan's unpopularity was contributing to these financial problems, the British government transferred the duty of organizing funding for American purchases to a special corps of Treasury employees, headed by Sir Hardman Lever, who sailed for New York in February. The severing of diplomatic relations between the United States and Germany, as a result of the latter's resumption of unrestricted submarine warfare, brought timely relief. Wilson approved a new British Treasury bond issue on 20 February and the Federal Reserve Board officially withdrew its warning against foreign loans on 8 March. Discussions in February between the Board and Lever's forces were heartening. Colonel House, speaking on behalf of the President, was cordiality itself. He assured the British officials that the United States wanted 'to be your reservoir for everything that America can supply – Food, Munitions, Money and Men'.[12]

In April it seemed as if the third of these at least had been settled during talks between the US Secretary of the Treasury, William McAdoo, and Balfour, who led a mission to the United States soon after America declared war on Germany. On 25 April, only three days after the mission arrived, Britain was awarded its first loan by the United States Treasury. Balfour took this to be a firm commitment for future funding of Allied dollar purchases, but this was being denied by the Americans as a misconception almost as soon as the mission set sail for home. It was not until August that the matter began to be sorted out. One factor contributing to the confusion was a misunderstanding by the Americans as to the purpose of Balfour's visit. Since Lloyd George had received full approval for the mission from Ambassador Page, with whom he had discussed matters in detail, the British assumed that President Wilson welcomed the opportunity to discuss formally the scope of the United States' future contributions to the war effort, including its financial assistance to the European Allies. Wilson, who disliked Page's pro-British attitude and who rarely read his despatches, had not, however, sanctioned official talks for the latter purpose. The President was initially unenthusiastic about Balfour's coming, fearing that the American public would interpret the visit as an attempt by the British to relegate the United States to a supporting role in the direction of the war effort. In the event, the Balfour mission, which consisted primarily of representatives of the purchasing departments rather than financial experts, received a warm welcome in the United States, from government officials, the press and the public. This in turn contributed to Balfour's mistaken belief that his financial negotiations had been successful.[13]

A major problem derived from the staggering size of the loans requested by the Allies and the difficulty of the Wilson administration in justifying these loans to Congress. The Americans were inexperienced in the realm of international finance at this time and the sums seemed unwarrantably enormous, especially those requested by the British, who were still financing the other Allies. By the beginning of July the United States had advanced Britain $685 million, yet it was constantly being asked for more. Further controversy surrounded Britain's request for help in settling the $400 million debt to J. P. Morgan and Company for purchases prior to April 1917 and the suggestion that the US Treasury take over responsibility for future dollar funding of the other European Allies. 'America's co-operation does not mean that America will assume the entire burden of financing the war,' McAddo responded ascerbically, if somewhat erroneously.[14] In an effort to elucidate Britain's position, Bonar Law sent McAdoo a long memorandum on 20 July pointing out that the credits requested were by no means excessive when compared to Britain's outlay in America. The Treasury was now spending some $280 million a month on all commodities. The American loans only just allowed trading to continue. Without an immediate guarantee of help, the Treasury feared that Britain would have to abandon the gold standard. 'Unless the United States government can meet in full our expenses in America, including exchange', the Chancellor of the Exchequer warned, 'the whole fabric of the alliance will collapse. This conclusion will be a matter not of months but of days.'[15]

In the face of these difficulties, the Wheat Commission's success in building up reserves was remarkable. However, the endeavour both contributed to the exchange crisis and was itself in constant danger of being undermined by the lack of dollar credits. Extra-large shipments of wheat were scheduled for June, the same month that American investors withdrew their deposits in British banks to participate in the Liberty Loan floated by the American government. This resulted in a $250 million deficit in the dollar credits needed that month. By dint of various stratagems and a small advance from Canada, the Treasury managed to reduce this substantially, but only the personal intervention of Colonel House, who persuaded McAdoo to bridge the gap, allowed the full programme of food exports to be carried out.[16]

To the British, McAdoo's reluctance to end this harassing cycle of last-minute reprieves made him appear vacillating and unreliable.[17] Yet his position was most difficult and was not made easier by the attitude of the British officials themselves. McAdoo's relationship with Congress was poor. The President's son-in-law and his chief advisor, McAdoo had been accused of being Wilson's 'evil genius'; it was now being said that he was spending the nation's wealth 'like a drunken sailor'.[18] McAdoo had to reassure both Congress and, as a presidential hopeful, the people that American largesse was not being distributed indiscriminately. He had asked the British and French governments on several occasions for details about their financial status rather than general statements of needs. The British Ambassador, Sir Cecil Spring-Rice, passed on similar complaints from congressmen.[19] It was only on 20 July, however, that Bonar Law obliged with figures that revealed the full extent of Britain's financial underwriting of the Allied cause. Even then the American authorities were not fully informed of the effect that the war was having on British life. It was not until 23 July, for example, that the War Cabinet agreed, in response to an urgent plea from Lord Northcliffe, to disclose to the American government the true consequences of the German submarine campaign.[20] News releases gave no indication that a food shortage existed despite Hoover's suggestion that the goodwill of Americans would be quickened if the Ministry of Food displayed 'more anxiety' in its announcements.[21] Northcliffe, who was sent to the United States in June to untangle the administrative chaos amidst which the various British missions were operating, found that the censorship of war news had gone to ludicrous lengths. Even some top United States officials were ignorant of the British burdens in the war. The British army, whose campaigns went virtually unreported in the American press, was believed by some to be still at home. 'We cannot expect sacrifices from our people,' Wilson told Northcliffe, 'unless they know that Great Britain is suffering too.' Little wonder that there was resistance to British requests for financial assistance. 'We have only ourselves to blame', Northcliffe reported back wryly. 'If there is ever any hanging from lamp-posts, those who are responsible for our form of censorship should be the first to be strung up.'[22]

Although Bonar Law was able to satisfy McAdoo personally that the Allies were not overstating their needs, the Wilson administration believed that there was only one way by which congressional approval of regular funding for the Allies could be assured. This was the creation of an inter-allied council, which would supervise all Allied spending in the United States and guarantee that the loans were used solely for American commodities necessary to the war effort. The United States Cabinet declared such a body a prerequisite of recurrent loans as early as 11 May.[23] Thinking that the CIR might fill the role, the Europeans at first favoured the idea, approving an inter-allied council in principle on 4 June. When the Americans made it clear that they wanted an entirely new organization, however, enthusiasm rapidly waned. Although the subsequent lack of progress was blamed on French and Italian dislike of the proposal, it was Britain that was most reluctant to proceed. The government was anxious to divest itself of some of the financial burden of the war, yet hesitated to relinquish the influence that its own control of the purse strings had given it over general Allied policy. In addition, the Treasury objected most strongly to conducting financial negotiations through a multinational intermediary, an obstacle subsequently overcome by special arrangements covering questions of exchange and the debt to Morgan's and by the appointment of Lord Reading as Britain's chief representative in the United States. The Admiralty and Ministry of Shipping were also unhappy with the initial proposals because they would have removed British control over Allied shipping, most of which belonged to Britain.[24] To speed things along, McAdoo made the emergency loan issued on 20 July contingent upon the holding of an inter-allied conference in London to draw up details of a council. Yet the end of July found the Europeans still equivocating. On 3 August McAdoo warned that credits to the Allies would be cut off after the 15th, the date of the last payments from the first Liberty Loan, unless agreement was reached. This prompted discussions but 15 August passed without a decision. As a last resort, Hoover informed the Europeans on 24 August that he would place an embargo on all exports of food if the matter was not brought to a swift conclusion. Northcliffe was authorized to agree to the council on 25 August; confirmation by the British and French governments, with the concurrence of the Italians and Russians, followed on the 31st.[25]

Once basic agreement was reached, the development of the machinery proceeded swiftly. Northcliffe signed the contract on behalf of the British government on 12 October, organizational details were worked out during meetings of the Allied nations in London and Paris in November, and by early December an Inter-Allied Council on War Purchases and Finance was functioning under the chairmanship of Oscar T. Crosby, Assistant Secretary of the United States Treasury. Like the military Supreme War Council, this body soon proved incapable of acting as an executive unit. Its ostensible duties were to scrutinize and approve the purchasing programmes of the member nations. In reality, it was too small to do more than discuss them in the most general terms. Keynes, who represented the British Treasury on the Council, initially found the meetings useless: 'the only possible analogy to government by Inter-Ally Council,' he commented on 15 December, 'is government by Bolsheviks, though judging by results the latter are more efficient.'[26] By the end of January, however, he had changed his mind. As McAdoo had hoped, the Council was fostering confidence that everything was 'above board and conducted with reasonable efficiency'.[27]

The real work of the inter-allied trading system was done by a maze of other agencies. In Britain the first step in the process was the monthly submission by departments of state of purchasing programmes covering the next three months to a new American Board chaired by Austen Chamberlain, which co-ordinated them and determined priorities. The inter-departmental co-operation that had been so regrettably lacking earlier in the war was thus developed without fuss in direct response to an external stimulus. After formal approval by the Inter-Allied Council, the combined national programme was passed on to the Allied Purchasing Commission, which had been formed at the end of August to handle all trading in the United States on behalf of the European governments. This organization was part of the War Industries Board, which was responsible for United States government purchases too. A Division of Co-ordination of Purchasing (DCP) then determined prices and allotted orders to specific suppliers. In the case of foodstuffs, the DCP worked closely with the Allied Provisions Export Commission (APEC), formed in October, which at last brought the European purchasing units in the United States under one roof. APEC was the official agent for the European Allies as a group; contracts for food supplies going to Britain were signed by a representative of the British Ministry of Food in New York. APEC consisted primarily of this branch of the ministry with the addition of representatives of the other Allied governments and was initially located in the same offices and headed by the same person.

The APEC/DCP arrangements covered all foodstuffs except grain and sugar. These, the most important foods in contemporary estimation, were directly controlled by the American Food Administrator, Herbert Hoover. As Hoover's participation in the final negotiations on the inter-allied trading system suggests, he had been closely involved with the matter from the start. The size of the Allied purchases of food and the effect that they were having on markets in the United States was one cause of congressional reluctance to approve recurrent loans. The price of bread and other staples had been forced up and disruptions to the flow of supplies had led to disorder in some American cities. In mid-February 1917 thousands of women in the lower east side of New York had rioted when stores ran out of bread.[28] It was Hoover who had raised the idea of co-ordinating Allied trading agencies in the first place. His views on how war agencies should be run crystallized during his term as head of the Belgian Relief Commission, which only at his insistence was managed as a single-multinational unit. Summoned home in April 1917 to take up the post of Food Administrator, he broke his journey in London on his own initiative to discuss with government officials his idea for an international board to channel the purchase and shipment of food from North America to Europe. Devonport, singled out in the official history as the cause of Britain's delay in ratifying the Inter-Allied Council, warmly seconded Hoover's suggestions in a memorandum to the Cabinet dated 11 April.[29] During the protracted discussions that followed, Hoover brought Wilson to agree to a comprehensive and unified control of foodstuffs in the United States instead of looser supervision by a conglomeration of separate boards and committees as the President wished. It was also Hoover's suggestion that the principle of co-ordinated purchases be extended to the full gamut of exports. 'From observation of the host of ... Allied failures in organisation,' he wrote in his memoirs, 'I felt there must be a single head to the food problem and that his authority must cover every phase of food administration from the soil to the stomach.'[30] Hoover was determined that the 'single head' in the international sphere, not just in the United States, would be himself.

The prior existence of the Wheat and Sugar Commissions allowed the Food Administrator to bring grain and sugar under his control without waiting for the Allies to agree on the inter-allied trading system. The European side was already co-ordinated; only supervision of the American markets remained. On 15 August the United

States Food Administration (USFA) formed the Grain Corporation, under Hoover's chairmanship, to handle the purchase, sale and distribution of all grain and flour in the United States. The Grain Corporation set prices, the same for both American and foreign buyers, and ended speculation in the American market by closing the grain exchanges for the duration. All of North America's exportable surplus was promised to the Wheat Executive, which in turn agreed to buy the entire supply available. Arrangements were made to treat the North American harvests as a whole, the Canadian surplus being moved south via the Great Lakes for export. Since the Grain Corporation became the clearing house for wheat grown in South America as well as the United States and Canada, its importance for Britain soon far transcended that of a body controlling a single national market. In 1918, with Australian wheat largely unobtainable due to lack of transport and Indian produce diverted to the closer ports of France and Italy, virtually all of Britain's imported breadstuffs flowed through the Grain Corporation.[31]

Hoover took equally firm steps with sugar. He was as dissatisfied as the British public with the record of the Sugar Commission and was particularly incensed by its inept negotiations with the Cuban growers in 1916 that resulted in unnecessarily high prices being paid by all of Cuba's customers. In June 1917 he formed his own International Sugar Commission, a five-man board of whom only two were Europeans. Before the latter had time to arrive in Washington, Hoover negotiated for the entire Cuban crop of 1917–18 on terms he personally deemed appropriate.[32] Even this scoop did not satisfy him. The arrangement had been voluntary. In July 1918 he formed the Sugar Equalization Board, which it was mandatory for the Europeans to join if they wanted Cuban sugar. The pill was sweetened, so to speak, by the full dollar credits offered by the United States Treasury to those countries that accepted these conditions. This was an inducement the British could not afford to resist; 70 per cent of the sugar allotted to Europe by the Board was assigned to Britain.[33] In 1918–19 the Board bought the entire sugar crops of the United States, Cuba, the West Indies and the Philippines.

Hoover also encouraged the extension of the co-operative principles of the Wheat Commission, which he greatly admired, to other foodstuffs. He wanted the Europeans to pool their transactions for various commodities in as many import executives as possible. National boundaries, ethnic rivalries, traditional ways of working did not detract him from his purpose. He displayed a determination to reorganize the marketing techniques of the European nations as if these latter were a federated association of states like his own country. A useful weapon for attaining his goal, applied several times in addition to August 1917, was the threat of embargo. The Europeans themselves had already discussed the establishment of more joint trading units before the United States entered the war, but the talks, conducted primarily between the French and British, dragged on inconclusively for month after month. Had Hoover not intervened, implementation of these plans would have taken considerably longer or perhaps even not have come to pass. Proposals to combine meat imports for civilians dated back to the beginning of 1917. Early in June Hoover asked if the Wheat Commission could take on the task, but the Ministry of Food would not agree to this. No visible progress having been made by the end of July, Hoover threatened to ban all exports of meat unless an Inter-Allied Meat and Fats Executive was established promptly. The executive agreement was signed 29 August. A temporary embargo in November on the export of vegetable and animal oils was similarly followed by the formation of an Inter-Allied Oil and Seed Executive.[34] The creation of these bodies had an impact on food legislation in Britain. Private importation of meat ended in August and after November dealings in butter, cheese and condensed milk proceeded only under requisition orders issued by the Ministry of Food until the executive machinery had been set up. This meant both an increase in the jurisdiction of the ministry and a reduction in the size of the free market. Because this development complemented the controls introduced by Rhondda in accordance with government policy formulated in the summer of 1917, the official history denied that it owed anything to pressure exerted from abroad. Although Hoover's determination to integrate Allied buying in the United States *could* have had such a result, it was maintained, Rhondda 'needed no outside influence to set him on the course of full control'.[35]

The streamlining of purchasing channels permitted Rhondda to bring more foodstuffs under the control of the ministry. Responsibility for oils and fats were transferred from the Ministry of Munitions and imports of cheese were taken over from the Board of Trade. The Wheat Commission gained control of oats and other grains from the War Office and the Board of Trade. Rhondda hoped that the development of inter-allied trading arrangements would also help him wrest control of imports for the army from the Board of Trade. On 25 August, the day after Hoover's ultimatum, an army spokesman told Rhondda that the War Office considered it 'extremely desirable' to comply with the Food Adminstrator's wishes to pool orders and would end separate purchases as soon as effective arrangements were made with the French and Italian governments.[36] The plan foundered on the War Office's wish to transfer intact to the Ministry of Food the Board of Trade's special purchasing unit, which the military had found highly satisfactory. A personality conflict prevented this. Wintour, himself recently recruited from War Office ranks, simply could not get along with the personnel involved and refused to take on the entire staff of the unit. A weakly conducted investigation by Milner and Barnes led to a compromise that left the Board of Trade in charge of military supplies from Australia and New Zealand and gave responsibility for transatlantic supplies to the Ministry of Food. Despite this, Hoover's intervention was needed before the Board of Trade relinquished its dealings in North America. The Food Administrator blocked several attempts by the Board to place orders independently of the APEC/DCP system before the War Office finally consented, in January 1918, to transact all future business in the United States and Canada through the inter-allied organization.[37]

Although these developments led to an expansion of the Ministry of Food's jurisdiction in some spheres, they caused a diminution of its powers, and those of the Wheat and Sugar commissions, in others. In the world's most important markets Britain could now trade only through a third party. It could no longer negotiate independently either prices or quantities bought. As one ministry official put it: 'instead of the purchasing Allies having had their organisation to which prospective vendors should come with their goods, the chief vendor . . . set up machinery whereby to dispose of his commodities.[38] The initiative had been seized by others and Britain's ability to protect its own interests had been weakened in the process.

The inter-allied trading system, instead of easing the exchange difficulties that predated it, seemed designed both to remove Treasury curbs on spending and to perpetuate and compound that dependency on the American market that caused the problems in the first place. The loans advanced by the United States could, for the most part, be spent only on American goods or those, like sugar, that were controlled by the American authorities. The high prices of these goods in a seller's market in turn swelled the exchange deficit, which could only be liquidated by further borrowing. Hoover's assiduity in arranging loans to persuade the Allies to take products such as bacon in larger quantities than they otherwise would have done exacerbated the problem. The expense of American produce made it difficult for the Ministry of Food to maintain its price control policy. The strain of subsidizing the public against the effect of importing large quantities of American foodstuffs made Rhondda anxious to see prices in North America reduced. Since Hoover had cited the rise in the cost of living there as one reason why inter-allied trading should be adopted, it was logical to expect that he would work to bring down American prices once the new system was in effect. It soon became clear, however, that the Food Administrator had no intention of allowing the price of agricultural produce to fall to any great extent. It has been alleged that he was swayed by 'economic nationalism', that is, by a determination to make the Allies pay for what they wanted.[39] Hoover himself claimed later that his approach had been based on the 'utter failure' of maximum price ventures in Europe, which had been 'a universal stimulant to waste, black market and violation of law'. The Food Administrator believed that it was crucial in the long run to stimulate production. He took care therefore that the American farmer was assured of an attractive return on his crops. Defending his policy at a conference of the Allied Food Controllers in July 1918, Hoover declared price to be a 'triviality' compared to hunger.[40]

Thanks to the bread subsidy, the British consumer did not suffer from the high cost of American wheat, although Hoover's policy gave ammunition to opponents of the 9d loaf. In the case of sugar and pork products, however, the high prices were passed on to the public. On 1 April 1917 sugar cost 172 per cent more than in July 1914. The index rose to 190 on 1 October, held steady for some months, then soared in the spring of 1918 to stand at 240 per cent on 1 July. The price of bacon rose almost 50 per cent between July 1917 and January 1918. The responsible department at the Ministry of Food, which tried to cushion the impact of the trade, was one of the few units to operate at a constant loss.[41]

The British were also unhappy with the effect that the new arrangements had on the supply flow of some products. They had least reason to complain about sugar. Lack of shipping forced Britain to abandon efforts to acquire supplies from Java and other distant markets in the spring of 1918 and to rely almost totally on the more costly sugar obtainable through Hoover's organization. The quantities available to the consumer therefore ostensibly depended on what the Sugar Commission could obtain from this source. Maintaining that supplies being shipped did not equal quantities being consumed, the Ministry of Food kept sugar rations low. While the public went short, however, reserves were built up rapidly, reaching 400,000 tons by the end of the war.[42] The efficiency of Hoover's outfit had enabled this. Given the poor record of the Sugar Commission prior to the autumn of 1917, it is highly unlikely that that unit could have achieved a similar result. Not surprisingly, an attempt by the Europeans to get the Sugar Equalization Board changed into an inter-allied executive with a seat of operations in London instead of Washington was blocked by the America government on Hoover's insistence.[43]

There was more cause to be dissatisfied with the trade in pork products. The Europeans found themselves the victims of a miscalculation by Hoover. From 1914 to September 1917 the production of pork in the United States was low. The high prices that farmers could get for grain abroad made it unprofitable to feed to hogs. Hoover promised to reverse this trend, a move that would satisfy a lively agricultural lobby and his own aim of increased food output. Special arrangements were made to provide hog raisers with the cheap grain they needed. At the same time, an energetic campaign was launched to get the American public to eat less pork so as to increase supplies for export. The result by the end of the year was a glut of pork so vast that the market was threatened with collapse unless Hoover could unload the surplus onto the Allies. As Britain was then in the middle of a severe meat shortage, the Ministry of Food at first welcomed the prospect of larger imports of bacon and other pork products, the more so since Hoover arranged for special loans to cover the transactions. Large scale buying began in January 1918. By March the situation had got out of hand. The USFA insisted that the British take shipment during March and April alone of 450,000 tons of bacon, 100,000 tons more than that bought in the whole of 1917. Most of this was mild-cured bacon that needed immediate cold storage or further curing on arrival. The ports had no facilities to handle such a huge amount of perishable food; consignments rotted on the quayside and blocked unloading of other imports. Refrigerated warehouse space in Britain was likewise totally inadequate. By the time the bacon reached its final destination much of it had gone bad. Consumers blamed the Ministry of Food for poor management. The pressure to take the excess pork nevertheless continued. Despite tremendous shipments during the early part of 1918 the United States still had a huge surplus of pigs. In July herds numbered 100 million animals compared to the normal 70 million. A further agreement by Britain, in response to repeated urging from Hoover, to take a minimum of 100,000 tons of bacon and ham a month starting in October provoked protests all over the country. So traumatic was the experience that in 1937 planners, citing the unfortunate situation in the First World War, advised no importation of bacon in a future war unless the country was absolutely desperate for tonnage to carry feed for its own animals.[44]

The establishment of the inter-allied trading system had far more serious consequences in the case of wheat. With bread the staple food of the population, the authorities considered control of grain supplies an essential element in their ability to maintain domestic order and national efficiency. This control was impaired once the Wheat Commission could no longer buy on its own account and the country became dependent on allocations. In mid-1917, just before the new system went into effect, the Wheat Commission predicted there would be few problems in the coming cereal year. Stocks were considered large enough to maintain the thirteen-week reserve easily. Their only reservation was whether it could be kept up during the usual slow period of imports after March, when the bulk of the American and Canadian crops would have been shipped. The Commission therefore asked that wheat imports be kept as the first charge on the resources of the country.[45] A month later all optimism had evaporated. Failure by the American authorities to deliver amounts previously promised and the shipment, under the terms of the new agreement, of Canadian supplies to France and Italy instead of to Britain as in normal years, had resulted in a grave risk of an immediate and severe depletion of stores. Stocks fell rapidly in the last four months of 1917. Imports were far lower than those of the previous year, down 35 per cent in September and October and 45 per cent in November. Consumption was double the amount being received and the net outflow from stock between 1 September and 1 January was half as much again as during the comparable period of 1916–17.[46]

Several reasons were given for the low shipments from North America. In September the USFA blamed organized opposition from the American grain trade, which was allegedly inducing farmers to hold their wheat back from market.[47] Two months later, Hoover reported unexpectedly small surpluses of exportable wheat in the United States and Canada due to early frosts, a theme on which his

friend and representative, Alonzo E. Taylor, expanded at a conference of Allied food officials held in London in November. Taylor told
the assembly that North America had only about 140 million bushels
of wheat to send to Europe as opposed to the 260 million the Allies
wanted. There was said to be a deficit of over 3 million tons of cereals
after taking into account some supplies of rye that could be substi-
tuted for wheat.[48] This announcement, although greeted with
dismay, was not challenged by the Europeans. But did the deficit
really exist? A study of Hoover's grain policies has cast doubt on the
matter. The harvest in North America had indeed produced a smaller
surplus than expected but, it is argued, Hoover exaggerated the
position from a ruthless determination to hold on to his domestic
supplies. He was after all the American Food Administrator and his
first duty was to feed the American public.[49]

Hoover's approach appears more devious than ruthless, however,
and even had its amusing aspects. After advising the Wheat Commission on 1 January 1918 that the United States' export surplus was
exhausted and that only 90 million bushels were available from
Canada, Hoover asked his representative in London, Louis P.
Sheldon, in a 'highly confidential' telegram, to get Rhondda to cable
him expressing the imperative necessity of sending the extra 75
million bushels of wheat the Europeans needed by then in addition to
the Canadian surplus.[50] This Rhondda did on 17 January. Unless the
United States could export this amount, the Food Controller advised,
he would not be able to reassure the British people that there was food
enough to win the war. He concluded dramatically: 'it now lies with
America to decide whether or not the Allies in Europe shall have
enough bread to hold out until the United States is able to throw its
force into the field'. On 5 February the French Ambassador delivered
to President Wilson a similarly worded joint appeal from the Prime
Ministers of France, Italy and Britain.[51] One cannot but suspect that
Hoover engineered the whole matter to make him appear in the best
light possible. A colleague of his, without any intent of levity,
described the reaction at the USFA to Rhondda's message: 'I remem-
ber very well the thrill and the shock that ran through the ... staff
when that cable came. It seemed as if no more could be done than was
already being done. The breathless question was: could Hoover do the
impossible?' The Food Administrator proved to the Allies, and to the
American electorate, that he could indeed. Still protesting that no
surplus existed, Hoover launched a great conservation drive and by

July had found an extra 85 million bushels of wheat, 10 million more than the Allies had asked for.[52]

In return he expected concessions. Warning that wheat shipments would still be short of the minimum necessary in the months to come, he argued in March the advantages of a blanket order for America's entire excess of pork products. 'It appears to me that, in this situation, food is food,' he told Lord Reading.[53] He also tried to persuade the other Allied food authorities to place a total ban on brewing. The War Cabinet agreed to reduce beer output, to lower the gravity of beer again and to end malting of barley. Further than this the British would not go. 'I feel sure you will appreciate,' Rhondda cabled Hoover, 'the difficulties and dangers of imposing upon the working classes any sweeping measures of prohibition especially at a moment when drastic compulsory rations are coming into force.'[54]

To encourage the Europeans to introduce compulsory rationing had been one of Hoover's motives in announcing a shortfall of wheat exports. His scientific advisors (headed by Alonzo E. Taylor) had suggested that the European Allies bring their food consumption more in line with Germany's. They estimated that the Allies were consuming on average 2,900 calories per person each day compared to 2,000 in Germany, and that of this cereals represented 1,650 calories compared to 900. There seemed no reason why the Europeans could not at least reduce food intake to 2,500 calories a day.[55] Experiments on soldiers and students (some made by R. H. Chittenden, another member of Hoover's staff) had persuaded the Americans that reduced calorie intake for several months resulted in no appreciable diminution of muscular or mental activity. If they acquiesced, the European Allies feared that they would in all probability be forced to endure the lower calorie levels for longer than a few months with a consequent threat to the war effort. The Americans claimed that the Germans were 'trained down hard like athletes' and had not only suffered no ill effects from their diet but had managed to increase industrial production. Reports reaching Britain from Germany, however, suggested that since the beginning of 1917 food shortages had been having a marked impact on the health and stamina of the population.[56] Although Taylor was able to return home from the November talks with a signed promise from the British, French and Italian governments that compulsory restrictions would soon be in effect, Hoover's manoeuverings had not been totally successful. Britain for one resisted the pressure to introduce bread rationing, although the Ministry of Food did prepare the documents, and at the first conference of the Inter-Allied Scientific Food Commission, a meeting of medical and scientific officials held in Paris towards the end of March, the Europeans outvoted the Americans in favour of a British proposal to adopt a minimum of 3,300 purchased calories as the rationing standard.[57]

On 13 June Hoover requested presidential approval for a trip to Europe the following month. He had called a joint meeting of the Allied Food Controllers for four reasons: a cereal programme for 1918–19 had to be drawn up, the Europeans needed extra persuasion to substitute pork for beef in their food programmes, the organization of the inter-allied executives had to be tightened, and finally, 'the psychology of the American production and consumption would be improved if the entire food resources of the Allied nations were pooled and a definite and clear statement of the position published to the American people'.[58] It was the last of these that was the real basis for the trip, although it was the food resources of the European Allies alone that Hoover intended to see pooled. His prime aim was to change British food policies, which both he and Wilson believed detrimental to the Allied war effort. They considered Britain to be displaying an unwillingness to share supplies and make domestic sacrifices that was preventing the possibility of a big breakthrough on the western front. Britain's 'lion's share' policy of building up reserves of cereals and sugar and maintaining large herds of animals while its European neighbours struggled to scrape together the bare minimum to feed their populations, they said, had created such a bitterness among the others that it was affecting the performance of the entire alliance. The whole subject, Hoover told an aide, made one question the Allies' moral superiority over its foes. It was contrary to the principles of liberty and equality to conceive of one nation accumulating a surplus while another, making equal or preponderant sacrifices, was in want merely because the first controlled the shipping.[59]

Not unnaturally, the British government viewed the matter in an entirely different light. The reserves had been amassed only after the near exhaustion of supplies during the submarine attacks of 1917, and the smallness of Britain's agricultural sector made the country the most vulnerable of the Allies to another such campaign. The German offensive in the spring of 1918 strengthened British fears for the security of the supply lines. It was thought at one point that the

German army might reach the French coast and impose a blockade on the Thames. For a while too the constant decline in shipping losses to enemy submarines slowed almost to a halt. Germany was building submarines faster than they could be destroyed, while until the second quarter of 1918 the Allies were still losing more tonnage than they replaced by new construction. When one considered too that over four hundred ships had to be withdrawn from Britain's merchant fleet to transport the American forces and their equipment to the front during this period, the wisdom of holding food reserves appeared unquestionable. Far from being willing to alter their policy, the War Cabinet decided in April to put even more effort into accumulating reserves in the event that a German victory made it temporarily impossible to ship in food.[60] To the British, reserves were not selfishness but sense. Besides serving the country's own interest, they had enabled assistance to be rendered to others. They had allowed British shipping to be temporarily transferred to the use of Italy, France, Belgium and Russia, none of whom had been able to fend for themselves, and had permitted supplies to be sent to the others during a number of emergencies. As far as the military situation was concerned, the British countered that far from hindering matters the reserves helped by giving the Allies the freedom to divert commercial tonnage to meet a sudden military necessity.[61]

Although some might consider Hoover's remarks about the moral aspects of Britain's reserves rather hypocritical in view of the abundant diet enjoyed by Americans compared to the meagre rations of the British in 1918, it was true that the sharing of supplies and resources had become an issue among the Europeans. The subject had first come up in October 1917 when the French government had turned to Britain for help in obtaining imports. The recent harvest in France had produced less than half of the wheat grown in 1914 and smaller crops of other cereals. Several large cities, including Paris, had been reduced to one day's supply of breadstuffs and there had been scattered outbreaks of disorder. The French Premier, Paul Painlevé, urged the adoption of a joint Anglo-French programme of minimum food needs and asked Britain to set aside priority tonnage, to be partly under French control, to serve the scheme.[62] The War Cabinet was ready to tide France over the emergency but hesitated to sign a long-term agreement to pool supplies. They were by no means inclined to hand over ships; France still had not imposed full requisitioning on its own tonnage. They also objected to British reserves, accumulated in conjunction with rigidly enforced conservation legislation, being drawn on regularly by a country that was extremely lax about food control. One foreign resident of France during the war later declared that the only trouble Parisians had had with the food supply arose from the fact that nobody could be persuaded to obey the spirit of any of the elaborate regulations drawn up for the general benefit of the community.[63] Out of fear that the people would revolt, the French authorities made no attempt to stop the rural population hoarding their produce and did not enforce restrictions placed on consumption in the towns. Colonel House, assessing the position for Wilson, noted that 'dinners are given in Paris that would be a scandal in America, not to mention England', and remarked on the general atmosphere of normality in the areas he visited.[64] A British official sent to evaluate the French situation in November reported: 'If we are to "pool" food, *we* should *receive* large supplies from south and southwestern France.' He found conditions there much better than in the northern industrial areas of France or in Britain as a whole.[65] Having received assurances that France would soon be subjected to the same food controls as Britain, the War Cabinet nevertheless agreed at the end of October to divert as much tonnage as possible to French and Italian use during the next two months, although the ships were to remain nominally under British control. A committee chaired by Milner was given the job of reviewing Britain's import programme to see what could be cut to permit this assistance.[66]

Helpful as this was, Britain's allies preferred a more permanent commitment. The possibility of increasing imports to the continental countries by pooling shipping and thereby making available to others transport hitherto used exclusively by Britain was discussed in November 1917 by the recently formed Inter-Allied Transport Council. Equality of access to supplies and resources was also the objective of a proposed modification of the new inter-allied trading practices in the spring of 1918. Carrying the concept of co-ordination of acquisitions a step further, it was suggested that the food supply systems of the participating nations be treated as a unit and imports administered by a series of multinational programme committees. Existing trading units would be incorporated into the scheme: the Wheat Commission forming a separate programme committee, for example. The drawback as far as Britain was concerned was that the committees would consist of equal numbers of representatives from the Allied nations and would be headed by independent chairmen.

This meant that the country's influence in bodies like the Wheat Commission, which Britain to all practical purposes ran, would be reduced. A committee led by Austen Chamberlain, who was deputed by the War Cabinet to assess the implications of the proposals, nevertheless recommended in May that Britain agree to the combination of the inter-allied food executives into one Allied Food Committee, methodical planning of needs based on uniform rations, a single Allied import programme and the use of tonnage in common.[67] The idea of pooling the country's food supply with those of France and Italy was strongly opposed by both the Treasury, which objected to interference by outsiders in supplies drawn from within the Empire and charged that it would 'play into the hands of France', and the Ministry of Food, which believed Britain's interests would be seriously damaged and feared a diminution of its own authority. But the War Cabinet deemed it essential to make concessions to the Allies. 'I am sure we are in for trouble if we cannot devise some system more satisfactory to them than that which now prevails', Chamberlain wrote to Wintour in defence of the government's decision.[68]

Although the Americans were notified of this in mid-June,[69] the Ministry of Food remained convinced that the government had no real intention of going through with the plan. Nothing was done to implement the proposals before the conference of Allied Food Controllers opened in London on 23 July. This only served to discredit Britain further in the eyes of the American Food Administrator. Hoover, angered by the Ministry of Food's inactivity, arrived armed with an alternative scheme for a unit run solely by the United States, which would have rationed out transatlantic supplies to the European Allies without the latter having any say whatever. Despite the support voiced by all present at the conference for the immediate organization of a new inter-allied food body, the impression had already been given that Britain would not have agreed to share its resources with its friends in arms if it had not been forced to do so by the Americans.[70]

The delegates decided that in future the Food Controllers of Britain, France, Italy and the United States would constitute the Inter-Allied Food Council, which would meet at least once every three months to determine a joint food programme and decide general questions of policy. The day to day work would be handled by the Inter-Allied Food Council Committee of Representatives, made up of equal numbers of members from each country led by a neutral chairman. This body would consolidate the national programmes and act as the sole channel of communication between the various import executives, the Inter-Allied Maritime Council (which would allocate all shipping) and the Inter-Allied Finance Council. The committee was instructed to ensure that 'the morale of all Allies is kept up by the timely and equal distribution of Foods'.[71]

The creation of the Committee of Representatives was a blow for the Ministry of Food. Not only was its role in international trading further curtailed but it was also prevented from having direct contact with Britain's own Ministry of Shipping. In a sudden food emergency, such as had happened in the spring of 1917, the Food Controller would have to go a roundabout route via the Committee of Representatives to bring any pressure to bear on the shipping authorities to step up imports.[72] Nonetheless, the new arrangements offered the British a way to play a major role still in the running of affairs in the future, if the Ministry of Food was prepared to be flexible. The chairman of the Committee of Representatives was to be Sir John Beale, the current chairman of the Wheat Executive. Beale was a popular choice: he was well-liked within the government, was greatly respected by the Americans for his excellent work on the Executive, and was assessed as having 'the great gift of doing well by the United Kingdom while all the time he keeps France and Italy contented.[73] Clynes, who had succeeded Rhondda on the latter's death in July, proposed to make Beale chairman of a new Purchasing and Imports Board at the Ministry of Food with direct access to the Food Controller. The Board would supervise all activities of the ministry touching on shipping and international relations and would establish an import programme for Britain.[74] Through the judicious appointment of other members of the ministry to the Committee the views of Britain's food authorities could be effectively presented and, given the wider experience of the British in international trading, the British representatives might well be able to assume control of the new organization.

These objectives could not be achieved, however, unless a major change in personnel occurred at the ministry. Beale refused to take on the post at the Ministry of Food as long as Wintour remained as Permanent Secretary. A transfer for the latter was soon arranged. Beale's ultimatum had only finalized what had already been decided. Wilson and Hoover blamed Wintour for everything they considered obstructive and uncooperative about British food policy. According to Hoover's aide at the July conference, Lewis Strauss, Clynes regarded Wintour as 'the Oracle of the food control game' and the latter lived up to that reputation by opposing any opinion voiced by anyone else. 'If Alonzo Taylor were to propose that the export of pigs' noses be discontinued,' Strauss charged, 'he would meet immediate opposition from Clynes, who would present sixteen reasons drawn up by Wintour to show that the entire morale of the United Kingdom is dependent upon a steady flow of that prime foodstuff – pigs' noses.'[75] Hoover asked Lloyd George to dismiss Wintour at the end of July. The Prime Minister waited only for a suitable opportunity before doing so in September. Both he and Bonar Law had become highly dissatisfied with the Permanent Secretary's handling of affairs. Quite apart from the damage Wintour was doing to Anglo-American relations, they did not consider him capable enough for the sway he exerted over the Food Controller and the Ministry of Food. Wintour finally overreached himself. When Beale resigned from the Wheat Executive to take the chair of the Committee of Representatives, Wintour pressed Clynes to disband the Wheat Commission and transfer its duties to a department of the ministry headed by Wintour himself. His motive was partly personal jealousy of Beale, who had been promoted to a position of authority he thought unjustified, but he also hoped to counteract the ever-growing American influence over the inter-allied system. He believed the pooling agreement gave the United States an even greater say than before in British affairs and aimed to negate this in at least one important area by bringing cereals under his personal supervision. To bring an international unit under the aegis of a national food authority, however, was not only an impossibility now but an affront to the principles of co-operation that formed the basis for the latest inter-allied agreements. With a great joint offensive getting under way in France, the last thing the government wanted was any further suggestion that Allied harmony and morale were being undermined by Britain. Wintour was replaced as Permanent Secretary by Beale himself.[76]

Hoover's determination to get rid of Wintour was reinforced during the July conference by the adamant opposition of the Ministry of Food to one of the Food Administrator's most cherished proposals. This was an import quota system intended to whittle away Britain's reserves and force a reduction in the size of its herds. It rested on the premiss that people should be fed first, animals second – a principle that the Allies unanimously endorsed. There was similarly no disagreement about a priority import schedule that ranked in order of importance: 1) bread grains for civilians and military personnel, 2) army supplies (including fodder), 3) meat and fats for civilians, 4) fodder for dairy cattle, and 5) other cereals for civilians (not intended for bread). The problem arose from Hoover's suggestions for the import of non-priority foods. He proposed the allocation of shipping strictly by the five-class priority schedule. If no tonnage remained after loading these commodities, then other imports had to be dispensed with. This would not greatly affect France and Italy; they produced most of their own sugar plus maize for livestock. Britain, on the other hand, depended heavily on imports of both sugar and fodder and would most certainly have to face frequent interruptions of supply. Clynes, at Wintour's prompting, protested vehemently. Since – despite their alleged unhappiness with British policies – France and Italy refused to sanction such drastic measures, Hoover reluctantly agreed to a compromise. Priority tonnage was limited to 18.5 million tons of the 23.4 million tons of shipping currently available, leaving the remainder at the disposal of the individual nations to ship whatever they believed they needed most.[77] After expressing his disappointment freely to Lloyd George and engaging in an embarrassing argument with the Shipping Control Committee over grain imports, Hoover left England on 16 August in a rather disgruntled frame of mind.[78]

Although the Food Administrator had not succeded in placing formal restrictions on Britain's imports, his aims soon showed every likelihood of being achieved by other means. To prepare for a major military strike in September, the Allied leaders gave shipping priority to munitions for the next few months. Britain was asked to provide an extra 200,000 tons of shipping in September and October to transport American army personnel and supplies to Europe, with a probable 300,000 ton requisition thereafter. This meant that the food quotas drawn up at the Food Controllers' conference could not be met. Britain's share was reassessed at 10.5 million tons of imports in the coming year, the amount it would have got under Hoover's plan, instead of the 13.5 million tons allowed by the compromise plan and the 12.4 million tons actually shipped in 1917–18. At a meeting of the War Cabinet on 6 September Clynes begged that food imports not be reduced below the level of the previous year, but to no avail. The United States government had pledged to provide all its own transport by February 1919. Until then, the War Cabinet decided, Britain must live on its stocks. They gambled on an early end to the war and ordered that the country be rationed at the 13.5 million ton quota level even though this would mean the erosion of reserves.[79]

The effect of this decision was seen almost at once. Less than two weeks later grain shipments were falling so fast that there was talk in government circles of bread cards by the following spring and of an immediate cutback in imports of animal feed.[80] Even if transport had been available, fodder could not have been got. Despite an appeal from American representatives in Europe, Hoover refused both Britain and France supplies of cattle cake for milch cows in October. Citing the failure of the cotton crop in the United States, the Food Administrator told the Europeans that America was now importing oilcake instead of exporting it. The cessation of shipments was particularly effective. In contrast to 1917–18, British farmers started the cereal year 1918–19 with few or no stocks of feed on hand. The possibility of their being able to keep their animals back off the market, as they had done the previous winter, was therefore virtually eliminated. On 14 October the Ministry of Food announced that feed would be rationed from 17 November. A week later the size of herds was reported to be falling.[81]

Although Hoover had wanted the number of beef cattle to be reduced, the competition for fodder affected sheep most. By the end of 1918, after extremely heavy slaughtering in the autumn, there were 800,000 fewer sheep than at the beginning of the year. Beef cattle decreased by only 180,000. Herds still totalled 7.75 million, slightly more than prewar, and half of the loss in 1918 could be attributed to the Ministry of Food's own earlier pricing error. Dairy herds were maintained, although the lack of feed was reflected in lower milk yields.[82]

The sudden halt to the hostilities only a few weeks later left Britain in a generally satisfactory position with regard to food. There had not been time for stock levels to fall far and the threat to the herds was lifted with the armistice (the ministry rescinded rationing of feed on 13 November).[83] But what if the war had continued? The experiences of the last few months would suggest that 1919 might have been a difficult year, with reserves falling swiftly under the impact of the new inter-allied arrangements and, perhaps, shortages, further displays of popular disatisfaction and even more stringent controls over distribution. The Ministry of Food could have certainly expected a repetition of Hoover's efforts to mould British policies to his liking, forcing the Food Controller and his staff to become more conciliatory in their attitudes and to initiate further extensions of inter-allied co-operation if they wished to prevent more gains by the Americans in the realm of international food policy.

Notes: Chapter 7

1 J. M. Cooper, 'The command of gold reversed: American loans to Britain, 1915–1917.', Pacific Historical Review, vol. 45, no. 2 (May 1976), pp. 211, 230.
2 Quoted in *The Intimate Papers of Colonel House*, arranged by C. Seymour (ed.), vol. 3 (Boston, 1926–8), p. 213.
3 Ibid., p. 296.
4 Quoted in H. M. Hyde, *Lord Reading: The Life of Rufus Isaacs, First Marquess of Reading* (New York, 1967), p. 30.
5 C. Seymour (ed.), *Intimate Papers*, p. 213; F. H. Coller, *A State Trading Adventure* (London, 1925), pp. 190–1; Bonar Law to Prime Minister, 19 August 1918, F/30/2/40, Lloyd George Papers, House of Lords Record Office, London.
6 Lord E. Percy, Memorandum, 4 October 1916, FO 371/2795, Foreign Office Papers, Public Record Office. Quoted by Cooper, 'The command of gold reversed', pp. 219–20; Burk, 'The Treasury', in Burk (ed.), *War and the State: The Transformation of British Government 1914–1919* (London, 1982), p. 90.
7 R. McKenna, Our financial position in America, 24 October 1916, CAB 24/2/87 and CAB 37/157/40. Based on J. M. K., The financial dependence of the United Kingdom on the United States of America, 10 October 1916 in J. M. Keynes, *The Collected Writings of John Maynard Keynes*, E. Johnson (ed.), vol. 16 (Cambridge, 1971–1980), pp. 197–201.
8 Keynes, ibid.
9 Cooper, 'The command of gold reversed', pp. 222–5.
10 Remark made during discussions with Admiralty staff, 15 February 1917, quoted by editor, Keynes, *Collected Writings*, p. 210.
11 Colonel W. G. Lyddon, *British War Missions to the United States 1914–1918* (London, 1938), p. 126.
12 J. A. Baker to A. J. Balfour, 2 April 1917, FO 800/212.
13 W. B. Fowler, *British–American Relations 1917–1918: The Role of Sir William Wiseman* (Princeton, NJ, 1969), p. 25.
14 W. G. McAdoo, *Crowded Years: The Reminiscences of William G. McAdoo* (Boston, 1931), p. 394.
15 A. Bonar Law, Note for Mr McAdoo, 20 July 1917, T 172/434. Treasury Papers, Public Record Office. Also in Keynes, *Collected Writings*, pp. 245–252 (Keynes drafted the note); Editor's note, Keynes, ibid., p. 243; Undated Treasury memorandum, FO 800/208.
16 J. M. K., Minute to Sir R. Chalmers, 30 May 1917, T 172/427; Balfour to House, 28 June 1917, FO 800/209.
17 Editor's note, Keynes, *Collected Writings*, p. 239.
18 Lord Northcliffe, Report, 12 August 1917, *The Times* Archives, London.
19 Sir C. Spring-Rice to Foreign Office 3 August 1917, FO 800/242.
20 War Cabinet, Minutes, 23 July 1917, CAB 23/3/127.
21 H. Hoover to Sir W. Goode, 9 June 1917, Box 134, United States Food Administration (USFA) Papers, Hoover Institution, Stanford, California; Ministry of Food, *Weekly Reports*, 6 June 1917 and 13 June 1917.
22 Northcliffe to J. T. Davis, 20 June 1917, *The Times* Archives.
23 Lord Curzon to War Cabinet, Inter-Ally Council, 18 September 1917, PRO 30/68/9, Anderson Papers, Public Record Office, London; R. S. Baker (ed.),

Woodrow Wilson, Life and Letters, vol. 7 (University Microfilms edition) (New York, 1927–1939), p. 64.

24 Curzon, Purchases by the European and [sic] Allies in the USA, 30 June 1917, MAF 60/68; Keynes to Sir H. Lever, 21 July 1917, T 172/443. In Keynes, *Collected Writings*, pp. 252–3; War Cabinet, Minutes, 23 July 1917, CAB 23/3/127.

25 War Cabinet, Minutes, 23 July 1917, CAB 23/3/127; Spring-Rice to Foreign Office, 3 August 1917, MAF 60/68; Hoover to Surveyor General of Supply, War Office, 24 August 1917 (forwarded to Rhondda), MAF 60/59; Sir C. B. Gordon to C. J. Phillips, 25 August 1917, MAF 60/68; Baker, *Woodrow Wilson*, vol. 7, p. 247.

26 Keynes to his mother, 15 December 1917, Keynes, *Collected Writings*, p. 265.

27 Keynes to B. Blackett, 30 January 1918, Keynes, ibid., p. 269.

28 Mr Royden to Rhondda, 16 August 1917, MAF 60/68; S. Litman, *Prices and Price Control in Great Britain and the United States During the World War* (New York, 1920), pp. 188, 190, 199; T. H. Hall, 'Cheap bread from dear wheat: Herbert Hoover, the Wilson administration, and the management of wheat prices, 1916–1920', PhD thesis, University of California at Davis, 1970, p. 3.

29 Wheat Commission, Note of interview with Mr Hoover, 11 April, 1917, PRO 30/68/5 Anderson Papers; Lord R. Cecil to War Cabinet, 16 April 1917, forwarding H. Hoover, The food question, 14 April 1917, CAB 24/10; War Cabinet, Minutes, 18 April 1917, CAB 23/2/122. Appendix 2: Statement by Lord Devonport, CAB 23/2/124.

30 H. C. Hoover, *The Memoirs of Herbert Hoover*, vol. 1, *Years of Adventure 1874–1920* (New York, 1951–2), p. 241.

31 Coller, *State Trading*, p. 97; Burk, 'British war missions to the United States 1914–1918', Ph.D. thesis, Oxford University, 1976, p. 131.

32 W. C. Mullendore, *History of the United States Food Administration 1917–1919* (Stanford, CA, 1941), p. 169; Hoover to Rhondda, 31 August 1917. United States, Department of State, *Papers Relating to the Foreign Relations of the United States*, vol. 2, Part 2 (1917), p. 655.

33 F. M. Surface and R. L. Brand, *American Food in the World War and Reconstruction Period* (Stanford, CA, 1931), p. 20.

34 H. T. Robson to A. G. Anderson, 9 June 1917, PRO 30/68/11, Anderson Papers; A. Chamberlain to Prime Minister, 28 May 1918, AC 15/1/15, Chamberlain Papers, Spring-Rice to Foreign Office, 26 July 1917, MAF 60/68; Inter-Allied Meat and Fats Executive, Minutes, November 1917, Box 14, Inter-Allied Food Council Papers, Hoover Institution, Stanford, California.

35 Sir W. H. Beveridge, *British Food Control* (London, 1928), p. 117.

36 R. H. Brade to Rhondda, 25 August 1917, MAF 60/59.

37 Rhondda to Prime Minister, 10 October 1917, F/43/5/40, Lloyd George Papers; Report by Lord Milner and Mr Barnes, Transfer of Board of Trade organisation for purchase of meat and cheese, 13 December 1917, MAF 60/59; J. R. Brooke (Chairman, Inter-Allied Meat and Fats Executive) to Secretary, Board of Trade, 31 December 1917, BT 13/80/6 Board of Trade, Public Record Office, London; E. F. Wise, Note to Mr Tallboy, 15 January 1918, MAF 60/66.

38 W. W. Astor, Memorandum, 22 August 1918, GD 40/17/933, Lothian Papers, Scottish Record Office, Edinburgh.

39 Hall, 'Cheap bread from dear wheat', p. 194; Hoover, *Memoirs*, vol. 1, p. 245.

40 Hoover to Wilson, 10 July 1917. F. W. O'Brien (ed.), *The Hoover-Wilson Wartime Correspondence* (Ames, Iowa, 1974), p. 45; Conference of Allied Food Controllers, Minutes, July and August 1918, Food Files, Box 28, Beveridge Papers.

41 Coller, *State Trading*, pp. 344–5; Ministry of Food, *Monthly Office Report* (December, 1918), Table F: Percentage increase in retail food prices.

42 Ministry of Food, *Weekly Reports*, 28 November 1917; Ministry of Food, *Monthly Office Report* (London, December 1918), Table D: Stocks of the principle foods in the United Kingdom.

43 J. P. Cotton, Memorandum of conversation with Mr Rewcastle, Secretary, Royal Sugar Commission, 8 March 1918. Hoover to Sir C. Bathurst, 13 August 1918. Sugar Purchasing Body in the USA, n.d. All in Box 5, Inter-Allied Food Council Papers.

44 V. E. Kellogg, *Herbert Hoover, The Man and his Work* (New York, 1920), p. 240; N. Hill (Chairman, Port and Transit Executive Committee), to Hankey, 10 May 1918, MAF 60/256; Consumers' Council, Minutes, 24 July 1918, 42249, Ashley Papers; Lard, Summary, 1937, MAF 60/446; Professor E. K. Gonner, The meat organisation, 1937, p. 30, MAF 60/115.

45 Memorandum by the Royal Commission on Wheat Supplies for consideration by the Food Controller, no. 22, 11 August 1917, Food Files, Box 10, Beveridge Papers.

46 J. F. Beale to U. F. Wintour, September 1917, Food Files, Box 10, Beveridge Papers; Ministry of Food, *Monthly Office Report*, Table D: Stocks; War Cabinet, Minutes, 12 December 1917, CAB 23/4/245.

47 Memorandum on wheat shipments from the United States, September 1917, Food Files, Box 10, Beveridge Papers.

48 A. E. Taylor, Report of a conference on the Allied cereal situation, 12 November 1917, Taylor Papers, Hoover Institution, Stanford, California; A. E. Taylor, Report of a conference on the Allied cereal situation, 15 November 1917, Box 27, Hoover Papers, Hoover Institution.

49 Hall, 'Cheap bread from dear wheat', pp. 109–115.

50 Hoover to Sheldon, 15 January 1918, Box 133, USFA Papers.

51 Rhondda to Hoover, 17 January 1918, Box 131; USFA Papers *Woodrow Wilson*, p. 527.

52 Kellogg, *Herbert Hoover*, pp. 213, 215; Mullendore, *History of the USFA*, pp. 103–7.

53 Hoover to Reading, 1 March 1918, Box 131, USFA Papers.

54 Rhondda to Hoover, 1 March 1918 and 15 March 1918, Box 131, USFA Paper.

55 Notes taken at conference between Dr Taylor, Dr Chittenden and Dr Lusk, July 1917, Box 4, Inter-Allied Food Council Papers.

56 War Trade Intelligence Department, Daily notes and daily review of the foreign press, no. 771, Box 528, Royal Society Papers, Royal Society, London; Sir J. Crichton-Brown, 'Tuberculosis and the war', *Journal of State Medicine*, vol. , no. 5 (May 1917), pp. 144–6.

57 *Texte des resolutions adoptées par la Commission Scientifique Interalliée du Ravitaillement*, March 1918, Lusk Papers, Hoover Institution, Stanford, California.

58 Hoover to Wilson, 13 June 1918. O'Brien (ed.), *Hoover–Wilson Wartime Correspondence*, pp. 203–5.

59 Astor to Prime Minister, 14 August 1918 and 27 August 1918, F/2/7/1 and 2a, Lloyd George Papers; Lewis Strauss, Diary of visit to Europe, 8 July to 23 August 1918, p. 14, entry for 29 July 1918, Herbert Hoover Presidential Library, West Branch, Iowa.

60 Meeting with Ministry of Shipping, 17 April 1918, MAF 60/61; J. R. Clynes, *Memoirs*, vol. 1 (London, 1937), pp. 254–5.

61 Beale to Hoover, 13 August 1918, Box 132; USFA Papers; Inter-Allied Food Council Committee of Representatives, Minutes, 9 August 1918, Box 12, Inter-Allied Food Council Papers.

62 P. Pinot and M. Augé-Laribé, *Agriculture and Food Supply in France During the War* (New Haven, CT, 1927), p. 33; F. Bouillon to Lloyd George, 13 October 1917, CAB 21/123; War Cabinet, Minutes, 16 October 1917, CAB 23/4/100.

63 H. P. Adam, *Paris Sees It Through: A Diary 1914–1919*, quoted by J. Williams, *The Other Battleground: The Home Fronts – Britain, France and Germany 1914–18* (Chicago, IL, 1972), p. 140.

64 House to Wilson, 14 December 1917, United States, Department of State, *Papers Relating to the Foreign Relations of the United States*, no. 9037, vol. 2, part 2 (1917), p. 357.

65 War Cabinet, Minutes, 25 October 1917, CAB 23/4/122; Memorandum by W. A. Gill, Director of Information, recently returned from France, forwarded to the Cabinet by Sir Edward Carson, 29 November 1917, CAB 24/34.

66 J. A. Salter, *Allied Shipping Control* (London, 1921), pp. 148–9; War Cabinet, Minutes, 30 October 1917 and 31 October 1917, CAB 23/4/134 and CAB 23/4/136.

67 A. Chamberlain to War Cabinet, 3 May 1918, AC 34/1/6, Chamberlain Papers, University of Birmingham, Chamberlain to War Cabinet, 15 May 1918, AC 34/1/8, Chamberlain Papers; Extract of Minutes of War Cabinet, 23 May 1918, MAF 60/58; Laughlin to Secretary of State, 12 June 1918, United States, Department of State, *Foreign Relations Papers*, no. 9388, vol. 1, 1918, p. 587.

68 Keynes to Chamberlain, 19 April 1918, MAF 60/70; Wintour to Chamberlain, 2 May 1918, MAF 60/61; Chamberlain to Wintour, 8 May 1918, MAF 60/58; Astor, Memorandum, 22 August 1918, GD 40/17/933, Lothian Papers.

69 Foreign Office to Lord Reading, 14 June 1918, CAB 21/123.

70 Astor, Memorandum, 22 August 1918, GD 40/17/1933, Lothian Papers.

71 Ibid.

72 Ibid.

73 Astor to Clynes, 21 August 1918, GD 40/17/932, Lothian Papers.

74 Beveridge to Clynes, 13 September 1918, enclosing W. H. B., Ministry of Food imports organisation, 13 September 1918, IIa/64, Beveridge Papers.

75 Strauss, Diary, p. 15, entry for 30 July 1918.

76 Beveridge, Notes of Food Controllers' conference, 16–25 August 1918, Main Series, item 4, file 26, Beveridge Papers; Bonar Law to Prime Minister, 19 and 22 August 1918. Prime Minister to Bonar Law, 20 August 1918, F/30/2/40, 41 and 42, Lloyd George Papers.

77 Beveridge, *British Food Control*, pp. 250–1; Beveridge, Notes for Inter-Allied Food Council Committee of Representatives, Main Series, item 4, file 26, Beveridge Papers.

78 Strauss, Diary, pp. 34–5. Entry for 14 August 1918; Astor to Prime Minister, 14 August 1918 and 27 August 1918, F/2/7/1 and 2a, Lloyd George Papers.

79 Salter, *Allied Shipping Control*, pp. 206–7; Beveridge, *British Food Control*, p. 252; War Cabinet, Minutes, 6 September 1918, CAB 23/7/101.

80 J. P. Cotton to Hoover, 19 September 1918, Box 132, USFA Papers.

81 Cotton to Hoover, 25 October 1918, Box 131, USFA Papers; Beale to Dr Durand, 9 October 1918, enclosed copy of cable Sir W. Goode to Ministry of Food, 9 October 1918, Box 132, USFA Papers.

82 T. H. Middleton, *Production in War* (London, 1923), pp. 316–18.

83 Astor, Memorandum, 22 August 1918, GD 40/17/933, Lothian Papers; Astor, Memorandum, n.d. [August 1918], GD 40/17/938, Lothian Papers.

8

The Food Production Campaigns of 1917 and 1918

From the time the subject of food supply in wartime was first broached, the intensification of agriculture had seemed to many a logical solution to potential food problems. Dispute had ranged not so much over whether this *could* be done, to the point of self-sufficiency if necessary, but whether it *should* be done, keeping in mind the degree of state control that it would entail. Lord Milner was still firmly convinced in December 1916, it may be recalled, that development of the agricultural sector would be a major key to victory. Had he, however, been given his wish and been offered the post of President of the Board of Agriculture rather than that of Food Controller, which he dismissed as unworthy of his talents, he might rapidly have become disillusioned with his government career. Practical achievements in 1917 and 1918 proved earlier expectations unrealistic.

The subordinate position of the Board of Agriculture *vis-à-vis* the new Ministry of Food suggests that the Prime Minister for one had no faith that the respective contributions of domestic production and of importation to Britain's food supply would be reversed in the near future. The Food Controller was given general responsibility for all aspects of supply, including domestic production – 'much the most difficult of his tasks', according to one member of the ministry.[1] To a considerable degree the spheres of the Board of Agriculture and Ministry of Food remained separate. Farming methods were no concern of the Food Controller. His hand was felt as a purveyor of imported fodder and a setter of maximum prices for produce. The consequences of such powers for farming have been mentioned in previous chapters. For the first six months of the partnership there were few disputes between the two food authorities, but the consumerism of the Rhondda era, which led to farmers being included by extremists – even on occasion by the Food Controller himself – among the ranks of 'profiteer producers', gave rise to some hostility.[2]

Defending the farming community against such slurs was an able administrator but poor pugilist, R. E. Prothero (later Lord Ernle), who took over the Board of Agriculture in December. Although a relative newcomer to Parliament (he had held a seat for Oxford University only since 1914), Prothero had long figured as an informed spokesman on farming matters. He was an old friend of Milner's: the two had been at Balliol together and Milner had frequently consulted Prothero on agricultural questions over the years. Prothero served on both the Milner Committee of 1915 and the current Selborne Reconstruction Committee and belonged to Milner's British Empire Producers' Organisation. His association with these bodies allowed the new President to bring to his post well-defined plans for the future. At the Board of Agriculture there was none of the uncertainty about policy that marred the initial progress of the Ministry of Food. From the start, no one had any doubts as to what the Board's plans would be. Prothero's slogan was 'Back to the Seventies and Better!'; his aim was to turn the agricultural clock back to the period before the long decline set in in the last quarter of the nineteenth century.

Although it is an exaggeration to say, as one recent study has done, that the war 'exposed forty years of erroneous farming policy in an instant', and converted men 'overnight ... into protectionists and interventionists', opposition to the idea of state control and agriculture had been rapidly dissolving in the months before Prothero took office.[3] The harvest had been extremely disappointing in 1916. The previous year's bumper crops of cereals had not been repeated and production had fallen below the prewar average. Despite continuing high prices, 12 per cent fewer acres were planted with wheat in 1916 than in 1915. The area in potatoes was normal, but the crop was one of the worst for years, one third smaller than the year before. As a whole, food output was down 12 per cent compared to 1915 or 8 per cent compared to prewar.[4] Cereals and potatoes were staple foods. Given the fact that the nation was simultaneously facing the threat of another enemy submarine campaign and that shipping and finance for imports were both in short supply, it was generally conceded as imperative that firm action be taken to step up domestic agricultural production. Runciman surely spoke for many former opponents of intervention when he admitted in the Commons that the doctrine of *laissez-faire* could no longer be applied to this sector of the economy.[5]

What people could not agree on was the duration of the state's commitment to agriculture. Was it as with other controlled industries to be temporary, lasting only as long as the war did? Or should the wartime measures be the start of a permanent change of policy leading to a thorough transformation of farming methods? Just as traditionalists like Runciman had come to accept earlier arguments for temporary intervention, so those who had long advocated state action had moved on to a more extreme position. The prime vehicle for the latter's viewpoint was the first report of the Selborne Reconstruction Committee, drafted in December 1916. The Committee believed that it was perfectly feasible to so reorganize British agriculture that the nation would become self-sufficient in food and hence would never again be dependent on outside sources in a time of emergency. As always, the argument rested on the restoration of arable farming. If scientifically ordered, it was said, with improved patterns of rotation and the correct balance struck between arable and livestock on each farm, this would bring about not a decline in animal husbandry but a revolution in farming in general, allowing production of meat and dairy products to increase along with that of cereals. State guaranteed minimum prices for wheat and oats would provide farmers with the long-term financial security to alter land usage while the power to dispossess recalcitrant farmers would allow the Board of Agriculture to get the work done. The morale of the agricultural labour force was to be lifted by new district wages boards, who would fix minimum wages for a standard working week.[6] Although ostensibly a blueprint for the future, the atmosphere in which the report was prepared ensured that it was also taken as advice for the present. The outcome was the controversial Corn Production Act, passed into law on 21 August 1917 and described by Milner as 'one of the central pillars of Food Production policy'.[7]

The provisions of the Corn Production Act were similar to those recommended by the Selborne Reconstruction Committee: guaranteed prices for wheat and oats for six years, a minimum wage of 25/- for agricultural workers and the establishment of an Agricultural Wages Board, an injunction to prevent landlords raising rents in response to changed farming circumstances arising from the Act, and special authority for the Board of Agriculture to enforce cultivation. Minimum prices were set as follows: for wheat – 60/- per quarter in 1917, 55/- in 1918 and 1919, 45/- in 1920, 1921 and 1922; for oats – 38/6 per quarter in 1917, 32/- in 1918 and 1919, 24/- in 1920, 1921 and 1922. Although there were complaints from non-wheat growers in the

west and north that the government was showing regional favour-
itism, Lloyd George's announcement of the Bill in February was for
the most part well received by farmers. Many liked the idea of price
supports and welcomed an official show of appreciation of their
contributions to the war effort. Writing in favour of the state's
intervention later in the year, the *Mark Lane Express* observed that
'the Corn Production Act was a tardy recognition of the fact that
farmers were entitled to some security, and that they ought not to be
asked to undertake work of the highest national importance without
some guarantee against loss'.[8]

Although carried by a three to one vote, the Act was far from being a
popular piece of legislation. When introduced to Parliament on 5
April it met with immediate opposition, even from long-time supporters of the ploughing policy like Chaplin. There were several legitimate
reasons for unhappiness. The Selborne Reconstruction Committee
and earlier bodies had recommended guaranteed prices for grain
actually produced. To make things administratively easier, the Corn
Production Act took account of acres tilled: when the average market
price of grain fell below the guaranteed price, farmers were to receive
compensation calculated on assumed average yields of four quarters of
wheat or five quarters of oats per acre under those crops. With more
than 800,000 agricultural holdings over five acres in the United
Kingdom, all of whose sales records would have to be checked if
guaranteed prices applied to amounts marketed, the average yield/
acreage system seemed the only practical approach. However, this
meant that farmers whose land produced low yields would receive the
same bonus as those whose land was of above-average productivity.
Even worse, farmers who normally grew oats solely as fodder for their
own livestock would be eligible for the subsidy just like those producing for market. There were none of the conditions the Milner
Committee had proposed to ensure a good return for the taxpayers'
money. In sum, critics argued, the Corn Production Act would encourage the sowing of inferior land, carelessness about yields and
neglect of rotation crops.[9]

The potential cost of the subsidies was the major source of grievance in the Commons, especially among Liberal and Labour
members. Both groups objected to what they charged was the enrich-
ment of one sector of the community at the expense of the rest, and
they were not convinced by government assurances (correct as it
turned out) that in view of the prevailing high price for grain, the

guarantees would probably never come into effect. Runciman, stressing that the Bill departed from the rule that no controversial measures were to be introduced during the war, was concerned too that there would be no limit to the financial outlay. He feared that the subsidization of agriculture would have to be perpetuated indefinitely to prevent the land tilled from reverting to grass.[10] Although the independent Liberal leadership spoke out strongly against the Bill, however, they abstained from voting against it.

Resistance to the measure in the Lords focused on property rights. Part Four of the Corn Production Bill gave the Board of Agriculture the power not only to determine how the land should be used but also to interfere with leases and to replace tenants unwilling to comply with its orders. Many agreed with Lord Desborough that this was 'the most monstrous proposal . . . ever seen in any Bill that has ever been introduced into Parliament'.[11] It was feared that such freedom on the part of the Board would seriously alter the traditional relationship between landowner and tenant farmer and lead in due course to the nationalization of the land. The issue of compulsion also disturbed leading Conservatives in the lower house. One of the most alarming aspects of the matter was the absence of appeal to an independent adjudicator. If the Corn Production Act was indeed to be the cornerstone of future peacetime policy, serious ethical issues concerning a government's right to interfere with an individual's freedom of action in a non-emergency situation were at stake.

The Corn Production Act has so dominated discussion of agricultural developments in this period that it is often overlooked that, except in Ireland and then only partially, the food production campaigns of 1917 and 1918 were not actually carried out under its terms, but proceeded under amendments to the Defence of the Realm Act. Since one could hardly threaten large numbers of tenant farmers with eviction during an emergency, Part Four of the Act was postponed for a year and was not due to go into effect until August 1918. The President of the Board of Agriculture in fact already possessed adequate legal powers to carry out an extensive cultivation programme. Regulation 2L of DORA, introduced on 5 December 1916, gave the authorities access to unoccupied land. On 10 January 1917 Regulation 2M came into force. This conferred on the Boards of Agriculture in Britain the authority to inspect land, enforce cultivation orders and to take over the running of property if officials felt the occupier was unlikely or unable to comply. In Scotland these duties were carried out by government employees. In England and Wales the Board's powers were delegated to the local War Agricultural Committees, which Prothero made more efficient by the creation of Executive Committees of four to seven members. In Ireland, where there were far fewer tracts of permanent grassland to be transformed into arable, less stringent measures were necessary. Occupiers of land were allowed more leeway to decide their own farming programmes under a special Regulation 2P and the Compulsory Tilling Orders of 1917 and 1918, which set minimums. Regulation 2L and Part Four of the Corn Production Act gave the Irish Department of Agricultural and Technical Instruction the right to enter the land of defaulters and arrange for cultivation if necessary. Removing a major stumbling block to earlier efforts to induce farmers to plough grasslands, legal indemnity was extended to tenant farmers whose leases contained clauses forbidding an increase to arable. Landowners who wished to file suit against such infringement of leases could do so against a special Losses Commission. The agricultural authorities did not gain this unprecedented extension of their powers without protest. One opponent of the DORA amendments complained that 'the door is being opened wide to tyrannical action of the most serious kind', and Prothero later suggested that it was the Board's promise to repeal the amendments within a year of the Corn Production Act's passage that induced landowners to accept the latter measure. Despite DORA's unpopularity, however, only 251 of the 100,000 cultivation orders issued in 1917–18 were opposed to the point of litigation.[12]

To supervise the food production campaigns in England and Wales, Prothero formed a Food Production Department on 1 January 1917. Initially headed by T. H. Middleton, the senior civil servant at the Board, the Department was handed over on 14 February to an outside 'expert', Sir Arthur Lee, who was supposed to inject greater drive and efficiency into the project. Before Lee's arrival, a good deal of preparatory work had already been accomplished. Little could be done without a survey of current land usage. Carried out at remarkable speed by the War Agricultural Committees, this graded farms by quality, spotlighting those in need of improvement and identifying grasslands that could be ploughed. Based on this the first Cultivation of Land Order was issued on 18 January. Prothero had also established a staff of technical experts who were to offer advice of a scientific nature, and he had taken steps to provide the agricultural machinery, tools, fertilizer, seed and labour that farmers would need to fulfill their assignments.

One of the President's first actions had been to obtain funding from the Treasury for the purchase of equipment for lease to farmers who were under orders to plough their meadows. Just before he left office at the beginning of December 1916 Crawford had requested £50,000 to buy machinery from the United States, but only a £20,00 expenditure had been approved because of the exchange crisis. Prothero asked for and obtained a grant of £442,000, £350,000 of which was earmarked for American tractors.[13] The Food Production Department had high hopes that the mechanization of British agriculture would show quick returns and ordered large numbers of tractors from both British and American firms. Optimism quickly faded, however, for by the end of August 1917 only 929 of the 9,079 tractors ordered had been delivered. Private owners put a further 485 at the disposal of the department and 54 Caterpillar tractors built for military purposes were borrowed from the Russian government. This gave a total of about 1,500 machines available for hire that autumn. A major setback occurred in June when discussions with Ford for the assembly of American parts in Britain collapsed. The Ministry of Munitions had refused to provide factory space following a decision by the War Cabinet to double the output of planes.

The subsequent failure to plough as much grassland as was planned was later blamed partially on this lack of tractors, but in fact the technical quality of the machines made them the least efficient means of ploughing in Britain at that date. Practical as they were for the vast plains of America, tractors were frequently inoperable on the sloping fields and differing soil conditions of the United Kingdom. They could be used only for the lighter work, such as ploughing existing stubble or harvesting, and on the larger flat fields. A sudden check to its progress, caused perhaps by an attachment being caught by stones or roots, could overturn a tractor completely. The spikes in its solid iron rear wheels were also a drawback in Britain. Because of the damage tractors could do to a road's surface, they were not allowed on public thoroughfares, denying farmers road access to many fields. Suitable tool attachments, spare parts, clean water (for radiators) and petrol were not readily available in the countryside, while the great variety of models on the market bewildered potential customers and decreased chances of finding someone who knew how to repair a machine if it broke down. There were few farm workers who could both drive and service tractors. The Food Production Department tried to overcome this deficiency by opening training schools, and the War Office also set up courses for soldiers. Although more agriculturists came to appreciate the possibilities of mechanization during 1917 and 1918, most farmers were asking themselves – to quote the *Mark Lane Express* – 'Have tractors come to stay?'[14] Steam tackle and horse-drawn ploughs remained the farmers' best tools at this time. Steam engines stationed one on each side of a field would pull a plough hooked onto a connecting cable back and forth across the land. They were capable of breaking the most matted permanent grass and contributed heavily to the ploughing campaigns. The Food Production Department had a supply of these for hire as well, along with other farm equipment such as conventional plough teams, potato diggers and binders. Regrettably, many of these aids lay idle during 1917 because of lack of farm workers to use them. In October several thousand government-owned ploughs and horses were reported waiting for work.[15]

The need to find the extra labour for its food production campaign plunged the Board of Agriculture into protracted negotiations with the War Office. An agreement of October 1916 had protected general agricultural workers from the recruiters until 1 January 1917 and dairymen until 1 April. Early in January the War Office dealt the Food Production Department what Prothero deemed a 'staggering blow' by calling up 30,000 farm labourers in England and Wales. At Prothero's request, Lloyd George asked the military to 'go slow' on this drive. 'Unless we are able to increase the food supplies in this country,' the Prime Minister told Lord Derby, 'we shall be beaten by starvation.'[16] The War Office was co-operative; by the end of February fewer than 10,000 men had been drafted and the military authorities were providing substitutes. The Army formed Agricultural Companies of 15,000 men unsuited to overseas service, who could be released temporarily for farm work in the spring and autumn. Within a brief spell of time 11,500 of these men arrived on the farm. Unfortunately, few were skilled workers. Farmers complained that the men ran away from horses when there were problems, and one farmer reported finding his new help trying to harness a pony with tackle meant for a carthorse.[17] As a result of such incidents, the War Office was ordered by the War Cabinet on 12 March to furlough all skilled ploughmen in the Home Forces, a move that increased military assistance to a total of 40,000 men during the spring planting. Recruitment of skilled workers none the less continued in many rural areas, prompting an announcement by the War Cabinet on 24 May that the implementation of the Food Production Department's campaign for the coming agricultural year constituted 'a matter of the greatest national importance'. Call-ups declined thereafter while the number of men temporarily released from military duties grew. As of 14 June 1917 it was also established that no man employed on 1 June in full-time farm work could be recruited without the express permission of the War Agricultural Committees. In Lee's opinion, the sense of security this gave farmers contributed to their willingness to sign agreements in June and July to plough their permanent grasslands.[18]

Under the pressure of necessity, the farmers' prejudice against employing women on the land gradually diminished during 1917. The Board of Agriculture set up a Women's Branch in January 1917 staffed only by women to recruit women. Although this unit's best-known achievement was the 12,000-strong Women's Land Army, its greatest contribution was the recruitment of 230,000 village workers – a traditional source of extra seasonal labour. Since prisoners-of-war had to be guarded and were not allowed to work alongside the land-girls, their employment was initially problematic and they were used in large numbers only during the last few months of the war. When government-provided substitutes were not available, local War Agricultural Committees sometimes hired labour directly to undertake urgent projects on neglected lands chosen for improvement under the Board of Agriculture's cultivation orders. Recent estimates show manpower on farms in England and Wales during the last two years of the war to have been 95 per cent of normal levels in 1917 and 97 per cent in 1918, with replacement labour accounting for 6 per cent and 8 per cent respectively.[19]

A decline in the fertility of the land had been a major cause of poor yields in 1916. This was due partly to overcropping of grain in 1915 and partly to a shortage of fertilizers caused by the loss of potash imports from Germany and the diversion of other chemicals from agriculture to munitions. The Food Production Department, in co-operation with the Ministry of Munitions, made great efforts during the last two years of the war to remedy this problem. The price of sulphate of ammonia was lowered to a fixed £16 a ton throughout the country and the value of the chemical as a replacement for potash was assiduously publicized. Although the supplies channelled to agriculture could not satisfy the demand generated by these tactics, the tripling of agricultural usage of sulphate of ammonia between 1916 and 1918 contributed strongly to an improved harvest in 1918.[20]

To encourage farmers to use more fertilizer and to buy or hire extra machinery, horses and tools, the Board of Agriculture arranged early in 1918 for the commercial banks to extend special credit to the agricultural community. The resulting state-guaranteed, low interest loans (5 per cent for nine months) were not, however, taken up with much enthusiasm. As of 30 June 1918 only 750 applications for advances totalling £60,000 had been received, and those farmers seeking aid were not generally those whose land was in greatest need of improvement. The main point to the scheme, according to a contemporary, was that it allowed the authorities to order farmers to undertake projects that could hardly have been proposed if financial assistance had not been forthcoming.[21]

Middleton and Lee both left glowing descriptions of the food production campaigns of 1917 and 1918.[22] Both books suggest that a breakdown in the country's food supply, and by extension the war effort, was averted by a tremendous increase in the domestic output of food – one quarter higher in 1918 than prewar, according to Middleton.[23] As with so many of the other accounts of the period written by wartime functionaries, they provide a widely misleading picture.

Starting up as it did in the middle of the agricultural year, the Food Production Department proposed a rather modest programme for the 1917 harvest. Its goal was to do little more than confute Crawford's pessimistic forecast of continued agricultural decline. It was already too late in the year to do anything for wheat, which was an autumn-sown crop. The authorities therefore asked farmers to increase their acreage of spring-sown staples – oats, barley and potatoes. Compulsory ploughing orders led to only 250,000 acres of permanent grass being transformed into arable, but a large amount of temporary pasture was broken, especially in Ireland which contributed 638,000 of the 720,000 acres tilled. In terms of food produced, the results of the 1917 harvest were not impressive. In Britain, the 1,979,000 acres under wheat totalled only 4,000 more than in 1916 and because of poor weather and the shortage of fertilizer yields improved only slightly. Ireland increased both its acreage and production of wheat by 61 per cent, but owing to the small quantity grown there normally this did not add significantly to the overall food supply. The most notable improvements were seen in the crops of potatoes and oats, which together accounted for 88 per cent of the extra acres tilled between 1916 and 1917. The shortage of potatoes was transformed into a glut by a 50 per cent increase in production and despite a poor harvest in England fine crops in Scotland and Ireland gave a 15 per cent increase in the output of oats. These results surely do not constitute an achievement 'of major importance both in terms of yield per acre and amount of new land brought under the plough', as the editor of Lee's memoirs phrases it, especially since the larger arable crop were offset by a drop in the output of meat and dairy products, by 14 per cent and 11 per cent respectively. Total food production was 6 per cent higher in 1917 than in 1916, but it still remained below the prewar level.[24]

The programme for the 1918 harvest, drawn up in April 1917, was much more ambitious. Lee proposed that another 3 million acres of permanent grassland be broken up. If, because of geographic limitations and their contributions to the 1917 tilling programme, Scotland and Ireland could not increase their arable further, the entire 3 million acres would be sought in England and Wales. This meant, as Lee explained to the Agricultural Executive Committees on 15 May, that each county had to plough three quarters of the acreage put down to permanant grass since 1872. It was intended to use the extra arable for wheat, thus increasing the area under this crop by 150 per cent, from 2 million acres to 5 million. In an announcement of the new programme at the Guildhall on 27 April, Lloyd George said that this would make the country self-supporting.[25] In June, the Food Production Department revised its goals, blaming this necessity on delay by the War Cabinet in arranging for military furloughs for substitute agricultural labour. England and Wales were now to reduce permanent grassland by 2,050,000 acres and to raise 2,600,000 more acres of cereals than in 1916. These figures were closer to those suggested by leading agricultural experts, who had earlier advised that 2,200,000 acres would be the maximum addition to arable that could be expected.[26]

The Agricultural Executive Committees were asked to make a careful selection of the grassland to be ploughed and to try to obtain voluntary agreements with the farmers before issuing compulsory cultivation orders. In July the local authorities began to apportion among individual holdings the tillage requirement set for their county. This work was essentially complete by December. Because of the shortage of fertilizer, the Board of Agriculture emphasised that the grassland selected must be of superior quality. The local people generally evaded this order, however, and instead scheduled the least productive pastures to be ploughed. Even so, farmers responded slowly and heavy rains in early November did not help matters. On 19 November Prothero reported to the War Cabinet that only 600,000 of the proposed 2,600,000 acres had been tilled. By 12 December official observers noted little improvement and estimates of probable new acreage was put at 1,600,000, 1 million of which was likely to be sown with oats not wheat.[27] In fact, the tide had turned in mid-November. Farmers took advantage of a four-month bout of fine, dry weather to engage in extensive ploughing and sowing. The elation this progress caused among the personnel of the Food Production Department led to some rash and wildly over-optimistic statements the following spring. Lee told Lloyd George on 22 April 1918 that the original goal of 3 million acres of permanent grassland ploughed had been exceeded: officials now estimated that the total would be closer to 4 million acres and that the harvest would provide no less than a forty week supply of grain – a figure echoed by Middleton a few weeks later.[28] The Prime Minister passed on the good news to the War Cabinet and 'highly glowing telegrams' went speeding to the United States Food Administration. Hoover, kept up to date about European production figures by his own informants, sent a dampening reply: 'Recent announcement of the Director of Production that this year's harvest is 40 weeks supply is not only arrant nonsense,' he cabled, 'but will greatly weaken our ability to supply the great deficiencies in English production.[29]

The results had indeed been exaggerated. Final figures showed a total gain of 1,990,000 acres under crops in the United Kingdom as a whole in 1918 compared to 1917. Of this, 1,470,000 acres had been taken from permanent grassland and 520,000 from temporary pasture. When added to the figures for the year before (250,000 acres from permanent grassland and 720,000 acres from temporary pasture), the total addition to arable since 1916 was 2,960,000 acres. The authorities quoted this figure in support of their claim that they had met their goal, even though only half as much permanent grassland as planned had been broken in the course of two campaigns. More significantly, wheat acreage had increased by only 750,000 acres. Farmers in much of the country found the newly broken land unsuited for wheat: the soil was infested with pests and often had to be resown, sometimes twice. Moreover, the ploughing had once again begun too late in the year. As a result, farmers tended to sow wheat in the autumn on fields previously used for oats and used the newly-broken acres for this latter crop in the spring, increasing the area under oats by 1,529,000 acres. Some of the new arable was also used for potatoes.

Output of staples was nonetheless highly pleasing. The production of wheat in England and Wales was the highest since 1882 – 59 per cent greater than the average for 1904–1913. Scotland raised 54 per cent more and Ireland registered an impressive 390 per cent gain. The average increase for the United Kingdom as a whole was 65 per cent. Yields of oats and potatoes were the best on record. Because of the original smallness of the agricultural sector, however, the note-worthiness of these achievements shrinks dramatically when examined in the context of the overall food supply. Although a great improvement over the normal 10 weeks supply, home-grown grain still only satisfied 16 weeks of the year's needs. The oats primarily went for animal feed, in short supply in 1918 because of the decline in imports of cereals and fodder. Allowing for lower yields by dairy cattle caused by the shortage of feed, a continued decline in the amount of meat coming onto the market and the loss of root crops because of arable land having been turned over to cereals, the total amount of food produced in the United Kingdom in 1918 was not much greater than prewar. One independent study put the percentage of home-grown food to total supply in 1918 at 42 per cent, versus the prewar figure of 34 per cent. A more recent analysis, which is probably closer, found only a 1 per cent gain over prewar.[30] Although the larger quantities of wheat and potatoes grown in 1918 represented more staple foods for the mass of the population and were a welcome relief in view of the diversion of tonnage to military use in the autumn months, the gain was by no means large enough for the British to accept with equanimity the prospect of reduced import quotas in the year ahead. Not surprisingly, given the cost of the food production campaign to the nation – £9 million – and earlier promises of self-sufficiency, some observers were disappointed by the results.[31]

Equally dismaying was the fact that the achievements of 1918 could probably not be repeated in 1919. The raising of successive crops of grain in the same fields was exhausting the soil: to prevent crop failures in the future, the land had to be rotated. Officials estimated that present production levels could be maintained only if a further 1,300,000 acres of permanent grassland were broken. Since the lower-grade meadows had now gone, this would mean taking prime grazing lands. The great shortage of meat at the turn of 1917–18 had made livestock rearing an even more profitable occupation than before, however, and the pastures on which the animals were fattened had risen in value. There would be strong resistance to any effects to destroy them. Under the circumstances, a fresh ploughing campaign could succeed only if it were firmly backed by the War Cabinet, which would have to pledge its continued sanction of the Board of Agriculture's power to enforce cultivation.[32]

This support was not forthcoming. In March 1918 a new German offensive got under way and the War Office called up large numbers of men from agricultural areas to help counter it. In light of this, farmers took growing exception to the Board of Agriculture's ever-increasing demands for more arable. The improvement in the military situation by June then altered the political climate. With the possibility that the war was entering its final phase, Lloyd George deemed it judicious to repair his working relationship with the Conservatives, whose co-operation he would need if he were to retain his political position after the war. The Tory leadership's dislike of the government's land policy gave the Prime Minister his opportunity. Walter Long, Bonar Law, Curzon and other leading Conservatives had launched a campaign in the spring to get the Food Production Department's interference with traditional property rights curtailed. A formal request by Lee to the War Cabinet to have the Board of Agriculture's DORA powers extended for another year was turned down. Within a span of only a few days in July, the Board of Agriculture announced an important amendment to the Corn Production Act, the abandonment of the proposed ploughing programme for 1919 and the resignation of Sir Arthur Lee. In future, the Food Production Department would be able to intervene only if the land was neglected. If it wanted well cared for grassland to be ploughed, the Department had to serve a notice against which both owner and occupier now had the right to appeal before an arbitrator. In October the Food Production Department considered issuing a general order simply requiring farmers to maintain the same tillage area in 1919 as in 1918, but the prospect of having to cope with thousands of appeals caused even that modest proposal to be set aside.[33]

The food production campaigns and the war ended on a discouraging note for supporters of the thesis that Britain could be made self-sufficient in foodstuffs. Despite a magnificent harvest in 1918 it was clear that if the war had continued, the country's first line of defence against starvation would have remained the maintenance of imports, economy in food usage and the regulation of distribution and consumption – the work of the Ministry of Food. Moreover, far from inducing agriculturists to adopt a totally fresh approach to farming, the Board of Agriculture seemed to have provoked in them a determination to dig in heels and retreat, after only one major effort and before the war was even over. Although it was essential to have made the effort, the food production campaigns did not reduce to any significant degree the danger of defeat from inadequate food supply.

Notes: Chapter 8

1   E. M. H. Lloyd, *Experiments in State Control at the War Office and the Ministry of Food* (Oxford, 1924), p. 331.
2   Prothero to Prime Minister, 13 September 1917, F/15/8/22, Lloyd George Papers, House of Lords Record Office, London. Selborne to Milner, 26 September 1917, F/38/2/18; Lloyd George Papers, Prothero to War Cabinet, 14 May 1918 (copy), MAF 60/54; Deputation from the Unionist Business Committee to the Rt. Hon. Rowland E. Prothero, MP, MVO, 23 January 1918, MAF 53/8.
3   P. B. Johnson, *Land Fit for Heroes: The Planning of British Reconstruction, 1916–1919* (Chicago, Il, 1968), p. 26.
4   T. H. Middleton, *Production in War* (London, 1923), pp. 154–5; P. E. Dewey, 'Food production and policy in the United Kingdom 1914–1918', *Transactions of the Royal Historical Society*, no. 30 (1980), p. 84.
5   *Hansard*, vol. 92 HC Deb., 5s., 24 April 1917, col. 2277.
6   Reconstruction Committee, *Report of the Agricultural Policy Sub-Committee*, Part 1: Cd 8506 (1917–18), Part 2 and Evidence: Cd 9079 and Cd 9080 (1918).
7   Milner to Prime Minister, 17 August 1917, F/38/2/16, Lloyd George Papers.
8   *Mark Lane Express*, 31 December 1917.
9   Adams to Prime Minister, 31 March 1917 and 12 June 1917, F/70/15/2 and 4, Lloyd George Papers; Adams to Prothero, 12 May 1917, F/70/18/2, Lloyd George Papers; E. H. Whetham, *The Agrarian History of England and Wales*, vol. 8, *1914–1939* (Cambridge, 1978), p. 95.
10 *Hansard*, vol. 92 HC Deb., 5s., 24 April 1917, cols. 2263–2277; *Hansard*, vol. 94 HC Deb., 5s., 13 June 1917, col. 1019; B. Sacks, 'The Independent Labour Party and social amelioration in Great Britain during the war', *University of New Mexico Bulletin*, Sociological Series, vol. 2, no. 6 (1 August 1940); J. M. Winter, *Socialism and the challenge of war: Ideas and Politics in Britain 1912–1918* (London, 1974), p. 201.
11 *Hansard*, vol. 26 HL Deb., 5s., 9 August 1917, col. 278 and 10 August 1917 col. 323; *New Statesman*, 21 July 1917.
12 W. H. Long to Prime Minister, 17 August 1917, F/38/2/16, Lloyd George Papers, R. E. Prothero (Lord Ernle), *Whippingham to Westminster* (London, 1938), p. 307.
13 Notes of Treasury grant for stimulation of home food production, 23 December 1916, MAF 42/11.
14 A. Clark (ed.), *'A Good Innings': The Private Papers of Viscount Lee of Fareham*, (London, 1974), pp. 166–7; Middleton, *Food Production*, pp. 231–2; Whetham, *Agrarian History*, pp. 106–7, 206–7; Addison to Prime Minister, 22 June 1917,

enclosing memorandum from Lee, F/1/3/23; Lloyd George Papers; Adams to Prime Minister, Agricultural tractors, 21 August 1917. Lee, Agricultural tractors. The present position, 21 August 1917. Both in CAB 17/185; *Mark Lane Express*, 16 July 1917.

15 Whetham, *Agrarian History*, p. 107; Committee of Imperial Defence (CID), Food supply in war, p. 7, MAF 60/89.

16 Prothero, *Whippingham to Westminster*, p. 297; Prime Minister to Derby, 12 January 1917, F/14/4/16, Lloyd George Papers.

17 Deputation to Prime Minister from the Federation of County War Agricultural Committees, April 2, 1917, Re: recruiting in agricultural districts, F/226/2, Lloyd George Papers; Clark, Diaries. Entry for 31 March 1917, Bodleian Library, Oxford.

18 War Cabinet, Minutes, 24 May 1917, CAB 23/2/192; Agricultural programme for 1918, conference 6 June 1917, and meeting 22 June 1917, CAB 17/185; Lee, Memorandum on steps taken with reference to the programme for the 1918 harvest, No. 11, 16 August 1917, F/70/20/12, Lloyd George Papers.

19 Middleton, *Food Production*, pp. 222–3; Whetham, *Agrarian History*, p. 100; P. E. Dewey, 'Government provision of farm labour in England and Wales, 1914–18,' *Agricultural History Review*, vol. 27, part 2 (1979), pp. 120–1.

20 Middleton, *Food Production*, pp. 228–9; Whetham, *Agrarian History*, pp. 101–2.

21 Middleton, *Food Production*, p. 220; Credit for farmers, [early 1918], F/70/3/7, Lloyd George Papers; *Hansard*, vol. 108 HC Deb., 5s., 22 July 1918, col. 1437.

22 Middleton, *Food Production*; Clark (ed.), *'A Good Innings'*.

23 Middleton, *Food Production*, p. 322.

24 Middleton, ibid., pp. 154, 192, 312; Editor's note, Clark (ed.), *'A Good Innings'*, p. 168; Dewey, 'Food production and policy', p. 84.

25 Prothero, Programme of increased production of cereals and potatoes for 1918 in England and Wales, 20 April 1917, F/70/20/11, Lloyd George Papers; Board of Agriculture, Circular letter to County War Agricultural Executive Committees, 15 May 1917, F/70/12/1, Lloyd George Papers; Lloyd George, Speech at Guildhall, 27 April 1917, F/232, Lloyd George Papers.

26 Board of Agriculture, Circular letter to Agricultural Executive Committees, 14 June 1917, F/70/12/2, Lloyd George Papers; Lee, Memorandum on steps taken with reference to the programme for the 1918 harvest, No. 11, 16 August 1917, F/70/20/12, Lloyd George Papers.

27 Prothero, Food production, 19 November 1917, MAF 60/105; Adams to Prime Minister, 12 December 1917, F/70/22/2, Lloyd George Papers.

28 Lee to Prime Minister, 22 April 1918, F/31/2/9, Lloyd George Papers; Middleton, The food production campaign and the supply of breadstuffs in the cereal year 1918–19, 18 May 1918, F/70/33/3, Lloyd George Papers.

29 Hoover to Sheldon, 1 June 1918 (copy), F/70/20/14, Lloyd George Papers.

30 R. J. Hammond, 'British food supplies, 1914–1939', *Economic History Review*, vol. 16, no. 1 (1946), p. 2; Dewey, 'Food production and policy', p. 84.

31 Lord Harmsworth, Today's Cabinet discussion on food imports, 6 September 1918, F/87/1/13, Lloyd George Papers; S. J. Hurwitz, *State Intervention in Great Britain: A Study of Economic Control and Social Response*, 1914–1919 (New York, 1949), p. 221.

32 Middleton to Adams, 15 March 1918, F/70/33/1, Lloyd George Papers; Lee to Adams, 26 April 1918, F/70/33/4, Lloyd George Papers.

33 Food Production Department to Agricultural Executive Committees, The Corn Production (Amendment) Act 1918, 15 August 1918, MAF 42/4; Food Production Department, Maintenance of tillage area, 25 October 1918, MAF 42/5.

9

Afterword

Growing awareness in the late summer of 1918 that an Allied victory was only a matter of time made it necessary to decide what was to happen to the Ministry of Food and the state trading system after the war. Given predictions of a contraction in Britain's food supply in 1919, the food authorities anticipated that the ministry would be asked to keep at least some of its domestic operations going until the situation improved. They were less certain about the future of the international control network, and it was this which concerned them most.

Displaying a degree of urgency that contrasted sharply with its apathy when others had broached the subject of closer inter-allied relations only a few months earlier, the Ministry of Food appealed to the War Cabinet in August not only for an expansion of co-operative buying during what was left of the war but for the continuance of the inter-allied programmes after the war ended. The ministry justified this request partly as a concession to American feelings: Hoover was said to regard the recently formed Inter-Allied Food Council as an important step in the direction of a League of Nations, a basis for further international collectivism.[1] But although a memorandum on the subject spoke of 'effective association between nations in economic matters . . . being the strongest and most essential foundation for the re-establishment of permanent peace and order throughout the world', the ministry's policy makers did not share Hoover's reputed idealism.[2] Their main aim was to safeguard Britain's overseas sources of supply. Once the war was over, there was expected to be a public clamour in all the Allied countries for an end to rationing and other forms of food economy. Whether this demand could be met in Britain – and the food authorities considered it advisable for the social peace to try – was believed to depend on how effectively the Allies could dominate world markets and could restrict access to them by the present enemy states.[3] The ministry therefore proposed the formation of a new international purchasing board with responsibility for the acquisition of *all* the foodstuffs needed by the Allied and neutral nations. This would give the Allies almost complete control of the world's supply of food outside the Central Empires and Russia. The chairman of the new board – it went almost without saying – should be British.[4]

The ministry's views coincided with those of the reconstruction planners, who, stressing the probability of scarcity of raw materials in world markets for several years following an armistice, were advising the government to extend state economic controls in general into the postwar period.[5] It was argued that industry would need the protection of assured supplies and prices if the factories were to revert successfully to their original functions and absorb the millions of returning servicemen into their workforces in an orderly fashion. The War Cabinet were alive to the potential dangers of too-rapid decontrol. As a communique to the American government dated 15 October reveals, apprehension of the social consequences if food shortages coincided with industrial dislocation contributed to the War Cabinet's approval of the Ministry of Food's request that inter-allied trading arrangements be maintained. Citing the need to avoid social unrest, which could 'delay for an indefinite time the re-establishment of the peaceful international relations which it is the object of the War to safeguard and secure', the communique proposed the retention in peacetime of that 'close co-operation and mutual help which has been developed by the War among the Associated countries' with regard to foodstuffs, industrial raw materials and transport.[6] Two weeks later, on 1 November, Britain and France submitted to the Supreme War Council a joint recommendation that at the conclusion of hostilities the entire mercantile marine of the Central Powers be placed under the control of the Inter-Allied Maritime Council (to prevent independent access to markets) and that all supplies of food and other commodities needed by the former enemy nations be obtained through the inter-allied network.[7]

Only ten days before the war ended, therefore, it would seem to have been settled that the food control apparatus, both domestic and international, would be maintained virtually intact for some time, possibly for several years. Yet when peace was restored, food controls shared the same fate as the other special regulatory devices accumulated by government departments during the war – abandoned by their possessors with almost undignified haste. The fighting was officially over on the Western Front on 11 November; on the 10th the

Food Controller already had before him a memorandum detailing the course of decontrol.

This sudden reversal of policy was brought about in part by the refusal of the United States to participate in an inter-allied trading organization in peacetime. American attitudes had been misjudged. The original agreement entered into between the United States and the European Allies in August 1917 for the establishment of an international purchasing network in the United States had in fact specified that the arrangement would terminate with 'the war between the United States and its enemies'.[8] In possession of more than 50 per cent of the world's exportable surplus of food supplies, the United States in November 1918 saw every reason to stick to that stipulation. In unconscious parody of earlier British complaints about the short-comings of inter-allied trading, Hoover on 8 November declared it 'wholly inconceivable' that America's customers should be able (through majority representation on the Inter-Allied Food Council) to dictate to the producer of such vast quantities of foodstuffs as regards prices and distribution. With the intention of 'securing justice in distribution, proper appreciation abroad of the effort we make to assist foreign nations, and proper return for the service that we will perform', the United States government was to resume independent trading with the armistice, thus deliberately preventing 'the extension of the functions and life of the Inter-Allied Food and Maritime Councils either now or after peace'.[9]

Historians have suggested several other reasons for the change of course. In the case of food controls in particular, negative attitudes at the Ministry of Food (specifically on the part of Beale, the Permanent Secretary) are said to have contributed heavily to the decision to decontrol. The domestic aspects of peacetime food administration lacked appeal reportedly, and there was also a desire to sell off while prices remained high the huge reserves of food accumulated by the ministry during the war.[10] With respect to state economic controls in general, two quite different explanations have been tendered in recent years. One is that the strong support for continued regulation of the economy that existed in official circles during the last few months of the war rested on the assumption of an energetic economic challenge by a resurgent Germany as soon as the war was over. When Germany instead fell into total disarray, the rationale for a state-guided economy simply disappeared.[11] The second theory points to the economic situation in Britain soon after the armistice. With the armaments factories closed, wartime ministries disbanding and men being demobilized from the armed forces, unemployment began to rise. There was simultaneously a fall in prices and a lull in banking and currency operations. All were indicators, it was thought, of an imminent economic depression. The restoration of freedom of activity to trade and industry was done in the hope of instilling confidence in the business community.[12]

Domestic food controls in fact lasted rather longer than the other economic regulations introduced during the war. Decontrol at first proceeded swiftly. By the end of 1918 bread had returned to its prewar quality, fancy pastries were back in the shops, tea and meat other than beef, veal and mutton had been derationed, the meat coupon had been increased in value, and the orders affecting animal fodder had been rescinded. Early in the new year other foods were decontrolled and the coupon system gradually fell into disuse. The ration books expired in May. The Ministry of Food began disbanding immediately after the armistice and by June 1919 half of its staff had gone. In January 1919 both the Food Controller and the Permanent Secretary resigned to take up duties of greater interest to them. Their successors, the Labour MP George Roberts and W. H. Beveridge, expected to mop things up by 30 September. In July, however, the government issued a reprieve. Food prices, which had been falling steadily since the armistice, took a sudden turn upward, provoking demands from the unions for government action. Price controls were therefore reintroduced, along with coupons for meat, butter and sugar, in September. The meat and butter coupons were dispensed with fairly rapidly and sugar rationing ended in November 1920. On 31 March 1921 the Ministry of Food closed its doors. Although the Board of Trade assumed a few of the ministry's residual regulatory duties, as far as the British public could see food control had finally come to an end.

State support for agriculture ended a few months later. Although they had resented the Board of Agriculture's power to interfere in their affairs in 1917 and 1918, farmers had taken to the idea of government price cushions. Lloyd George's pledge to maintain guaranteed grain prices – easy to give in view of the high price for grain at the end of the war – assured him the farming vote in the postwar elections. The Agricultural Act of 1920 reaffirmed the financial security offered by the Corn Production Act of 1917. In 1921, however, agricultural prices slumped suddenly to half of those prevailing in 1920, threatening the state for the first time with large compensatory payments. Rather than endure the political consequences of mass disapproval by the rest of the electorate if these were made, the government repudiated agricultural subsidies.

Notwithstanding delays, false starts, mistakes and vacillation in policy, wartime food administration in Britain proved in retrospect far more satisfactory than in other belligerent nations. It finally resulted in a system in which controls were more comprehensive, the application of legislation was more efficient, supplies were higher and distribution was fairer. That the authorities had finally found the right formula was evident in the high degree of public acceptance of food controls and in the unimportance of the black market in Britain compared to the situation elsewhere. This was no mean achievement and bolstered national morale at a crucial point in the war.

Paradoxically, the factors that had made Britain the most vulnerable of the belligerent nations to seaborne attack on its trade facilitated the development and imposition of food controls. The large proportion of imported foodstuffs in the national diet allowed the state to identify and regulate with a minimum of difficulty two thirds of the total supply; The smallness of the agricultural sector reduced the headache of dealing with producers while, conversely, the concentration of the bulk of the population in urban centres made it easier to control distribution and consumption through the wholesaler/retailer/customer registration technique. The existence of great numbers of 'self-producers' intent on circumventing the rules was not a problem in Britain as it was, for example, in France. It was also an advantage for the Ministry of Food and the various agricultural authorities to be dealing with a smaller geographic area than France or Germany. Although not recognized as such by postwar critics, prevailing *laissez-faire* traditions in Britain before the war were beneficial in ensuring that the state did not rush in with controls too soon, as in Germany, and in the process wreck both the supply flow and the chances of consumer co-operation. Certain measures, such as compulsory rationing, should have come earlier, but the gradual introduction of food controls to a public with no prior concept or experience of them was an essential element in the success of British food policy in the First World War. The state's reluctance to take over the duties of the normal traders in foodstuffs moreover produced the eminently workable arrangement whereby the existing business network was incorporated into the centrally administered control system rather than superceded. Where state trading units replaced the original mechanism entirely, the results were not always satisfactory.

Other elements contributing to Britain's successful organization of food supplies were more obvious. The country possessed the great advantage of a huge mercantile fleet and immense wealth, which made it easier to seek out alternative sources of supply and pay for and transport these supplies in the face of highly effective submarine offensives by the enemy, increasing international competition for foodstuffs and rising commodity prices around the world. One important factor, the productive and organizational capacity of the United States, was, of course, shared by all of the Allies. The assistance from this source was invaluable and it is hard to see how the Europeans could have prevailed without it. Towards the end of the war it could be argued that the Americans were undermining British efforts to safeguard supplies, but the efficiency of the American system had enabled the food administrators to fulfill the policies that made the American pressure less effective, notably the extension of state jurisdiction over supply and the acquisition of food reserves.

Despite concrete achievements by the food authorities and widespread public satisfaction with affairs in the closing months of the war, positive attitudes towards food control did not last long into the postwar period. There were temporary displays of approval – as when labour called for a return of price controls in mid-1919, for example – but the popular mood turned steadily against it. When the Ministry of Food was finally dismantled, there was a communal sigh of relief. In a later editorial, *The Times* recalled the general feeling in 1921: indispensable though the ministry had been during the war, 'the net result of its history was to furnish an overwhelming argument against state trading in normal times'.[13] Sensibility of the unprecedented horror of the First World War was manifested in a general aversion throughout the 1920s to the very topics of war and of state intervention in the civilian economy. This attitude was even evident in the official history of food control written by one of the former officials of the Ministry of Food, W. H. Beveridge, which appeared in 1928. After a highly complimentary account of the ministry's activities, the book ended on a negative note. The work of the war years had been barren: food control 'opened no way of permanent advance'.[14]

Beveridge was looking at the question from too close a perspective. The bureaucratic and financial lessons of emergency food administration, which in the 1920s appeared of no use to a society that had decreed perpetual peace, were of course applied in the Second World War, providing guidelines for both paths to follow and paths to avoid. The greater understanding gained of the factors involved in the feeding of masses of people, beyond the logistic aspects of acquisition and distribution, are still useful to governments and relief agencies – factors such as the psychological, social and political ramifications of food shortages and high prices and stumbling blocks to organization and the provision of alternative foodstuffs stemming from eating habits and dietary prejudices.

Taken in a broader context, food administration in the First World War contributed to a number of other long term developments generally considered beneficial. Among the more important consequences of the war was a lessening of class distinctions. Food control played a part in this. Concern about the negative impact of poor working class diets on national efficiency had been growing for some time before the war, but government efforts to do something about the situation had been modest and were focused primarily on infants and children. By 1917 the great disparity of diet that existed between rich and poor could not be allowed to continue unmodified. Unequal distribution in time of scarcity threatened the morale and stamina of the labourforce and consequently the ability of the nation to survive a war of endurance. In addition, it could not be morally justified given the sacrifices of the working classes in the factories and at the front. The outcry over this issue lent force to the more diffuse movement for social reconstruction. By limiting the purchases of the rich while leaving those of the working classes much the same, rationing made food problems a shared experience in 1918. Rigorous enforcement of controls gave the privileged classes in Britain fewer opportunities than their continental counterparts to use their wealth to maintain old standards. At the other end of the social scale, regular employment during the war allowed unskilled labourers to bridge the nutritional gap between themselves and skilled workers. Although differentials in consumption increased again with peace, the range lacked the extremes of the prewar era. Surveys taken in the 1930s revealed that despite continued malnourishment among the lowest paid, the trend towards better and more homogenous standards of nutrition in Britain was maintained in the interwar years.[15]

Their involvement with the food question enhanced the prestige of labour representatives both in Parliament and on the local level and contributed to the development of Labour into a broad-based party of popular appeal. J. R. Clynes and his successor George Roberts gained valuable administrative experience at the Ministry of Food and bettered their reputations in the process. The inclusion of working class members on the municipal food committees and County War Agricultural Committees provided an opportunity for labour to show that it was competent to share in the running of local and regional affairs. Trades councils experienced a noticeable change in attitudes to them by local dignitaries and officials as their services to the community increased.[16] By linking their campaigns for food controls with consumer rights the WNC similarly gave socialism a great boost. Through focusing on questions of general public interest rather than on issues of concern only to the unions, they reached out to a wider sector of the electorate than Labour had previously represented.

The transformation that took place during the war in concepts of government and in opinions about the extent to which the state should be responsible for the well-being of the people was, as we have seen, assisted by the necessity to impose controls over food supply. Although some may feel that the process ultimately went too far, surely few would deny that the growth of the state's role had many beneficial results for the ordinary citizen. Like other wartime excursions by the state into collectivism, the Ministry of Food and the Food Production Department of the Board of Agriculture expanded the acceptable limits and directions of government intervention in civilian affairs and thus paved the way for postwar social legislation in such areas as health, education and housing. The change in outlook had incalculable results for agriculture too. Despite the reaction that set in in the 1920s, the authorities looked to the war years to find solutions to the ills of the Depression. The Wheat Act of 1932 restored the guaranteed grain price. Other legislation such as the Import Duties Act of 1932, the Agricultural Marketing Acts of 1931 and 1933 and various Marketing Boards established in 1933 and 1934, extended the subsidization of agriculture and brought to an end a century of *laissez-faire* in this sector of the economy.[17] The intervention was timely: it provided incentive for a revival of British farming in the years immediately preceding the Second World War.

One aspect of the food question that had had only marginal significance for policy during the war itself showed some of the most rapid advance in the postwar years – the understanding and application of scientific principles of nutrition. The newness of the field at the onset of the war, the paucity of the scientists' own knowledge and the lack of appreciation by government officials of how the information that was available fitted in with their work frustrated the efforts of scientists to contribute much to the formulation of food policy. This very frustration, however, as well the general highlighting of food issues by the war, helped foster interest in nutritional research by both the international scientific community and, later by national governments. The postwar years saw the fruition of many scientific and technical investigations that originated in wartime food problems. For example, the difficulties experienced with the shipment and storage of perishable foods (such as the American bacon) led to more sophisticated methods of refrigeration that brought an improvement in the quality and variety of imported foods in the interwar years. The low-grade frozen meat of the prewar era gave way to more wholesome chilled meat, and fresh produce began to be available throughout the year. By 1934 the British public was eating nearly twice as much fruit as prewar and about two thirds more vegetables. Discoveries came quickly. Vitamins replaced calories as the basis for good nutrition in the 1920s, and by the 1930s techniques had been developed that permitted the addition of vitamin supplements to commonly-used foods such as bread and margarine. This work provided the basis for the scientifically-planned onslaught on eating patterns in Britain during the Second World War and for the national welfare programmes introduced after 1945.

Wartime food policy, then, turned out to be far from a simple matter of reconciling supply and demand. The issues that had to be considered in its formulation proved considerably more varied and complex than either prewar government planners or private pressure groups had imagined. The food authorities found their attention claimed by far-reaching social and political trends, international diplomacy, high finance, popular psychology, science and evolving techniques of bureacratic administration in addition to the more mundane matters of supply sources, trade patterns, transport and distribution. Food supply served as a mirror of both a changing national society and of a readjustment in the balance of world power. One can agree with Lloyd George that civilian food administration, seen before the war was at best of minor concern to war strategy, emerged during the First World War as a central element of a successful war effort.

Notes: Afterword

1 W. W. Astor, Memorandum, 22 August 1918, GD 40/17/933, Lothian Papers, Scottish Record Office, Edinburgh.
2 Astor, draft memorandum for Clynes to War Cabinet, n.d. [August or September 1918], GD 40/17/934/3, Lothian Papers.
3 Astor, draft memorandum, n.d. [mid-October 1918], GD 40/17/937/2, Lothian Papers.
4 Astor, memorandum GD 40/17/934/3, Lothian Papers.
5 For a more detailed discussion of this theme see P. Cline, 'Winding down the war economy: British plans for peacetime recovery, 1916–19', in Burk (ed.), *War and the State: The Transformation of British Government 1914–1919* (London, 1982), pp. 157–181.
6 Commercial Advisor of British Embassy, Washington [R. Crawford] to Counselor for the Department of State [Polk], 15 October 1918, United States, Department of State, *Papers Relating to the Foreign Relations of the United States*, No. 9388, vol. 1, Part 1 (1918), pp. 613–15.
7 Telegramme, Cotton to Hoover, 30 October 1918, United States, Department of State, *Foreign Relations Papers*, No. 9388, vol. 1, Part 1 (1918), p. 615.
8 Anglo–American agreement respecting a purchasing commission in the United States, August 1917, AC 12/198, Chamberlain Papers, University of Birmingham.
9 Telegramme, Hoover to Cotton, 8 November 1918, United States, Department of State, *Foreign Relations Papers*, No. 9388, vol. 1, Part 1 (1918), pp. 616–17.
10 J. Harris, 'Bureaucrats and businessmen in British food control, 1916–19', in Burk (ed.), *War and the State*, p. 146.
11 P. Cline, 'Winding down the war economy', in Burk (ed.), *War and the State*, p. 159.
12 E. V. Morgan, *Studies in British Financial Policy, 1914–25* (London, 1952), pp. 374–5.
13 *The Times*, 14 October 1924.
14 Sir W. H. Beveridge, *British Food Control* (London, 1928), p. 344.
15 C. L. Mowat, *Britain Between the Wars 1918–1940* (Chicago, 1955), p. 505.
16 A. Clinton, *Trade Union Rank and File: Trades Councils in Britain, 1900–40* (Manchester, 1977), p. 70.
17 S. Pollard, *Development of the British Economy 1914–1967* (London, 1969), pp. 138–141.

Appendices

Appendix 1 Stocks of Food in the United Kingdom, '000 tons (selected items)

	Wheat and wheat flour	Oats	Bacon and ham	Other meat	Sugar	Cheese	Butter	Margarine
1 Oct 1914	2,710	2,335	15.9	48.3	n.a.	13.0	13.5	3.2
1 Jan 1915	2,166	1,486	14.9	61.9	*427	12.3	5.5	2.9
1 Apr 1915	1,459	672	30.0	75.3	379	7.4	7.7	4.0
1 July 1915	1,200	359	37.1	64.7	151	9.8	12.2	4.0
1 Oct 1915	2,602	2,658	28.6	88.6	94	19.1	15.0	4.3
1 Jan 1916	1,904	1,625	15.8	80.1	99	13.2	26.6	5.1
1 Apr 1916	1,481	890	37.0	59.5	92	9.6	15.4	4.3
1 July 1916	1,486	245	62.9	53.3	98	9.7	12.2	4.4
1 Oct 1916	2,399	2,749	31.3	56.2	62	14.7	8.9	4.1
1 Jan 1917	1,815	1,612	26.8	62.4	79	12.9	5.8	5.3
1 Apr 1917	1,237	584	29.2	61.2	34	4.9	6.7	2.6
1 July 1917	1,360	264	60.1	57.9	62	11.0	20.9	4.1
1 Oct 1917	3,078	3,224	18.6	69.9	192	17.4	8.1	5.0
1 Jan 1918	2,117	2,087	9.3	87.5	209	17.1	1.2	2.6
1 Apr 1918	1,512	682	9.3	90.0	218	9.7	3.3	2.4
1 July 1918	1,714	216	99.3	98.4	247	11.6	23.5	1.7
1 Oct 1918	3,296	3,773	92.2	74.8	382	24.7	12.7	1.8

* 1 March
Source: Ministry of Food, Monthly Office Reports (December 1918), Table D: Stocks of the principal foods in the United Kingdom.

Appendix 2 Net imports of food into the United Kingdom, '000 tons (selected items)

	Wheat and wheat flour	Oats	Bacon and ham	Other meat	Sugar	Cheese	Butter	Margarine
4th quarter 1914	1,348	119	71.4	184.6	760	32.2	44.2	19.6
1st quarter 1915	1,101	202	96.4	180.8	438	26.2	55.3	22.2
2nd quarter 1915	1,323	253	105.5	204.9	268	31.6	44.7	21.9
3rd quarter 1915	1,328	173	103.3	252.4	385	47.2	39.2	24.4
4th quarter 1915	1,265	145	81.4	161.5	385	28.6	50.6	34.1
1st quarter 1916	1,389	220	121.3	139.0	366	21.3	31.9	30.9
2nd quarter 1916	1,752	109	126.3	179.8	455	27.5	24.0	30.9
3rd quarter 1916	1,214	211	84.7	179.4	455	44.9	24.0	33.7
4th quarter 1916	1,252	68	107.0	176.5	350	34.0	27.0	41.2
1st quarter 1917	1,292	66	109.1	133.7	276	30.1	32.5	32.6
2nd quarter 1917	1,777	137	138.3	124.4	341	33.7	39.2	23.3
3rd quarter 1917	1,275	319	78.8	148.3	453	50.9	13.1	21.7
4th quarter 1917	670	106	62.7	165.4	319	33.0	5.7	13.9
1st quarter 1918	783	30	78.2	151.4	273	22.6	23.2	15.1
2nd quarter 1918	1,438	98	246.4	183.9	360	25.2	36.7	n.a.
3rd quarter 1918	982	201	167.7	133.5	455	50.5	7.1	n.a.
4th quarter 1918	1,402	207	104.6	158.5	223	19.3	13.5	n.a.

Source: Ministry of Food, *Monthly Office Reports* (December 1918), Table E: Net imports of the principal foods in the United Kingdom.

Appendix 3 *Percentage increase in retail food prices, United Kingdom*

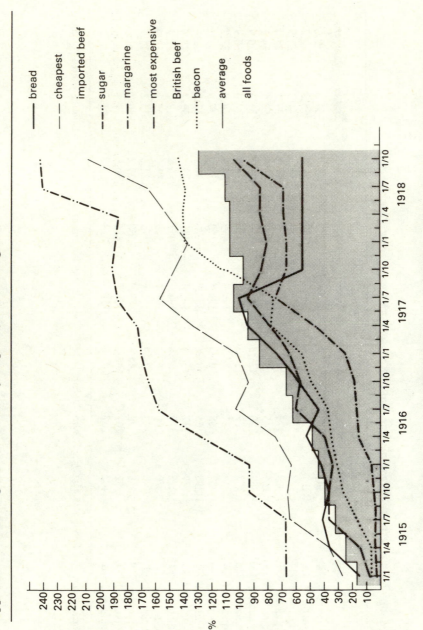

Sources: Ministry of Food, *Monthly Office Reports* (December 1918), Percentage increase in retail food prices; Table F: N. B. Dearle, *An Economic Chronicle of the Great War*, passim.

Appendix 4 *Cultivated area and acreage and production of staples, United Kingdom*

Year	Total cultivated area	Permanent grass	Arable	Wheat		Oats		Potatoes	
	million acres	million acres	million acres	million acres	million quarters	million acres	million quarters	million acres	million tons
Average 1904-13	47.08	27.63	19.45	1.78	7.09	4.11	21.56	1.17	6.59
1914	46.76	27.35	19.41	1.91	7.80	3.90	20.66	1.21	7.48
1915	46.67	27.33	19.35	2.33	9.24	4.18	22.31	1.21	7.54
1916	46.69	27.19	19.50	2.05	7.47	4.17	21.33	1.12	5.47
1917	46.34	26.59	19.75	2.11	8.04	4.79	26.02	1.38	8.60
1918	46.27	25.05	21.22	2.80	11.64	5.71	31.31	1.51	9.22

Source: T. H. Middleton, *Food Production in Wartime* (London, 1923), pp. 312, 315.

Sources

Manuscripts

Public Documents, Public Record Office (PRO), London
  Board of Trade (BT)
  Cabinet (CAB)
  Foreign Office (FO)
  Ministry of Agriculture, Fisheries and Food (MAF)
  Ministry of Reconstruction (RECO)
  Treasury (T)

Papers and Diaries of Individuals
  Christopher Addison (Bodleian Library, Oxford).
  Alan G. Anderson (Public Record Office, London).
  Sir William Ashley (British Library, London).
  H. H. Asquith (Bodleian Library, Oxford).
  W. W. Astor (Reading University).
  A. J. Balfour (British Library, Public Record Office, London).
  W. H. Beveridge (British Library of Political and Economic Science, London).
  Lady Beveridge (British Library of Political and Economic Science, London).
  Andrew Bonar Law (House of Lords Record Office, London).
  John Burns (British Library, London).
  Austen Chamberlain (University of Birmingham).
  Reverend Andrew Clark (Bodleian Library, Oxford).
  Lord Crewe (University College, Cambridge).
  David Lloyd George (House of Lords Record Office, London).
  Major Adrian Grant-Duff (Churchill College, Cambridge).
  M. P. A. Hankey (Churchill College, Cambridge).
  L. H. Harcourt (Bodleian Library, Oxford).
  Arthur Henderson (Transport House, London).
  Herbert Hoover (Hoover Institution, Stanford, California).
  E. M. H. Lloyd (British Library of Political and Economic Science, London).
  Lord Lothian (Scottish Record Office, Edinburgh).
  Graham Lusk (Hoover Institution, Stanford, California).
  Ramsay MacDonald (Public Record Office, London).
  Reginald McKenna (Churchill College, Cambridge).
  Lord Milner (Bodleian Library, Oxford, Public Record Office, London).
  E. S. Montagu (Trinity College, Cambridge).
  Lord Mottistone (Nuffield College, Oxford).
  Sir George Newman (Ministry of Health Library, London).
  Lord Northcliffe (*The Times'* Archives, London).

Sir Horace Plunkett (The Plunkett Foundation for Co-operative Studies, Oxford).
Walter Runciman (University of Newcastle-upon-Tyne).
Colonel Sir Robert Sandars (Conservative and Unionist Offices, London).
Lord Selborne (Bodleian Library, Oxford).
Lewis Strauss (Herbert Hoover Presidential Library, West Branch, Iowa).
Alonzo E. Taylor (Hoover Institution, Stanford, California).

Other

Central Land Association, Executive Committee Minutes (Reading University).
Consumers' Council (Transport House, London).
Inter-Allied Food Council (Hoover Institution, Stanford, California).
National Farmers Union (Reading University).
Royal Agricultural Society of England, War Emergency Committee Minutes (Reading University).
Royal Society Food (War) Committee (Royal Society, London).
United States Food Administration (Hoover Institution, Stanford, California).
War Emergency Workers' National Committee (Transport House, London).

Parliamentary Papers and Reports

House of Commons, Debates

House of Lords, Debates

Command Papers
Board of Agriculture and Fisheries
Annual Report of the Education Branch on the Distribution of Grants for Agricultural Education and Research 1914–1915, Cd 8066 (1914–16).
Departmental Committee on the Home Production of Food (England and Wales). *Interim Report*, Cd 8048; *Final Report*, Cd 8095 (1914–16).
The Recent Development of German Agriculture, Cd 8305 (1916).
Board of Trade
Departmental Committee on Prices. *Interim Report*, Cd 8358 (1916); *Second and Third Reports*, Cd 8483 (1917–18).
Report of the Physiology (War) Committee of the Royal Society on the Food Supply of the United Kingdom, Cd 8421 (1916).
Commission of Enquiry into Industrial Unrest. Local *Reports* and *Summary*, Cd 8662–9, Cd 8696 (1917–18).
Committee on the Production and Distribution of Milk. *Interim Report*, Cd 8606 (1917–18); *Second Interim Report*, Cd 8886 (1917–18); *Final Report*, Cmd 483 (1919).

Department of Agriculture and Technical Instruction for Ireland. *Report of the Departmental Committee on Food Production in Ireland*, Cd 8046, Cd 8158 (1914–16).

Dominions Royal Commission. *Food and Raw Material Requirements of the United Kingdom*, Cd 8123 (1914–16).

Inter-Departmental Committee on Meat Supplies. *Report*, Cmd 456 (1919).

Reconstruction Committee (later Ministry of Reconstruction). *Report of the Agricultural Policy Sub-Committee*, Part 1: Cd 8506 (1917–18); Part 2 and Evidence: Cd 9079 (1918) and Cd 9080 (1918).

Registrar-General for England and Wales. *Annual Report for 1918*, Cmd 608 (1920).

Royal Commission on the Sugar Supply. *Memorandum as to the Distribution of Sugar, July to December 1916*, Cd 8395 (1916); *First Interim Report*, Cd 8728 (1917–18).

Royal Commission on the Supply of Food and Raw Material in Time of War. *Report*, Cd 2643, *Evidence*, Cd 2644, *Appendices*, Cd 2645 (1905).

Working Classes Cost of Living Committee. *Report*, Cd 8980 (1918).

Reports

Board of Trade. Industrial (War Inquiries) Branch, *Report on the State of Employment in Agriculture in Great Britain at the End of January 1917* (and subsequent reports) (HMSO, London).

London Chamber of Commerce. *Report of the Special Committee to the Council of the Chamber: Food Supplies in Time of War* (London, 1914).

National Health Insurance, Medical Research Committee. Special report no. 68, H. Corry Mann, *Rickets* (London, 1922).

Scottish Departmental Committee on Food Production. *Report on the Question of Maintaining and if possible Increasing the Present Production of Food in Scotland. First Report*, August 1915; *Second Report*, December 1916; *Third Report*, April 1917 (HMSO, London).

Select committee on high prices and profits. *Special Report* and *Report* (Parliamentary Papers, 1919, vol. 5).

Select committee on national expenditure. *Eighth Report, 1918: Financial Relations with Allies, War Office, Board of Trade, Ministry of Food* (Parliamentary Papers, 1918, vol. 4); *Second Report, 1919: Wheat Commission* (Parliamentary Papers, 1919, vol. 5).

Official Publications

Board of Agriculture

Food Production Leaflets Nos. 1–62 (1917–1919).

Journal (1914–1919).

Special Leaflets Nos 1–78 (August 1914–June 1917).

Board of Education *Economy in Food* (HMSO, 1915).

Ministry of Food

Food Economy Handbook (HMSO, 1917).

Food Supply Manual (revised to 31 July 1918).

Handbook of National Kitchens and Restaurants (1918).

List of Food Control Divisions in England, Scotland and Wales (1917).
Monthly Office Report (September 1917–December 1918).
National Food Journal (12 September 1917–19 June 1920).
Report on the Constitution and Work of the Consumers' Council. n.d.
Weekly Bulletin (Food Control Campaign) (2 May 1917–20 June 1917).
Weekly Enforcement Guide (3 August 1918–21 September 1918).
Weekly Reports (24 January 1917–29 December 1917).

Other
  United States, Department of State
  Papers Relating to the Foreign Relations of the United States
  No. 9037, 1917. vol. 1; vol. 2, part 2.
  No. 9388, 1918. vol. 1, part 1.

Memoirs, Diaries and Collected Works

Addison, C., *Four and a Half Years*, 2 Vols (London, 1934).
Addison, C., *Politics From Within 1911–1918*, 2 Vols (London, 1924).
Asquith, H. H., *Memories and Reflections 1852–1927*, 2 Vols (Boston, 1928).
Baker, R. S. (ed.), *Woodrow Wilson, Life and Letters*, 8 Vols (New York, 1927–1939).
Barnes, J. and Nicholson D. (eds), *The Leo Amery Diaries*, vol. 1: *1896–1929* (London, 1980).
Beaverbrook, Lord, *Men and Power: 1917–1918* (London, 1956).
Beaverbrook, Lord, *Politicians and the War* (London, 1960).
Beveridge, W. H., *Power and Influence* (London, 1953).
Chamberlain, A., *Down The Years* (London, 1935).
Chamberlain, A., *Politics From Inside* (New Haven, CT, 1937).
Clark, A. (ed.), *'A Good Innings': The Private Papers of Viscount Lee of Fareham* (London, 1974).
Clynes, J. R., *Memoirs*, 2 Vols (London, 1937).
David, E. (ed.), *Inside Asquith's Cabinet: From the Diaries of Charles Hobhouse* (London, 1977).
George, D. Lloyd, *War Memoirs*, 6 Vols (London, 1933–6).
Grey, E., *Twenty–Five Years 1892–1916*, 2 Vols. (New York, 1925).
Gwynn, S. (ed.), *The Anvil of War: Letters between F. S. Oliver and his Brother 1914–1918* (London, 1936).
Hankey, M. P. A., *The Supreme Command 1914–1918*, 2 Vols (London, 1961).
Hendrick, B. J. (ed.), *The Life and Letters of Walter H. Page*, 3 Vols (New York, 1922–5).
Hewins, W. A. S., *The Apologia of an Imperialist: Forty Years of Empire Policy*, 2 Vols (London, 1929).
Hoover, H. G., *The Memoirs of Herbert Hoover* 3 Vols (New York, 1951–2).
Keynes, J. M., *The Collected Writings of John Maynard Keynes*, E. Johnson (ed.), vol. 16: *Activities 1914–1919: The Treasury and Versailles* (Cambridge, 1971–1980).

Kearley, H. E. (Lord Devonport), *The Travelled Road: Some Memoirs of a Busy Life* (Rochester, Kent, 1935).

McAdoo, W. G., *Crowded Years: the Reminiscences of William G. McAdoo* (Boston, 1931).

Middlemas, K. (ed.), *Thomas Jones' Whitehall Diary* (London, 1969).

Mottistone, Lord (J. E. B. Seely), *Adventure* (London, 1930).

O'Brien, F. W. (ed.), *The Hoover–Wilson Wartime Correspondence* (Ames, Iowa, 1974).

Patterson, A. T. (ed.), *The Jellicoe Papers*, 2 Vols (London, 1966–8).

Peel, C. S., *A Year in Public Life* (London, 1919).

Prothero, R. E. (Lord Ernle), *Whippingham to Westminster* (London, 1938).

Rodd, Sir J. Rennell, *Social and Diplomatic Memories*, 3 Vols (London, 1922–5).

Salter, A., *Slave of the Lamp* (London, 1967).

Seymour, C. (ed.), *The Intimate Papers of Colonel House*, 4 Vols (Boston, 1926–8).

Smillie, R., *My Life for Labour* (London, 1924).

Tallents, Sir S., *Man and Boy* (London, 1943).

Taylor, A. J. P. (ed.), *Lloyd George: A Diary by Frances Stevenson* (New York, 1971).

Webb, B. P., *Diaries, 1873–1943*, microfiche edition (Cambridge, 1978).

Wilson, T. (ed.), *The Political Diaries of C. P. Scott 1911–1928* (London, 1970).

Contemporary Works

Akers, A., *The War and the World's Wheat: The Risks of a Shortage Next Harvest* (London, 1914).

Angier, T. V. S., *Our Food Supplies in the Time of War* (London, 1903).

Bathurst, C., *To Avoid National Starvation* (London, 1912).

Benedict, F. G., 'Physiological effects of a prolonged reduction in diet on twenty-five men', *Symposium on Food Problems in Relation to the War* (New York, 1918).

Beveridge, Sir W. H., *British Food Control* (London, 1928).

Bowley, A. L., *Prices and Wages in the United Kingdom 1914–1920* (Oxford, 1921).

Carnegie Institution of Washington, *Annual Report of the Director* (1909–1920).

Clemesha, H. W., *Food Control in the North-Western Division* (Manchester, 1922).

Coller, F. H., *A State Trading Adventure* (London, 1925).

Co-operative Union Ltd, *Co-operative National Emergency Conference, October 17 and 18, 1917* and *Report of the Deputation to the Prime Minister, October 31, 1917* (London, 1917).

Crichton-Brown, Sir J., 'Tuberculosis and the war', *Journal of State Medicine*, vol. 25, no. 5 (May 1917), pp. 144–6.

Crookes, Sir W., *The Wheat Problem* (London, 1918).

Dearle, N. B., *An Economic Chronicle of the Great War for Great Britain and Ireland 1914–1919* (New Haven, CT, 1929).

Doyle, Sir A. Conan, 'Danger', *Strand Magazine* (July 1914).

Doyle, Sir A., Conan, *Great Britain and the Next War* (London, 1913).

Edsall, E. W., *England Must Be Fed: The Reply to the U-Boat Menace* (London, 1916).

Eltzbacher, Professor P., *Germany's Food: Can It Last?*, English version edited by S. R. Wells, MD, with critical introduction by Professor A. D. Waller (London, 1915).

Evans, D., *'D. A.': Viscount Rhondda: A Memoir* (South Wales Journal of Commerce, 1920).

Fairlee, J. A., *British War Administration* (New York, 1919).

Ferguson, M., 'The family budgets and dietaries of forty labouring class families in Glasgow in war time', *Proceedings of the Royal Society of Edinburgh*, vol. 37 (November 1916–July 1917), pp. 117–136.

Fielding, Sir C., *Food* (London, 1923).

Firth, C.H., *Then and Now: or A Comparison Between the War With Napoleon and the Present War* (London, 1918).

Gardiner, A. G., *Pillars of Society* (London, 1916).

General Federation of Trade Unions, *Food Prices* (London, 1916).

George, D. Lloyd, *The Great Crusade*, arranged by F. L. Stevenson (New York, 1918).

Hall, Sir A. D., *Agriculture After The War* (London, 1920).

Harpenden Local Food Control Committee, *To the People of Harpenden* (London, 1917).

Hibbard, B. H., *Effects of the Great War upon Agriculture in the United States and Great Britain* (New York, 1919).

Hirst, F. W. and J. E. Allen, *British War Budgets* (London, 1926).

Hoover, H. C., *Food in War* (London, 1918).

H.S., 'Early phases of food control', *The Edinburgh Review*, vol. 227 (January 1918), pp. 108–130.

Hyndman, R. T., *The Last Years of H. M. Hyndman* (London, 1923).

Jones, D. T., Duncan, J. F., Conacher, H. M., and Scott, W. R., *Rural Scotland During the War* (New Haven, 1926).

Jones, Sir. T. G., *The Unbroken Front: Ministry of Food, 1916–1944* (London, 1944).

Kellogg, V. E., *Herbert Hoover, the Man and his Work* (New York, 1920).

Kellogg, V. and Taylor, A. E., *The Food Problem* (New York, 1917).

Kenderine, C. H., *Food Supply in War Time* (London, 1913).

King's Lynn and District Central War Savings Committee, Food Economy Section, *The Voice of King's Lynn on the Subject of the Food Economy Campaign* (September 1917).

Labour Party Information Bureau, *Bulletin No. 10* (London, 1917).

Litman, S., *Prices and Price Control in Great Britain and the United States During the World War* (New York, 1920).

Lloyd, E. M. H., *Experiments in State Control at the War Office and the Ministry of Food* (Oxford, 1924).

Londonderry, Marchioness of, *Henry Chaplin: A Memoir* (London, 1926).

Lusk, G., *Food in Wartime* (London, 1918).

Middleton, T. H., *Production in War* (London, 1923).

Morgan, Reverend J. V., *Life of Viscount Rhondda* (London, 1919).

National Farmers' Union, *The Food of the People* (London, 1920).

National Food Reform Association, *Leaflets* (1917).

Orwin, C. S., 'The reports of the departmental committees on the home production of food', *Economic Journal*, vol. 26 (March 1916), pp. 105–13.

Paish, Sir G., 'Prices of commodites in 1915', *Journal of the Royal Statistical Society*, vol. 79 (March 1916), pp. 189–206.

Pankhurst, E. S., *The Home Front* (London, 1932).

Peel, C. S., *How We Lived Then 1914–1918* (London, 1929).

Philip, A. J., *Rations, Rationing, and Food Control* (London, 1918).

Pinot, P. and Augé-Laribé, M., *Agriculture and Food Supply in France During the War* (New Haven, CT, 1927).

Playne, C. E., *Society at War 1914–1916* (London, 1931).

Prothero, R. E. (Lord Ernle), *English Farming, Past and Present*, Revised edition (London, 1961).

Prothero, R. E. (Lord Ernle), 'The food campaign of 1916–1918', *Journal of the Royal Agricultural Society of England*, vol. 82 (1921), pp. 1–48.

Prothero, R. E. (Lord Ernle), *Speech*, Federation of War Agricultural Committees, Middlesex Guildhall (London, 20 December 1916).

Prothero, R. E. (Lord Ernle), *Speech*, Meeting of agriculturists, Mechanics Institute, Darlington (London, 5 October 1917).

Repington, C. A., *The First World War 1914–1918*, 2 Vols (London, 1920).

Rew, Sir R. H., *Food Supplies in Peace and War* (London, 1920).

Rew, Sir R. H., *Food Supplies in War Time* (London, 1914).

Rew, Sir R. H., 'The prospects of the world's food supplies after the war', *Journal of the Royal Statistical Society*, vol. 81 (March 1918), pp. 41–63.

Rewcastle, C. S., *Sugar Distribution* (London, 19 October, 1916).

Rhondda, Viscountess *et al.*, *D. A. Thomas, Viscount Rhondda* (London, 1921).

Roorbach, G. B., 'The world's food supply', *Annals of the American Academy of Political and Social Science*, vol. 74 (November 1917), pp. 1–33.

Salter, J. A., *Allied Shipping Control* (London, 1921).

Spencer, A. J., *The Agricultural Holding Acts 1908 to 1921 and the Corn Production Acts 1917 and 1920* (London, 1921).

Spriggs, E. I., *Food and How to Save It* (London, 1918).

Starling, E. H., *The Feeding of Nations* (London, 1919).

Surface, F. M., and Bland, R. L., *American Food in the World War and Reconstruction Period* (Stanford, CA, 1931).

The Times History of the War, 22 Vols (London, 1914–1921).

Turner, F. L., *National Kitchens and National Health: A Great Public Work* (London, 1917).

War Emergency Workers' National Committee, *Publications* (London, 1914–1918).

Webb, A. D. (ed.), *The New Dictionary of Statistics*, microfilm edition (London, 1964).

Wood, F., 'The increase in the cost of food for different classes of society since the outbreak of war', *Journal of the Royal Statistical Society*, vol. 79 (July 1916), pp. 501–7.

Wood, H. M., 'Methods of food control in war-time', *Journal of the Society of Comparative Legislation and International Law*, vol. 18 (April 1918), pp. 100–10.

Wood, T. B., *The National Food Supply in Peace and War* (Cambridge, 1917).

Secondary Works

Bentley, M., *The Liberal Mind 1914–1929* (Cambridge, 1977).

Brand, C. F., 'British labor and the International during the great War', *Journal of Modern History*, vol. 8, no. 1 (March 1936), pp. 40–63.

Burk, K. M., 'British war missions to the United States 1914–1918', PhD thesis, Oxford University, 1976.

Burk, K. M., 'The diplomacy of finance: British financial missions to the United States, 1914–1918', *Historical Journal*, vol. 22, no. 2 (1979), pp. 351–72.

Burk, K. M. (ed.), *War and the State: The Transformation of British Government 1914–1919* (London, 1982).

Chambers, F. P., *The War Behind the War 1914–1918* (New York, 1939).

Churchill, R. S., *Winston S. Churchill*, vol. 2: *Young Statesman, 1901–1914* (Boston, 1966–7).

Clinton, A., *The Trade Union Rank and File: Trades Councils in Britain, 1900–40* (Manchester, 1977).

Clinton, A., 'Trade councils during the First World War', *International Review of Social History*, vol. 15 (1970), part 2, pp. 202–34.

Cooper, J. M., 'The command of gold reversed: American loans to Britain, 1915–1917', *Pacific Historical Review*, vol. 45, no. 2 (May 1976), pp. 209–30.

Curtis–Bennett, Sir N., *The Food of the People: being the History of Industrial Feeding* (London, 1949).

Dayer, R. A., 'Strange bedfellows: J. P. Morgan & Co., Whitehall and the Wilson Administration during World War 1', *Business History*, vol. 18, no. 2 (July 1976), pp. 127–51.

Dewey, P. E., 'Agricultural labour supply in England and Wales during the first World War', *Economic History Review*, vol. 28, no. 1 (February 1975), pp. 100–12.

Dewey, P. E., 'Food production and policy in the United Kingdom 1914–1918', *Transactions of the Royal Historical Society*, no. 30 (1980), pp. 71–89.

Dewey, P. E., 'Government provision of farm labour in England and Wales, 1914–18', *Agricultural History Review*, vol. 27, part 2 (1979), pp. 110–21.

D'Ombrain, N., *War Machinery and High Policy: Defence Administration in Peacetime Britain, 1902–1914* (London, 1973).

Drummond, J. C. and Wilbraham, A., *The Englishman's Food*, revised edition by D. Hollingsworth (London, 1957).

Easterling, V. R., 'Great Britain's peril and the convoy controversy: a study of the intended effects of unrestricted U-boat warfare and the convoy system as a countermeasure, World War One', PhD thesis, University of Colorado, 1951.

Fowler, W. B., *British–American Relations 1917–1918: The Role of Sir William Wiseman* (Princeton, NJ, 1969).

French, D., *British Economic and Strategic Planning, 1905–1915* (London, 1982).

French, D., 'Some aspects of social and economic planning for war in Great Britain, c. 1905–1915', PhD thesis, London University, 1979.

Gilbert, M., *Winston S. Churchill* (Boston, 1971).

Gollin, A. M., *Proconsul in Politics: A Study of Lord Milner in Opposition and in Power* (London, 1964).

Gooch, J., *The Plans of War* (New York, 1974).

Grady, H. F., *British War Finance*, revised edition (New York, 1968).

Hall, T. G., 'Cheap bread from dear wheat: Herbert Hoover, the Wilson administration, and the management of wheat prices, 1916–1920', PhD thesis, University of California at Davis, 1970.

Hammond, R. J., 'British food supplies, 1914–1939', *Economic History Review*, vol. 16, no. 1 (1946), pp. 1–14.

Hammond, R. J., *Food*, 3 Vols (London, 1951–1962).

Hammond, R. J., *Food and Agriculture in Britain 1939–45: Aspects of Wartime Control* (Stanford, CA, 1954).

Hardach, G., *The First World War 1914–1918* (Berkeley, CA, 1977).

Harkness, D. A. E., *War and British Agriculture* (London, 1941).

Harris, J., *William Beveridge* (Oxford, 1977).

Hazlehurst, C., 'Asquith as prime minister, 1908–1916', *English Historical Review*, vol. 85 (1970), pp. 502–31.

Hurwitz, S. J., *State Intervention in Great Britain: A Study of Economic Control and Social Response, 1914–1919* (New York, 1949).

Hyde, H. M., *Lord Reading: The Life of Rufus Isaacs, First Marquess of Reading* (New York, 1967).

Jenkins, R., *Asquith* (London, 1964).

Johnson, P. B., *Land Fit for Heroes: The Planning of British Reconstruction, 1916–1919* (Chicago, IL, 1968).

Koss, S., *Asquith* (London, 1976).

Lyddon, Colonel W. G., *British War Missions to the United States 1914–1918* (London, 1938).

McGree, D. H., *Herbert Hoover: Engineer, Humanitarian, and Statesman* (New York, 1965).

McKenna, S., *Reginald McKenna 1863–1943* (London, 1948).

Mackintosh, J. P., *The British Cabinet* (London, 1962).

Marrack, J. R., *Food and Food Planning* (London, 1943).

Marwick, A., *The Deluge: British Society and the First World War* (London, 1965).

Mathias, P., *Retailing Revolution* (London, 1967).

Middlemas, K., *Politics in Industrial Society* (London, 1979).

Morgan, E. V., *Studies in British Financial Policy, 1914–25* (London, 1952).

Morgan, K. O., *Consensus and Disunity: The Lloyd George Coalition Government 1918–1922* (Oxford, 1979).

Morgan, K. O. and Morgan J., *Portrait of a Progressive: The Political Career of Christopher, Viscount Addison* (Oxford, 1980).

Morris, A. J. A., *Radicalism Against War 1906–14* (London, 1972).

Mowat, C. L., *Britain Between the Wars 1918–1940* (Chicago, 1955).

Mullendore, C. W., *History of the United States Food Administration 1917–1919* (Stanford, CA, 1941).

Oddy, D. and Miller, D. (eds), *The Making of the Modern British Diet* (London, 1976).

Orr, Sir J. B., *Food and the People* (London, 1943).

Peacock, A. T. and Wiseman, J., *The Growth of Public Expenditure in the United Kingdom* (Princeton, New Jersey, 1961).

Pollard, S., *The Development of the British Economy 1914–1967* (London, 1969).

Pound, R. and Harmsworth, G., *Northcliffe* (New York, 1960).

Ramsden, J., *The Age of Balfour and Baldwin 1902–1940* (London, 1978).

Roseveare, H., *The Treasury: The Evolution of a British Institution* (New York, 1969).

Roskill, S., *Hankey: Man of Secrets*, 3 Vols (New York, 1970–4).

Russell, Sir E. J., *A History of Agricultural Science in Great Britain 1620–1954* (London, 1966).

Sacks, B., 'The Independent Labour Party and social amelioration in Great Britain during the war', *University of New Mexico Bulletin*, Sociological Series, vol. 2, no. 6 (August 1940).

Sykes, A., *Tariff Reform in British Politics 1903–13* (Oxford, 1979).

Taylor, A. J. P., *English History, 1914–1945* (Oxford, 1965).

Taylor, A. J. P., *The First World War* (Penguin Books edition, Harmondsworth, 1976).

Taylor, A. J. P., *Politics in Wartime* (London, 1964).

Turner, J., *Lloyd George's Secretariat* (Cambridge, 1980).

Waley, S. D., *Edwin Montagu* (Bombay, 1964).

Whetham, E. H., *The Agrarian History of England and Wales*, vol. 8: *1914–1939* (Cambridge, 1978).

Williams, J., *The Other Battleground: The Home Fronts – Britain, France and Germany 1914–18* (Chicago, IL 1972).

Wilson, J. H., *Herbert Hoover: Forgotten Progressive* (Boston, Massachusetts, 1975).

Wilson, T., *The Downfall of the Liberal Party 1914–1935* (London, 1966).

Winter, J. M., *Socialism and the Challenge of War: Ideas and Politics in Britain 1912–1918* (London, 1974).

Woodward, Sir L., *Great Britain and the War of 1914–1918* (London, 1967).

Wrigley, C., *David Lloyd George and the British Labour Movement* (Brighton, 1976).

Young, K., *Arthur James Balfour* (London, 1963).

Newspapers and Periodicals

Clarion
Daily Mirror
Herald
Justice
Labour Year Book
Liberal Magazine
Manchester Guardian
Mark Lane Express Agricultural Journal and Live Stock Record
Morning Post
Municipal Journal
Nation
New Statesman
Observer
Spectator
The Times

Index